Skeptics
vs.
Scripture
Book I

Julie Fuller,
God Bless
Daniel Riddel
Heb 6:10

SKEPTICS
VS.
SCRIPTURE
BOOK I

A RESPONSE TO 25 SKEPTIC QUESTIONS ABOUT GOD, CHRISTIANITY, AND THE BIBLE

BY DAVID KIDD

XULON PRESS

Xulon Press
2301 Lucien Way #415
Maitland, FL 32751
407.339.4217
www.xulonpress.com

Unless otherwise indicated, Scripture quotations are taken from the King James version of the Bible. Bold type and plain text followed by page numbers in parentheses, as well as chapter titles, are taken from *50 simple questions for every christian,* by Guy P Harrison, Prometheus Books, © 2013. Used by permission.

Printed in the United States of America.

ISBN-13: 9781545634967

This book is dedicated to the memory of my father
Rev. Richard M. Kidd
Sept. 24, 1924 - July 9, 2017

"The greatest friend of truth is time."

And I will set up
shepherds over them
which shall feed them...
Jer. 23:4a

Acknowledgments

W hen you have a wife and children, plus a full time job, writing a book is an imposition on the time needed to be a husband and father. I want to first thank my wife, Leaann, for her assistance and patience in critiquing and editing, and my two children still at home, David and Laura, for tolerating the hundreds of hours spent writing this book while supporting my vision for the need it represents. Thank you for years of patience. I love you.

My good friend, Troy Wolfe, who is a kindred spirit when it comes to this subject matter, was kind enough to devote many hours to reading the manuscript and offer his insights. Even where he disagreed with me theologically, he did so with respect and grace. On the ninety-nine percent where we were agreed, his encouraging words were inspiring and motivating.

Emily Sisson offered her professional evaluation for chapter one without charge. Her suggestions there were extremely helpful in editing the remainder of the book. Mistakes that were missed are entirely mine.

Finally, I would be remiss if I did not acknowledge the lifetime of help I have received from my father, Richard M. Kidd. Dad is with the Lord now, but the many books I received from him, his love of uncompromising truth, and the godly men I have been able to associate with throughout his forty years of ministry were the most significant factors of all in the writing of this book. His influence is on every page. I wish he were here to read it, but then, I guess by now he knows what it says anyway.

TABLE OF CONTENTS

INTRODUCTION

When someone asks you a question the polite thing to do is answer if you can. In 2013, Prometheus Books published *50 simple questions for every christian,* by Guy P. Harrison (capitals omitted intentionally). I learned of this book in the spring of 2015 and bought it immediately. It was just what I was looking for.

I grew up a preacher's kid and attended Christian schools all the way through college. While I am thankful for the education I received, it did not provide much opportunity to entertain questions or answer objections to my Christian faith. When I became a young adult and was confronted with people whose education was entirely secular and sometimes very anti-Christian, questions arose which I was not prepared to answer. I started reading — a lot.

To someone who wanted to see how Christianity and the Bible fare against articulate skepticism, *50 simple questions for every christian* was like a gold mine. Finally, here were well thought-out and sincere questions which challenged my own Christian beliefs. I wondered if I would have answers. I devoured the book, making prolific notes along the way and began to mentally compose responses to the skeptic's questions and reasoning. Soon I was researching and writing these responses down. A manuscript began to take shape.

I'm not a theologian and have never spent a single day in seminary. I was ordained by an independent committee of seasoned ministers and Bible teachers and pastored a small house church for 15 years. The prime objective for writing this book became a mission to demonstrate that one does not have to be a trained theologian to answer skeptic questions. My apprehension that an educated skeptic might have arguments against Christianity that could not be logically answered quickly vanished. Though some questions required digging into the scripture in a way I had not done before, answers leaped from its pages and from the reservoir of logic and rationality upon which the Bible is based.

If a skeptic says he really wants to understand something about the Bible or Christianity that to him makes no sense, I'll take his word and try to give an honest, reasonable, and biblical answer. If skeptics think most Christians have not thought very deeply about their own faith, I agree. A second reason for this book is to help Christians do what skeptics say many have not done, think and reason through their own Christian belief. You can't do that unless your belief is challenged, which is a biblical concept. I Peter 3:15 says *But sanctify the Lord God in your hearts: and be ready always to give an answer to every man that asketh you a reason of the hope that is in you with meekness and fear.*

In *50 simple questions for every christian*, the author has spoken for skeptics everywhere. The introduction states, **These are the questions non-Christians ask aloud or in the privacy of their thoughts when they think about Christianity... This book presents a skeptic's perspective, the view many Christians never hear. (9) I'm not arguing; I'm explaining what many skeptics, right or wrong, honestly think about Christian claims. (10)**

Christians who have never thought through the logic of their professed belief often feel impotent in the face of powerful questions posed by confident and educated unbelievers. This book is written for them. Many churchgoers listen weekly to sermons from a book they have never read through and often do not understand. They believe, but their belief hangs by a thread that can be unraveled by atheist arguments. This book is written for them. Like some Christians, many skeptics have a skewed knowledge of the Bible and Christian doctrine. They know enough to speak articulately but not enough to understand accurately. This book is written for them. And finally, there are those whose once Christian faith has been shattered by what they thought were questions for which Christianity and the Bible do not have answers. This book is especially written for them.

If you are inclined toward unbelief, these responses probably will not make a believer out of you, but I hope it will at least make you more informed of what biblical Christianity is really all about and why it has endured thousands of years of skeptic critique. I also hope the answers provided here will help the Christian to recognize that many questions which superficially seem to bury Christianity are not the mortal blows they appear to be. Truth always sides with reality. It is our own misperceptions that lead to wrong conclusions.

As you begin this book, allow me to explain the format. First, since it is a response to a book with fifty questions, you have already noticed that only half of those are included. When you set out to address someone else's questions you must not only focus on the answer, but include a representative portion of the reasoning behind each question in order to give the reader a fair idea of just what is being answered. There are generous quotations from *50 simple questions for every christian*. These are in bold text followed by the page number in parentheses where they are found. In some cases, a passage may be summarized. These are not in bold type but are similarly notated.

Then there are the answers, which of necessity must be concise enough to fit into a readable sized book, yet thoroughly address the question at hand. To do this with fifty questions in one volume would result in a cumbersome text too intimidating in size for the target audience. So I have decided to break it into two separate volumes. A preview of Book II is provided at the end of this book.

Secondly, I refer repeatedly to "the skeptic" or "a skeptic." These references are not merely directed at the author whose questions I am addressing but to skeptics in general. As we have noted, the skeptic acknowledges that the questions he proposes are not just his but are typical of skeptics everywhere.

Thirdly, I have not attempted to answer every question, objection, or criticism of the Bible and Christianity raised by the skeptic. To stay on message, the main question is addressed along with significant points the author has made to justify that question. The chapters of this book are enumerated and titled the same as *50 simple questions for every christian* by permission of the author and publisher. Their cooperation is greatly appreciated.

Finally, answers to each of these questions are based on foundational doctrines of Christianity. I am not expounding on the many variants of denominational diversity that collects itself under the Christian umbrella. It is simple, fundamental, evangelical, New Testament Christianity, that provides the framework for this discussion. Therefore, this is not a deeply theological book but one of logic and reason supported by rational argument and ordinary common sense based on an accurate understanding of scripture. I have attempted to expose, not defend Christianity and the Bible. As the nineteenth-century British preacher Charles Spurgeon said,

"Defend the Bible? You might as well defend a lion. Unchain it, it will defend itself."

In the past few years, honest, open, and civil debate has been replaced by angry, agenda-driven rhetoric. The art of logical and rational argument has been sacrificed for simply shouting down those with whom you disagree. Nowhere has this been more obvious than in the political arena where policy is too often determined by who can protest the loudest or the most violent. Religion also ranks high on the list of topics where differences cannot be discussed reasonably and rationally.

Though occasionally disingenuous, Guy Harrison, in my opinion, made an effort to fairly present the skeptic's case in *50 simple questions for every christian*. Of course, I strongly disagree with his perspective, some of which simply misrepresents the Bible and true New Testament Christianity. I hope this response will be received as fair, polite, rational, reasonable, and most of all, a biblical reflection of Christian doctrine.

Introductions to books are a necessary evil, full of information that is not what interested the reader at the time of purchase. You bought this book either because you are a skeptic and were curious how a Christian would answer your questions, or you are a Christian, seeking answers to such questions. Perhaps you are somewhere in-between. Whatever the case, let's get on with examining twenty-five questions skeptics ask about God, Christianity, and the Bible.

The truth will set you free, but first it will make you miserable.

- James A. Garfield

ONE

DOES CHRISTIANITY MAKE SENSE?

The first question is prefaced with a fairly acceptable skeptic definition of Christianity. You might find something similar in the statement of faith of many evangelical churches.

> **God sent his son, Jesus, into the world so that he could die for us. His sacrifice was a pardon for our sins that allows us to be saved from death and enjoy eternal life in heaven. Without Jesus, we would all be doomed because of our inherently sinful nature. In this great act of mercy, God saved us from ourselves. And all we have to do in return to accept this gift is to repent our sins and embrace Jesus as our only lord [*sic*] and savior.** (13)

However, the skeptic insists that probing more deeply into the Christian faith leaves one perplexed by doctrines and concepts that are confusing or even irrational. The essence of these objections could be summarized as follows.

1. The Trinity, coupled with Christ's atoning death on the cross, makes no sense. **It** [the Trinity] **can't be reasonably ignored in any serious discussion about Christianity because, if true, it means that God sent himself to Earth, sacrificed himself to himself, and then returned to be with himself. The skeptic can only ask how any of this makes sense?** (14)

1

2. **If Jesus was God and knew that he would return to heaven after his death, where is the big sacrifice? What did Jesus/God give up? These are the things skeptics wonder about when trying to understand Christianity.** (14)

3. The sacrifice of Christ was senseless and inhumane. **If the crucifixion of Jesus did happen and was even fractionally as inhumane and cruel as Christians claim, then the obvious question that comes to the skeptic's mind is "why?" Why did Jesus or anyone else, god or human, have to suffer and die? Human sacrifice? Really? If this did happen, as Christians say it did and for the reasons they say it did, there needs to be some better reasoning, some rational explanation for why it was necessary. Why would a god need to rely on such a disgusting and primitive act to forgive us and save us from judgment?** (15)

Why would he [Jesus] have to do anything to provide us with a route to salvation and heaven? Couldn't he simply have skipped the whole slow agonizing death of Jesus and just forgiven us? (15)

4. Skeptics are frustrated by the notion of giving praise to any person or god who saves people from something that exists only because of that person or god. **We are inherently guilty? Condemned before we even learn to walk and talk? What sort of justice is that?** (16) **If a firefighter intentionally sets a house on fire and then rescues half the family inside while the other half burns to death, is he or she really a hero?** (16)

5. God's method is ineffective. **Why would any god who wished to share himself and his message with the world make himself invisible and silent to billions?** (18)

With the main objections summarized, let's address the core question. Does Christianity make sense?

First, Christianity cannot make sense to a skeptic because he does not acknowledge three fundamental Christian concepts.

1) Holiness - The state belonging to God alone of being without sin, and having absolute purity of thought, motive, word, and deed
2) Sin - Any thought, motive, word or action that violates a command or prohibition of God
3) Redemption - The act of God buying back his relationship with mankind entirely at his own cost

There is more, but these three concepts are foundational to understanding Christianity and we will unpack them later. Skeptics often acknowledge sin only as a Christian term, not as any sort of real thing. Holiness and redemption, central to Christian doctrine, are generally not even considered.

Immediately, we have a problem. How can someone who does not think there is enough evidence to believe in God, make sense of a belief system that revolves around God? How can a belief system that centers on this God make sense to someone who does not accept that this God even exists, much less that he is holy and has injected himself into human experience in some way? Some skeptics seem to genuinely want to understand Christian doctrines but just can't get past the "it makes no sense" barrier. **We all have to share this planet, so we should make the effort to understand one another. To that end, it is necessary for Christians to grasp why so many people think Christianity doesn't make sense.** (10) By the same reasoning, a skeptic should be willing to at least try and understand when the Christian offers logical and reasonable answers.

That doesn't mean he/she has to agree with Christian teaching, but there is a big difference between not agreeing and not understanding. Christians don't expect anyone to agree without good reason, at least we shouldn't. Understanding however, only requires intellectual honesty, the ability to reason through abstract thoughts and arrive at logical conclusions. One may do all this and still reject the idea that Jesus died on the cross for our sins and the only way to heaven is by accepting his substitutionary atonement. Faith is still an element of Christian doctrine, even after all the intellectual and theological explanations are understood.

One of the biggest obstacles to Christianity is the doctrine of the Trinity. How can one God exist in three persons? Skeptics exploit the difficulty of understanding this doctrine by making the fundamental Christian concept of Christ dying for our sins seem like a senseless exercise of God sacrificing himself to himself then returning to be with himself. Before examining the particulars of this perspective, let's try to grasp some basic understanding of the Trinity.

For centuries scholars have offered many ways of looking at this doctrine. The idea of an eternal being existing in three persons while remaining one entity may seem difficult at first glance, but it is not so far outside our experience as we may think. The Trinity can be understood, but it does not have to be in order to be accepted. I accept cell phone capability, and use it, but do not understand it in the least.

Despite growing up in a Christian home, going to church every Sunday, and graduating from Christian high school and a Christian university,

I was never taught the explanations of the Trinity I am about to offer. They are neither perfect, nor theologically profound, but they are rational, useful, and compelling.

The Bible tells us in Genesis that God created man in his own image, meaning that man bears some manner of resemblance to God. The Bible also teaches that God created the entire universe and everything it contains. It is understandable to us when something is produced, say a work of art, or a particular architectural structure, that it bears the designers image. That is, something of the designer can be seen in what is created.

A serious student of art can recognize a Picasso or a Rembrandt because the painting bears the artist's particular style, we might say, his fingerprint. Most people today who know anything about Thomas Kinkaide, "The painter of light," can recognize his paintings. They bear his trademark of light. Norman Rockwell's style is so unique to him that even the most casual observers today could pick out his work. A "creation" bears some mark of its creator. In art or architecture we can easily understand this premise. It should come as no surprise then that if a triune God really did create the universe, it might have trinitarian characteristics. But does it?

Our entire universe has just three aspects: time, space and matter. Take any one of these three away and you destroy the whole universe. We could not even describe or comprehend the idea of a universe without all three of these very separate entities coexisting as one. Remove time and all reference points are gone. A hundred billion light years has no meaning without time. Remove space and matter has nothing to occupy. Without matter, of course, there is nothing at all. Some scientists include energy as a fourth aspect. But energy is really a subset of matter. The universe is a trinity.

If that does not at least prick your curiosity, it gets even more interesting. Each of these three aspects of our universe is itself a trinity. Time is composed of past, present, and future. Space is three-dimensional having height, width, and depth. Likewise, matter is made up of individual atoms which are also a trinity of protons, neutrons, and electrons. These are the basic building blocks of all matter and they are trinitarian in nature.

Everything we see in terms of color is also trinitarian. The primary colors are red, blue and yellow. All other colors come from these primary three. Of course, each of the primary colors in its purest form can exist on its own, so this is perhaps not as good an example as the others, but in practical terms, we don't identify a color as "pure red." We see a menagerie of colors each having a single name and characteristic hue we recognize as purple, orange, pink, red etc... but existing as a trinity of three colors combined. Color is trinitarian.

These examples provide basic evidence that our universe has character-istics of trinitarian existence. Christians believe the universe is a magnif-icent work of art. It even inspires awe in the mind of the atheist. Is it not appropriate to wonder if the triune nature of our world possibly reflects the nature of its designer? The Christian view of the trinitarian universe matches reality and science's analysis of it, once we take an objective look.

Let's dispense with arguments that the trinity makes no sense. Our universe is full of sense. In fact, without its trinitarian nature it would make no sense. I fully understand that trying to comprehend the Trinity as it applies to God is different from understanding time, space and matter, or height, width, and depth. But just because it is harder to understand, or that we do not yet have all the information we need to understand it fully, does not make it unreasonable to accept. Science is constantly trying to unravel mysteries that it recognizes and accepts but does not yet fully understand. Theology does the same.

In the nationally televised debate between Ken Ham of Answers in Genesis, and Bill Nye the Science Guy, Nye responded to a question about where the atoms came from that produced the Big Bang by saying,

> This is a great mystery. You hit the nail on the head. What was there before the Big Bang? This is what drives us. This is what we want to know, let's keep looking. Let's keep searching.[1]

The Trinity is a most basic Christian doctrine and remains a mystery, but we can still believe it, just as scientists who deny the existence of God cannot explain the most basic question of their own evolutionary doctrine. Where did the original material of the universe come from? Being unable to answer that does not deter them from holding onto their belief that the universe came into being spontaneously.

All this is to offer some practical examples of how we can begin to accept trinitarian existence. However, this does not really answer the notion that according to Christianity, God sacrificed himself to himself then returned to be with himself. So with perhaps a little better grasp of trinitarian existence, let's further analyze this objection.

There is another example of the Trinity in our world that I did not mention earlier. The foundational building block of every society on earth is the nuclear family. In its most simple form it consists of a man, his wife, and a child. When a man and woman get married they are not recognized as a family but as a married couple. Once a child comes into the picture the term "family" is appropriate. You probably see where this is going: man + wife + child = trinity. Just like the basic building block of our material universe is trinitarian, so is the basic building block of social structure.

Let's say the child is a son who goes off to join the military. He is apart from his mother and father but is still in the family. The family unit is intact, still a distinctive entity. He can communicate with his father and mother even if he is on the other side of the world. The family continues to exist even though one member has separated himself. Additionally, though separated from proximity to his family, he bears the image of it in his manners, habits, characteristics, language, appearance, etc... Others may get a picture of what his family is like by watching and listening to him. Jesus gives this same image of his "family." God the Father and the Holy Spirit could be seen in him. He says, *He that hath seen me hath seen the Father.* (John 14:9)

Phil. 2:5-11 elaborates that Jesus was equal with God, but voluntarily separated himself from the other members of the Godhead and took on the form of a man. Now it gets very interesting. Jesus claimed to be God. That's one of the things that angered the religious Pharisees of his day. Unless he was a liar and a fraud, he actually was God in human flesh. The theological term for this is incarnation.

This is one of the proofs of his deity. I don't mean proof in the sense of empirical evidence that you can put your hands on, but in the sense of a logical consistency between what he said and what others said about him. The testimony of those who lived in his time does not corroborate the notion that he was egotistical or irrational.

An unbeliever may question his existence, and certainly his divinity, but if we can agree that Jesus did exist, it remains indefensible historically to relegate him, because of his proclamations, to the domain of the insane. If one who makes such audacious claims as he did is not considered the least bit deranged, or even just plain silly, especially by his detractors, then we have to ask, Why not?

So we begin to see the rational sensibility of Christian claims about Jesus Christ and the logical fallacy of skepticism about the authenticity of his existence, and the truthfulness of his claims. If we put aside personal bias and examine Jesus objectively, we discover that we cannot reasonably and logically dismiss him as just another in a long list of deluded religious zealots. There must be something legitimate about him.

Now the stage is set for addressing the misunderstanding that **God sent himself to Earth, sacrificed himself to himself, and then returned to be with himself.** (14) According to the Christian story in the Bible, Jesus was both human and divine, yet he never sinned. Even secular historians who were contemporaries of some of the apostles acknowledge Jesus as doing wonderful works and being undeserving of execution. I know this sounds like fantasy to some, and that's OK for now. I am just explaining what the Bible teaches and Christianity believes.

The problem with the view that Christianity actually teaches that God sacrificed himself to himself, is that it is a straw man argument. For those unfamiliar with debate terminology, a straw man argument is a way of minimizing or misrepresenting your opponent's position so you can more easily defeat it. I don't think the skeptic does this intentionally, but the point reflects the straw man strategy nonetheless. Here's why.

According to Christian teaching, when Jesus was nailed to the cross he was God the Son, still holy, without sin, still perfect in the eyes of his Father, and still part of the holy, sinless trinity. From the cross Jesus said, *Father, forgive them, for they know not what they do.* (Luke 23:34) His relationship within the Trinity was still intact. But there was a point on the cross when the trinitarian relationship was broken, or at least altered from its previous state of perfect harmony and unity. Jesus ceased to be holy in the eyes of his Father. He was no longer sinless.

The Bible teaches that Jesus became sin on the cross, not that he overtly sinned, but that God made him the very embodiment of sin. II Corinthians 5:21 says, *For he hath made him to be sin for us, who knew no sin; that we might be made the righteousness of God in him.* We know when this happened because when it did, Jesus no longer calls God his Father but his God. *My God, My God, why hast thou forsaken me.* (Matt. 27:46) What happened?

For Jesus, the nightmare of the cross was not the physical torture, as bad as it was, but for him to actually become a liar, a thief, a child molester, a Hitler, Stalin, and Pol Pot. In the eyes of his Father, he became the most vile, filthy, calloused, perverted sinner in the universe. It cost him not just the human part of his life, but more importantly, his holy nature. On the cross, Jesus became sin.

So did God put the sins of all mankind on himself? Yes, he did. He put all the sins of mankind on that part of himself that had been incarnated in human flesh. Did he sacrifice himself to himself? No. In becoming sin, that part of the Trinity called God the Son, Jesus, was now forsaken by God the Father, because holiness cannot coexist with sin. They are mutually exclusive. The relationship between God the Father and God the Son was altered. I cannot say for certain to what degree, but it was to the extent that Jesus felt abandoned by his Father. Hence, the one who had called out to his Father, now calls out to his God. Apparently, this altered state lasted for at least a few hours. Before Jesus died, he said, *Father, into thy hands I commend my spirit.* (Luke 23:46) Some theologians may disagree with this view, but it makes sense and is consistent with the biblical teaching of the trinity.

The central element of Jesus' relationship to God the Father is what unbelievers miss when discussing the Trinity and the death of Christ on the cross. Jesus did not sacrifice himself to himself, he sacrificed his holy nature and the perfect relationship with his Father.

The skeptic asks, **If Jesus was God and knew that he would return to heaven after his death, where is the big sacrifice? What did Jesus/God give up?**(14) On the cross, Jesus willingly forfeited his sinless nature to become sin in the eyes of God the Father. What would that have been like? Once God put the guilt of all mankind's sin on him, and as Paul wrote in II Cor. 5:21 *he hath made him to be sin for us...*, did Jesus sacrifice actually being God for the sake of being made sin? He was forsaken by his own Father, and the reason was because of sin, not committed sin, but imputed sin. This distinction is central to Christian doctrine.

Whatever happened within the Trinity in those hours on the cross we cannot really say with authority, at least I cannot. We are not entitled to enter into a discussion of what Christ personally experienced on the cross beyond what we are told. It is like having lived comfortably through World War II, trying to discuss and debate with one who was there and lived what it was like to be a POW or storm the beaches of Normandy. We cannot relate. We have not earned the right to question or inject our own pathetically irrelevant ideas of what it might have been like. We can only listen in silence and honor.

I had an elderly friend who was in the invasion of Normandy. I asked him once if I could do a story on him for the local paper. He did not want to talk about it. The horror was too much, even 60 years later. He was there, but the only "proof" I had was his word. It is somewhat similar as the perspective we have been addressing, except the horror Christ would have endured on the cross must be extrapolated to unimaginable proportions before we even begin to scratch the surface of its reality. The magnitude of the spiritual horror of the crucifixion, suffered along with the physical pain, is the backbone of the Christian teaching that Christ died for our sins.

In trying to entertain the thought of a holy, omnipotent, omniscient, God becoming a human, we might listen to Oxford scholar and former atheist, C.S. Lewis, who wrote in his landmark work, *Mere Christianity*, "If you want to get the hang of it, think of how you would like to become a slug or a crab."[2] We have to get a sense of the scale of difference between a holy God and sinful man. The chasm between the created and most intelligent mortal and the omniscient eternally existent creator God is infinitely wider than that between a genius and a slug.

So then we come to the question, **Why would a god need to rely on such a disgusting and primitive act to forgive us and save us from his judgment?** (15) The question reflects a lack of appreciation for the seriousness of sin. I'm not trying to be critical here, but it seems that some easier, more palatable method is expected without offering a clue as to what that alternative could have been. To help with that sense of scale, let's use a couple real-world examples of the horror of sin God put upon Jesus and which he willingly accepted.

As I write this, two convicted murderers have escaped from Clinton Correctional facility in upstate NY. One had shot a police officer 22 times, the other killed and dismembered his boss. They did not get the death penalty but life in prison. As monstrous as these men were, someone thought they deserved the chance to be free and helped them escape. I'll explain how this melds into the skeptic's philosophy in a moment. But one more example that hit pretty close to home helps to put into perspective what it meant for Christ to take our sin as the Bible teaches.

Less than a mile from where I live, a father rigged a pickup truck on jacks, had his son get under it to do some repair, then knocked the truck off the jacks and walked away, leaving his son to die. A few weeks earlier he had taken out a large life insurance policy on his son. He pretended the murder was an accident, collected the money, and lived well for several years before his suspicious second wife secretly recorded his confession. His first wife had died mysteriously in a fire years earlier. He collected insurance then as well and had just taken out a large policy on his second wife. At the sentencing, the judge said to this smirking murderer, who showed no remorse or emotion, that if he were ever brought up for parole, everything in the judge's power would be done to ensure he never sees the free light of day for the rest of his life.

Such heinous crimes as these should earn the death penalty if any crime could. And these examples are just two of millions of such hideous acts perpetrated throughout history. Now imagine if all these brutal and calloused acts were committed by one man. Would he not be considered the very epitome of evil, the absolute worst human being mankind has ever produced? If anyone deserved severe punishment, would not such a monster be the top candidate?

I'm not trying to be melodramatic. The Christian doctrine is that Jesus took the guilt and punishment for all the vile, corrupt, maniacs of history, along with the everyday liar, thief, slanderer, extortioner, and bigot, down to the homeless man who steals from someone even poorer than himself. Jesus became all of these, sacrificing his divine perfection to become sin for us and suffer the wrath of God as the just consequence for such an unimaginable magnitude of sin.

So how does this shed light on a skeptic philosophy that says, **Couldn't he simply have skipped the whole slow agonizing death of Jesus and just forgiven us?**(15) Suppose the president of the United States, for some unknown reason, decides to pardon such monsters as I have described. He has the power to pardon the undeserving, so why doesn't he? The answer of course, is that justice must be satisfied. It would be entirely unjust to simply pardon such maniacs simply because he can.

Does reading about these hideous criminals who could kill in such a bloodthirsty, calloused fashion, not strike at your own sense of justice? Do you not hear the demand for it calling out from the blood-drenched ground on which these victims were murdered? Do you not feel the agonizing pain of friends and family for their lost loved ones? Can you not at least acknowledge that according to Christian theology, Jesus willingly took responsibility for these and all other acts of selfish, brutal, hatred piled up throughout the centuries of time, past and future? The sense of revulsion you feel, the natural demand for justice and the inability to compose thoughts or call up words sufficient to reflect the repulsive nature of such heinous acts are but only a pinprick in comparison to the wrath of God against the enormity of what Jesus took upon himself on the cross. The disgusting and primitive act the skeptic objects to was required by God to satisfy a sense of justice for millions of such treacherous, and nauseating deeds throughout history. God is a God of justice, but he is also a God of love, and love sacrifices itself for others.

The skeptic may not believe or like the biblical account of how God chose to pay for the forgiveness of the sin of mankind, but his own demand for justice on a microscopically smaller scale betrays his true belief. Crime, as well as sin, requires punishment. The Christian story is that Jesus took the punishment for us so that we could be forgiven and declared innocent in the eyes of God because justice has been satisfied. However, this pardon is granted by God for the eternal consequence of sin, not the natural course of human justice.

The skeptic adds, **And that this human sacrifice was necessary because we are all guilty of a crime we did not commit. Adam tasted the forbidden fruit, remember, not I and you.** (19) Here we see the absence of acknowledgment of personal sin. I suppose that is understandable for someone who does not really believe in God, and consequently offenses against him he calls sin. But if a skeptic is honestly trying to understand Christianity for what it really is, and not just what he thinks it is, he cannot erect a shield of innocence around himself. Romans 5:12 says, *Wherefore, as by one man sin entered into the world, and death by sin; and so death passed upon all men, for that all have sinned.*

I realize we are quoting the Bible to prove the Christian doctrine of the sinfulness of man. This may appear to be circular reasoning, but if we are really trying to make sense of Christianity, even the unbeliever must acknowledge that it is not reasonable to tie the hands of the Christian by prohibiting him from referencing the book from which his belief arises. So the Christian position is that all people are sinners, not just Adam and Eve.

A final illustration of a very personal story may help us understand the Christian one. On a day in 1968, when I was in 5th grade, the principal called an assembly of all boys from 3rd to 8th grade. Our school only went to 8th grade at the time. Someone had vandalized the walls of the boys bathroom with handwritten graffiti. Students below 3rd grade had not yet learned cursive writing, which the graffiti was, and all boys were in attendance on this day, so the principal knew the guilty one stood in the room. He asked the guilty one to raise his hand. No one did. He lined us up shoulder to shoulder and went down the line asking each of us if we wrote on the walls. We all said, "No."

"Someone in this room is a vandal and a liar," the principal thundered, "and is unwilling to face the consequences of his actions." Then he asked a very odd question. "Is there someone who will take the punishment for the guilty one?" To my disbelief, an 8th-grade boy said, "Sir, I did not write on the walls, but I'll take the punishment for whoever did." He stepped forward, put his hands on the back of a chair, and the principal paddled him in front of all of us. Spankings were common in schools in the 60's. He then turned to the rest of us and said, "Whichever of you is guilty, this boy took your punishment. Even if you confess now, you will not be punished because the punishment has already been taken for you." I have forgotten many things of my elementary school days, but that day is as clear in my mind as if it happened yesterday.

The principal had the authority to just forgive the guilty one and dismiss the assembly and be done with it. Why the need for allowing an innocent student to suffer for the guilty? It is an elementary truth, crime demands punishment, even small ones. The principal allowed an innocent substitute to voluntarily take a punishment he did not deserve in order to pay the debt for the guilty one.

Extrapolate that little offense in 1968 to the hideous, ruthless, selfish and dishonest acts of the entire world throughout all of human history and out into the future of mankind, and multiply the punishment by 10 trillion, and you may begin to get an inkling of the sacrifice of Christ and the core message of Christianity. On that day when I was a 5th grader, just like that day we now call Good Friday, an innocent substitute took the punishment for the guilty to satisfy justice.

As with many things in real life, like cell phones, it does not have to be fully understood to accept. But if the punishment must fit the crime, then the punishment Jesus accepted for every sin that ever was and ever will be committed had to be very harsh indeed. If the principal had punished the willing substitute by having him stand in the corner, or miss recess for a couple days, or just tell the unknown guilty one he was forgiven, the impact of the lesson taught would have been meaningless and long since forgotten. The act of vandalism would have been viewed by all of us as no big deal. You may forget much of what you read in this book, but you will not likely forget this story. God did not intend for us to forget the salvation story either. Sin, and the price paid for us to be pardoned from its eternal consequence is a very big deal indeed.

Skeptics also consider God's method of revealing himself to man as ineffective. **Why would any god who wished to share himself and his message with the world make himself invisible and silent to billions?** (18) However, the question ignores fundamental Christian doctrine that for 33 years God walked the earth as a human being, interacting with others, teaching, rebuking and revealing himself for who he is. It also ignores the fact that in every observable instance, order, precision, and complexity only come from an intelligent source. These characteristics in the universe, and all of life, are hardly invisible or silent.

Before leaving the question of whether Christianity makes sense, we should answer one other point skeptics make to illustrate the injustice of original sin and the unfairness of sinners being judged for their own sin. ...**thoughtful Christians who pause to think about this idea for a moment are likely to recognize that something doesn't add up. We are inherently guilty? Condemned before we even learn to walk and talk?**

What sort of justice is that? To skeptics of Christianity, it seems crazy to view newborn babies as defective and doomed forever without spiritual intervention. Of course all people are imperfect, but hopelessly flawed at birth and deserving of endless agony in hell? Really? (16)

Once again, to a skeptic the insensibility of Christianity is rooted in the fact that he does not accept the concept of sin, original or otherwise, since sin is disobedience to a God he does not believe exists. If there is no God, or at least not enough evidence of God to warrant believing in him, then it is perfectly logical to also not believe that violating laws attributed to him produce a sentence of guilt.

Consequently, condemnation for violating laws from a God that does not exist would be very perplexing. The inability to make sense of sin and its consequence also prohibits an unbeliever from understanding the concept of redemption, another essential component of Christianity. Redemption is the self-sacrificing act of buying back, entirely at one's own expense, someone who has willingly rejected you. But a skeptic reasons, **If a firefighter intentionally sets a house on fire and then rescues half the family inside while the other half burns to death, is he or she really a hero?** (16)

The problem with this parallel is that according to the Christian story as it is given in the Bible, God did not "set the house on fire," nor does he "rescue half the family." Man is the one who chose to sin, that is to reject God, so man is the one that starts the fire. And God does not rescue half the human family, he makes a way of escape (redemption) for the entire family at enormous cost to himself. Some just choose not to take advantage of the escape provided.

Here again is the creation of a straw man version of Christianity to illustrate its insensibility. But the argument is against a misunderstood concept, not something that is real. Until we get further on in our discussion about God and Christian doctrine we will have to leave these arguments for now, but the pattern of arguing against a misconstrued version of Christianity repeats itself, as we shall see.

TWO

WHAT IS A GOD?

In any discussion of the Christian God, the term "god," lower case "g," does not usually come into play because while Christianity has God, it has no "god." It is not until you consider human inventions as alternatives to God that you can begin to discuss lower case "g" gods. Of course, there is much in the Bible about these kinds of gods, especially in the Old Testament.

When it comes to modern New Testament Christianity, the idea of a "god" is generally thought of as anything that displaces the God of the Bible from first priority in the life of the believer regarding worship and devotion. This kind of "god" can be a car, a job, a hobby, even another person. If you are a Christian, but voluntarily don't go to church, whatever it is that keeps you away is your god. That is, it is more important to you than God. Probably the biggest god many people have today is themselves. The "god" of humanism is mankind.

But I don't think skeptics are interested in the idea of a god in this context. A skeptic asks questions like these about gods.

Are they all supernatural? Are they all immortal? Can all of them fly, or only some? Can they walk through walls? Can they read our thoughts? Do they know the future? Can a god have mental and physical frailties? Can a human become a god? Can a god become a human? (21)

Most Christians perform terribly when asked to define god... In my experience, most non-Christian religious people and atheists stumble when defining gods. This is probably why so many simply skip the issue completely. Let's not bother being clear about what we are talking about, let's just talk about it. (21)

Since we are addressing questions relative to Christianity and the Christian God, we might start by defining God. At the beginning of their famous 1948 debate on the existence of God, theologian Father Frederic C. Copleston and atheist Bertrand Russell agreed to the following definition of God.

> Copleston: As we are going to discuss the existence of God, it might perhaps be as well to come to some provisional agreement as to what we understand by the term "God." I presume that we mean a supreme personal Being -- distinct from the world and Creator of the world. Would you agree -- provisionally at least -- to accept this statement as the meaning of the term God?
>
> Russell: Yes, I accept this definition.[1]

Skeptics muddy the water however, by grouping the Christian God with all other concepts of god, from the many gods of ancient Egyptians to the perception that Alexander the Great was a god. Interestingly, Julius Caesar gets godhood conferred upon him posthumously. **After his death, Roman general and dictator Julius Caesar was officially declared a god in 42 BCE. Any definition of god must accommodate Caesar.** (23)

There have been many such gods, but formulating a definition for "god" in this context is not really a Christian concern. If a skeptic wants to ask, "Who is God," then we have a discussion starter. Copleston's definition, accepted by atheist Bertrand Russell for purposes of the debate, is simple, straightforward, and accurate.

There is a particular quirk about skepticism that is both obvious and interesting and which surfaces in this discussion. Skeptics seem to deify doubt. In fact, it could be argued that doubt is the skeptic's god. This doubt becomes particularly obvious regarding any evidence that seems to support the biblical record and Christian claims regardless of what answers may be provided by the believer or what evidence there is for those answers. We will be getting into more of these later, but let's observe how this plays out regarding the question of what makes a god?

Apparently, many people during the time of Alexander the Great, thought he was a god. **Alexander the Great was a man who changed the world by conquering the Persian Empire and spreading Greek culture deep into Asia. He was also a god — at least that's what many people said at the time. Of course Alexander was probably just a flesh-and-blood man, but how can we know for sure more than two thousand** years after his reign? Maybe he was a god. (22) **We have to keep in mind that most religions are not based on proof, good evidence, and scientifically verifiable claims. They are instead based on shared stories, personal experiences, claims of divine revelation, and the words of authority figures.** (23)

The skeptic quirk can be seen in the words, "how can we know for sure." As time separates us from historical events, what was personally experienced by some is now relegated to the status of a shared story and the words of authority figures, (i.e., historians and /or documents written by eyewitnesses). The "how can we know for sure" mentality could, if applied consistently, call into question any event of history that occurred before our lifetime. It could be used to doubt any claim that relies on a shared story or personal experience of eyewitnesses who were there as well as the words of authority figures, like historians who research, document, and study events of the distant past.

Was William Bradford really the governor of Plymouth Plantation? William Bradford wrote, "Of Plymouth Plantation," documenting events he witnessed and experienced himself. Or did he? How can we be sure this first-person account was not fabricated, or at least embellished?

Did 1000 Jewish men and women really commit suicide at Masada in A.D.74 rather than be taken by the Tenth Legion of the Roman army? How can we know for sure? Flavius Josephus is the only source of this memorialized event in Jewish history. He got his information from two women who survived the self-inflicted massacre.[2]

How can we know for sure about any events hundreds or thousands of years after they are said to have occurred? Can we trust the authors? The documents? The books written during the time period? Supposed first-person accounts? We can play the skeptic game too by asking, "How do we know Julius Caesar was officially declared a god in 42 BCE?" Some people today doubt the Holocaust. This game can be played endlessly and pointlessly until everything in the distant past is doubted.

While these historical examples may not rise to the level of divine revelation, they do share characteristics the skeptic says are the basis of religion, and in particular, Christianity - shared stories, personal experiences, and words of authority figures. What we know about God from the Bible comes from just such sources. Why are other historical events and personalities accepted while biblical events, personalities and claims are not? The answer might likely be the lack of "good evidence," or "scientifically verifiable claims," but there is much more of this than skeptics would have us believe.

THREE

IS IT RUDE TO ASK?

The polite skeptic wonders if it is rude to ask a Christian who publicly announces his belief to justify that belief. Why shouldn't prominent and influential people be asked about their religious beliefs and how they might affect public policy?

If a president says he believes the Bible, or quotes from it regularly, then why can't someone ask if he really expects the apocalypse to occur as described in Revelation? Does he believe we are in the 'End Times?' If so does this influence the president's attitude toward environmental policy or the use of nuclear weapons? (25) **Why can't we just get it all out in the open and talk about religion?** (25) The skeptic wonders why, when Obama often brought up God and the Bible, he was not asked if he thinks **the Bible is wrong in declaring that gay men should be put to death,** (28) as it states in Lev. 20:13?

The skeptic also stresses the need for polite discourse and mutual respect for others even if you disagree with their beliefs. **Over the years, I am sure many religious people wrongly assumed that I am only interested in trying to beat up their ideas and belittle their beliefs. But the truth is that I have only ever wanted to help make the world a little more rational, more sensible, and safer for all. My ideas and suggestions, every one of them on this topic, are offered with only kindness and optimism in mind. And I am hardly unique among skeptics. Virtually every one of us wants a better world for everyone.** (31) A fair summation is that skeptics think Christians, no matter what walk of life they may be in, should not think it rude to be asked specific questions about what the Bible says and what they believe. Christians should agree. That is one reason for writing this book.

Let's examine the point that Christians are often not asked difficult questions about what the Bible we quote from says and whether we really believe it — all of it. This may be seen in the case of politicians who frequently evoke Christian ideology or biblical references. I think it is a fair question to raise and one I have often wondered myself.

During Jimmy Carter's presidential campaign, he "wowed" evangelical Christians by his political popularizing of the biblical term "born again." Strangely however, many of his policies then and his views yet today clash with evangelical Christianity and clear biblical prohibitions, such as homosexuality. So I agree with the skeptic. Asking an outspoken public figure to justify or explain his views as they relate to Christianity is not at all unreasonable.

In a July 2015 interview with The Atlantic, Carter said, "I personally have always been in favor of people who are gay being permitted to marry legally."[1] President Obama also shared this view. Though Carter and Obama are no longer president of the United States, would it not be fair to ask how this position squares with the Bible, which both quoted from occasionally. Romans 1:26-28 says:

> ... for even their women did change the natural use into that which is against nature: And likewise also the men, leaving the natural use of the woman, burned in their lust one toward another; men with men working that which is unseemly, and receiving in themselves that recompence of their error which was meet.

The context of this passage is in reference to those who *changed the truth of God into a lie,* (v.25) and who God, *gave over to a reprobate mind,* (v. 28) and is followed by a long list of other behaviors which are characterized as *unrighteousness.* Wouldn't it be entirely reasonable to ask public figures who quote the Bible as if they believe it, then support positions which contradict it, how they decide which parts of the Bible inspire their ideology and which are archaic or just plain wrong?

And while we are contemplating the question of whether or not it is rude to ask Bible-quoting politicians to come out in the open about their religious beliefs, we should consider it from the opposite perspective. When a skeptic wonders why Obama wasn't asked if he believes the Bible is wrong in declaring that gay men should be put to death, we should apply this same expectation to the politician or other public figure who announces he or she is gay.

No one ever asks exactly what it means to be gay. Maybe it is just assumed, but since it is now so public, is it rude to ask? If so, why? Why can't we just get this "coming out" business into the open and talk about what it actually means to say you are gay? Modern dictionaries define gay as "homosexual," and "homosexual" as " sexually attracted to people of one's own sex."[2] Being gay has been cloaked in the mantle of two people of the same gender who love each other, but is that all it really means?

I had an aunt who lived her entire adult life with the same female companion. They shared a house, car, and living expenses. They were lifetime companions and dearly loved each other until my aunt died, but they were not lesbians. They were horrified at the notion of same-sex marriage and homosexuality in general. The difference is, while they truly loved each other, they repudiated sexual contact with members of the same gender. They were simply two ladies who had no desire to marry or just never met a man they wanted to marry. Loving someone of the same gender isn't what makes you gay.

If presidential candidate Mitt Romney, a Mormon, should have been asked to explain **if temple garments (underwear) provide literal or symbolic protection for Mormon's who wear them**, (28) then shouldn't an openly homosexual Congressman be asked if he believes sodomy is natural and healthy? Shouldn't he, and other politicians who are outspoken advocates of homosexuality, be asked to comment on the 2012 Centers for Disease Control report entitled "HIV Among Youth in the US".

> "Gay and bisexual men are 40 times more likely to have HIV than other men," and that of the 50,000 new HIV infections annually, "about 87% of young males got HIV from male to male sex."[3]

Why weren't politicians aggressively questioned about or asked to comment on this report? Why haven't reporters deluged same-sex marriage advocates with questions about the implications of such devastating statistics? Why haven't political leaders, who are informed by our own Centers for Disease Control about a behavior that precipitates 50,000 new HIV infections annually, initiated a massive education program to warn youth about the dangers of this deadly attraction?

When studies confirmed the connection between smoking and lung cancer, such an ad campaign was started and it continues today. Why should we allow people to believe that homosexual behavior is not equally harmful, as these statistics demonstrate? Beside the horrific human toll, the health care cost to treat those who are HIV positive is astronomical.

A CBS NEWS article from 2006 reported findings of a Cornell/Johns Hopkins/Harvard/Boston University study which pegs the cost of treating an HIV patient at over $600,000.[4] If all of those 50,000 newly infected patients received treatment, that's a mind-numbing cost of 30 billion dollars to treat just one year's worth of new infections, most of which were acquired by voluntary homosexual sex! And that's not even taking into account successive years of inflation and higher health care costs since 2006. Using just CDC facts, homosexuality has far too high a human cost and financial price tag to be nationally sustainable.

An April 19, 2016, Fox News report entitled, "Deserting ObamaCare: UnitedHealth, nation's largest health insurer, bolts, fears huge losses," examines why health care providers are losing massive amounts of money under the Affordable Care Act.

> A recent study by the Blue Cross Blue Shield Association detailed how many new customers nationwide under ObamaCare are higher-risk. It found new enrollees in individual health plans in 2014 and 2015 had higher rates of hypertension, diabetes, depression, coronary artery disease, HIV and Hepatitis C than those enrolled before ObamaCare.[5]

Would it not be fair to ask politicians who support same-sex marriage how they can endorse its associated life-threatening behavior in light of these facts? Such statistics and obvious questions generated by them should not be viewed as offensive, hateful, or intolerant. They are based on purely neutral facts. The real concern should be the well-being of 50,000 people each year. There is no hateful motivation involved. When Paul had some hard things to say to the Galatians he concluded with, *Am I become your enemy, because I tell you the truth.* (Gal. 4:16)

The skeptic says **I have only ever wanted to help make the world a little more rational, more sensible, and safer for all. My ideas and suggestions, every one of them on this topic, are offered with only kindness and optimism in mind. And I am hardly unique among skeptics. Virtually every one of us wants a better world for everyone.** (31) Is it unreasonable or impolite to ask if support for such documented, self-destructive behavior is sensible, rational, and makes the world safer for everyone? These are not just "turnabout is fair play" type of questions. They are logical and obvious questions that should be center stage in any debate over the normalization of homosexuality. Why aren't they being asked?

In a truly fair world, the Christian should expect to be asked difficult questions about his or her beliefs. As noted in the introduction, I Peter 3:15 tells the believer, *But sanctify the Lord God in your hearts: and be ready always to give an answer to every man that asketh you a reason of the hope that is in you with meekness and fear.* The very reason for this book is to answer sincere and difficult questions about Christianity and the Bible. By the same sense of openness expected from the Christian, the skeptic should be willing to have his or her belief system challenged and be prepared to defend positions necessitated by it. No, it is not rude to politely ask difficult but legitimate questions, no matter which side of "religion" you are on.

To see how this could play out in the political world, let's create an imaginary scenario of a president, who is also a Bible-believing Christian, being asked a potentially explosive question which the skeptic has already suggested. What if this president were publicly asked if he thinks **the Bible is wrong** (in Lev. 20:13) **in declaring that gay men should be put to death?** (28)

The scene is a White House press conference. Dozens of TV networks allow millions of people to see and hear the president answer any question. A reporter, who only wants a better and more tolerant world for everyone, gets the nod and seizes the opportunity.

"Mr. President, you frequently cite Bible passages and openly speak of your Christian beliefs. You have also been very adamant about your lack of support for same-sex marriage and even the gay rights issue in general. Considering your high regard for the Bible, do you believe the Bible is wrong in declaring that gay men should be put to death as Lev. 20:13 says?" The room goes deathly silent.

"You ask a difficult but fair question, one that conveys what I believe is a common perspective and misunderstanding by those who support the agenda of the homosexual community toward those of us who oppose that lifestyle. The answer to your question is neither short nor simple.

First of all, we must acknowledge that the Bible does not say that gay men should be put to death, at least not if you accept the prevailing view that being gay refers to two men who love each other. Leviticus 20:13 says, *If a man also lie with mankind, as he lieth with a woman, both of them have committed an abomination: they shall surely be put to death; their blood shall be upon them.*

We have allowed the term "gay" in our culture to be defined in terms of love. A favorite question of same-sex marriage supporters is, Why shouldn't two people who love each other be able to marry? Love is not the issue. It could hardly be more clear what the Bible is talking about in this passage. This is not a reference to two men who love each other, but two men who engage in sodomy. This is an unnatural act that perverts the normal use of body systems and precipitates disease. For the Jews to whom this was written, it was a threat to their national survival. I'll explain why in a moment.

The second thing that must be understood is that this was written to the fledgling nation of Israel at a time when they were without a homeland and wandering in the wilderness. Most of the Old Testament is the record of God's dealings with the nation of Israel. If you do not agree or believe that, the rest of my answer will be meaningless to you, but it is the answer you asked for nonetheless.

God had promised Abraham he would father a great nation. If you follow biblical genealogies that promised nation was, and still is, Israel. According to the Bible, by the time of Leviticus, some of the Israelites were forsaking the God that brought them out of bondage in Egypt and began adopting practices of other nations, including homosexuality. The same Bible you are questioning says God created humans male and female and commanded them to *be fruitful and multiply and replenish the earth.* Homosexuality is impotent to fulfill that command. Those Jews who practiced it were in direct violation of one of God's first decrees.

Is it not obvious that an entirely heterosexual nation can replenish itself, while an entirely homosexual nation would vanish in one generation? Homosexuality is not nationally sustainable on a large scale. It must either be vanquished entirely, or somehow contained to a small percentage of the population. The more it spreads, the greater the detrimental effect on the country that hosts it.

America has decided to normalize homosexuality, paving the way for it to spread unchecked throughout the nation. The accompanying consequences have already been devastating to one of our core constitutional values — religious freedom. Christian business owners are being sued because they do not want to violate their own personally held religious convictions by accommodating same-sex weddings. Photographers, bakers, wedding planners, city clerks, and others have all been caught in the dragnet of persecution for what their Bible-based convictions tells them is an abomination.

In addition, the fiscal demands to treat increasing numbers of HIV positive patients as a result of homosexuality are another factor producing an economic train wreck for our health care system, as 50,000 people per year, by a voluntary act, become infected with a debilitating disease. The Leviticus 20:13 decree was God's way of ensuring that the health-destroying reality of homosexuality would not happen to the people of Israel, crippling it before it even obtained its national identity.

Being the creator and designer of both genders of the human family, God knew that misuse would result in gross malfunction. God's command to put to death those whose actions prevented the nation from fully developing, and which would have allowed a disease to spread rampant, as statistics show it now is in America, was intended to prevent Israel from self-destructing while still in its infancy.

At the time Leviticus was written, about 3400 years ago, there was no treatment for diseases like AIDS. They would not have even known what it was. As the designer of human beings, God knew that if mankind engaged in sodomy it would set in motion incurable disease that would devastate those who practice it and those nations that embrace it. For the Jewish people at the time, it was an act of treason because it inhibited the procreation necessary to strengthen the nation while at the same time weakening it, as more and more homosexuality would foster more and more disease that would produce increasing numbers of weakened men unable to fight or even care for themselves. This would require that others divert their attention from matters of national survival to caring for those who rendered themselves disease-ridden and militarily impotent. In addition, at the time this was written, the Israelites were profoundly vulnerable.

When HIV was first identified it was so prevalent among homosexual (gay) men that the illness it produced was called GRID (Gay Related Immune Deficiency).[6] Initially, it was a statistically accurate acronym as it was discovered almost exclusively in homosexual men. Although subsequent infections were found among a broader demographic, thus prompting the change to AIDS (Acquired Immune Deficiency Syndrome), it remains disproportionately prevalent among those who engage in male to male sex. CDC.gov posts the following data on their website relating to HIV/AIDS.

> In 2015, gay and bisexual men aged 13 to 24 accounted for 92% of new HIV diagnoses among all men in their age group.[7]

When AIDS became a national issue, some prominent evangelical television preachers said they believed it was a judgment from God for homosexuality. I have never believed that. I do believe the HIV virus is nothing new. It was not created by God to punish homosexuals. It has always existed. Of course, 3400 years ago, during the time of Leviticus, it was not known except by God.

The divine prohibition against homosexuality, and the death penalty for violating it, were given to protect the Jewish people from the ravages of a disease that could decimate their nation if permitted to go unchecked. Effects of bacteria were also unknown at the time. God gave Israel strict guidelines to protect them, like not touching a dead animal, the use of latrines for dealing with human waste, and how to disinfect a house after an infectious illness. These laws, which must have seemed bizarre to surrounding nations, protected Israel from illness, as did the prohibition and severe consequence for sodomy. Given the stakes for Israel at the time, the treasonous nature of the act, and the disastrous consequences it would produce for the people, my answer is no, I do not believe God was wrong to issue such a decree for the protection of the Israelite people.

I am sure the follow-up question will be do I think that homosexuals should be killed today? My answer again is no, I do not. I have elaborated long on the Leviticus question. If you want to know why I do not think the passage applies to our time, you may refer to the book of John, chapter 8, verses 1-11. After forgiving an adulterer, an offense punishable by death for both men and women in the Old Testament, Jesus told the offender to sin no more. I think that is very good and healthy advice regarding homosexuality today."

So is it rude to ask a Christian about his or her beliefs? No. But I wonder if the playing field is truly level on this question. If a skeptic ran for president, should he be asked how his worldview would influence his decisions? Since he believes humans are just more highly evolved animals and does not believe there is a God, how important would it be for him to protect the religious freedoms guaranteed by the first amendment? Would freedom of speech in the public sector be censored if it was religious in nature but conflicted with social mores? Would Christian organizations, churches, schools, and universities, be forced to accept members/students whose behavior conflicts with its own core values? Could a pastor be indicted for using the Bible's clear denunciation of sodomy when counseling a homosexual? The questions would be endless and speak to the very core of our American constitution. But would it be rude to ask?

FOUR

DOES JESUS ANSWER PRAYERS?

I f Jesus really answers prayer, then a skeptic's gut-wrenching scenario provides the ultimate test. A mother cradles her dying baby. **I beg you, God, save my baby. Please, God, don't let her die.** (33) **This is a prayer for a young child, easily the most innocent and worthy of rescue of anyone. It's about as sincere and unselfish as any prayer could be. I think this is the prayer that provides us with an ideal way to judge whether or not God answers prayers.** (33)

Children all over the world endure unimaginable suffering through disease, hunger, and the ravages of humans preying upon the weakest and most vulnerable. Across the world there are horrific scenes of such suffering. People beg whatever god they believe in for relief while skeptics insist, **A god who ignores those prayers has no business answering any others.** (36) And then there is Matthew 21:22 *And all things, whatsoever ye shall ask in prayer, believing, ye shall receive.* If that verse is true, then why doesn't God answer the prayers of those most deserving of divine intervention?

To an unbeliever, the reality is obvious. **In the end, I believe we can all be honest and mature enough to confront what is most likely the truth about prayer. Either no gods are there to listen, or, if there are, the gods do not respond to us in the way many religious people claim they do. If Jesus really is listening and really does fulfill the wishes of Christians, then wouldn't the entire world have noticed by now?** (39) So what can a Christian say to such arguments? Does Jesus really answer prayers?

The Christian will never be able to answer this question to a skeptic's satisfaction. Here's why. There have been times when a Mother's prayer for her dying baby has been answered, at least the child had what appeared to be a miraculous recovery against all doctor's prognoses to the contrary. A skeptic can merely say, "How do you know the child wouldn't have recovered anyway?" Or, "Sounds like the treatment the baby received worked." This is an argument skeptics cannot lose. If the mother's prayer is answered, then it would have happened anyway. Prayer had nothing to do with it. If the baby dies, then it is proof that either there is no God, or if there is, he doesn't answer prayers the way we think he does. The skeptic argument prevails either way. Such reasoning however, though accurate, does not answer the sincerity of the question, so let's consider the scenario of this praying mother with her dying baby.

On the surface, anyone who does not really believe there is a God has good reason to question the efficacy of prayers at all if Jesus does not answer this woman's prayer. The "good reason" however, has a caveat. The unbeliever does not recognize that he has limited knowledge of the situation. The assertion that if Jesus really answered prayers he would have to answer this one if he has any sense of justice, brings God down to a human level and demands he respond as any reasonable human would.

Let's expand the scenario larger than it appears on the surface we have been provided and examine it in terms of biblical teaching on prayer. This is not just an evasive maneuver. It is based on the Christian teaching regarding prayer, which is what the question is really all about. The unbeliever does not get to define the question, set the limits of discussion, and expect the Christian to answer within those predefined limits. Jesus, prayer, and biblical teaching are larger than the limited scenario we have been given.

Here is just one passage on what the Bible says about prayer. James 4:3 *Ye ask, and receive not, because ye ask amiss, that ye may consume it upon your lusts.* Am I saying that a mother begging God for the life of her child is lust? Am I out of my mind?

What we are doing in this book is answering skeptic questions about God, Christianity and the Bible. To do that, we have to state what the Bible says, I mean what it actually says and what it really means. Once we are talking accurately with legitimate definitions, we are in a position to have an intelligent discussion void of presumed meanings and preferred interpretations. I know this seems like a long way around to get to a point, but as C.S. Lewis famously said, "Sometimes the longest way round is the shortest way home."

The Greek word translated "lust," as used in James 4:3, literally means, "a desire for pleasure." What is the basis for the mother's desire for God to save her dying baby? Is it the good of the baby, or to escape the agony of not having her baby with her? Don't think I am being calloused and uncaring here. I have six children and would have prayed just the same as this mother if any one of them faced a life-threatening situation. There is no fault in the mother's prayer. But is it, after all, a selfish prayer motivated more by her own desire for the pleasure of having her baby to love, hold, and watch grow, than for the ultimate good of the child? Presuming the mother in this scenario is a God-fearing, Christian woman, the Bible teaches that if her baby dies it will go to heaven — a far better place than any thing on earth according to what the praying mother believes. Have I crossed the line of reason and sanity? Let's continue with the expansion of the scenario so we can more fully understand the concept of asking God to do something out of selfish motivation.

Suppose the baby is now grown and is a 17-year-old young lady who was just offered the opportunity to travel and study abroad. She will get to see the world, learn from masters, and experience the very best of education, culture, food, and natural beauty. But it will take her from her mother. The mother prays, "God please don't allow my precious daughter to be taken away from me. I know this is a wonderful opportunity for her, but I do not want to lose her. She could marry someone from a far country. I may never see her again. Please don't let her go!"

Does this now sound like a loving, caring mother, or a controlling, selfish woman who does not want to lose her daughter to places and experiences the mother has only ever dreamed about? Do you see how selfish the mother seems now? The prayer is much the same. Although the daughter will live in the second scenario, she will be separated from her mother, perhaps forever, at least on earth, which is really what the mother is praying will not happen in both situations.

If she actually believes her dying baby will be taken to a place of great beauty, comfort, wonder, and knowledge, as the Bible she believes says heaven will be, the only real reason to pray for her baby not to die is that she wants to have it with her. Again, it is a normal emotion that no reasonable person would object to, but it still is based on the mother's desire for the pleasure of having her baby in her arms. At its root, it is a selfish prayer. The baby, according to the mother's own belief, would be far better off in heaven. And after all, according to what she believes, she will see her baby again.

The point of all this is not to be critical of the prayer or maternal love, but to recognize that this "ultimate prayer," no matter how it may sound, is actually a selfish prayer. The James 4:3 passage says this is one kind of prayer that may not be answered. Not that it is never answered, many such prayers have been. But the presumption that God, if he cares at all, has to answer this prayer, is based on the skeptic's own definition of what is best for the baby and the mother regardless of the eternal peace and comfort Christianity says awaits the deceased child. The only way God can be charged with injustice if he does not answer the prayer is to define in limited and purely human terms what is best, then accuse God of not providing it.

Here is a far less dramatic example where I believe God answered a prayer of mine. In the summer of 1984 we had just bought our first house and needed a lawn mower, nothing fancy, just a simple push mower. It was at the time when safety regulations required new mowers to be equipped with a kill bar built into the handle. You couldn't start the mower or leave it running without this handle being engaged. It dramatically raised the price of the most basic mower. We had looked all over and couldn't find a used one for sale anywhere, and a new one was expensive.

But our grass needed mowing, so I decided I was just going to bite the bullet and buy a new one anyway. I don't remember if it was my wife's idea or mine, but we decided to pray about it, asking God to provide us with a mower. No one else knew we had prayed. It was a prayer of little faith and great doubt. I was planning to buy one the next day. God had 24 hours.

The next morning when I went outside there was a brand new mower on our back porch with a card attached that said, *That was a little short notice, but thanks for asking. Hope you like the color.* Just kidding! No, there was no magical appearance of a mower from heaven with a note from God. I went to the hardware store next door to where my brother lived and bought a brand new mower. "Go buy a new one." That was God's answer to my prayer as far as I was concerned.

While the store owner was checking everything out on the mower, I went outside. My brother was in his backyard. He walked over to me and asked what I was doing. "I just bought a mower," I told him. "Dave, I know where there is a perfectly good mower people will give you free," he said. The mower I had just bought was over $200! I went back inside and told the owner that I had just been given a used mower. I still remember his words after losing this sale. "A free mower is better than one you have to pay for any day, no problem."

So did God answer our pathetic, unbelieving, faithless prayer? Well, within 24 hours we had a mower that cost us nothing and came from someone who I didn't know and who didn't know we had prayed for one. Coincidence? Perhaps. Any apparent answer to prayer that comes in precision timing can be chalked up to coincidence. It is an easy and predictable out for anyone who can cite examples of similar "coincidences," minus the prayer, in the lives of non-believers. Skeptics "believe" in coincidences. Christians "believe" in answers to prayer.

And what about Matthew 21:22 which skeptics cite as evidence that the Bible teaches if you just believe you can have all your prayers answered? *And all things, whatsoever ye shall ask in prayer, believing, ye shall receive.* Our lawn mower prayer certainly wasn't a believing prayer. But it wasn't a totally unbelieving prayer either. The very act of praying implies some minutiae of belief. In fact, I have often felt that my prayers were more characterized by doubt than belief. But again, doubt is not the same as unbelief. Unbelief closes and locks the door, expecting nothing. Doubt may close the door but leaves it unlocked and the porch light on, just in case.

So let's be honest and reasonable enough to acknowledge that prayer is not a guarantee of getting whatever you ask for and that is not what Matthew 21:22 is really saying. There is not sufficient space in this book to go into a long discourse on the biblical teaching on prayer, but if conjuring up enough belief was the secret to getting whatever you ask for, the world would be full of self-indulgent, praying Christian gluttons who could gorge themselves then simply pray away the calories and come out looking like an Olympic athlete. This is childish thinking.

When I was a boy in Sunday school I used to think this verse was a way for me to get whatever I wanted. All I had to do was learn how to believe and I could have a go-cart, a pony, a swimming pool, anything! It may have been sincere, but it was childish, ignorant, and selfish.

However, in Matthew 17:20, Jesus himself said that if you have faith as small as a grain of mustard seed you could move a mountain. I guess that mustard seed-sized faith would look like a mountain next to my doubt-filled, obligatory prayer for a mower. I never saw myself as a man of mountain-moving faith.

I did hear testimony once from someone who actually took this promise literally, prayed, and saw a mountain moved. He was a preacher at a small town church. They needed space to expand and there were no suitable buildings nearby to which they could move. The large hill at the back of their property was too close to where they would need to add on.

Moving the mountain of dirt that would be required made the project too costly. They were stuck.

The pastor met with his people and they decided to pray that God would "move the mountain." After some time praying, I'm not sure if it was a few days or several weeks, the pastor was approached by a stranger and asked if he was the pastor of this church. When the pastor said he was, the man told him he was foreman for a municipal project. He needed fill dirt and a lot of it. "Would you be interested in allowing us to excavate that hill at the back of your property," the man asked. The pastor agreed. When they were finished the church had obtained free excavation of their "mountain" and had plenty of room for their building project.

So did God answer this prayer, or was it just another amazing coincidence? What you believe about that will be determined by your presupposition about God and prayer. But I would say that believing it was just a coincidence is just as much a faith-based belief as believing that God arranged the circumstances. Would it have happened anyway? We'll never know, but it doesn't really matter. The pastor led the people in an exercise of faith and the mountain was moved. Such amazing coincidental circumstances, even if they occur for a non-praying but wishful-thinking skeptic, should at the very least inspire some degree of curiosity.

However, our miracle mower and the mountain that was moved are small potatoes compared to the mother praying for her dying baby. There is simply no comparison in scale or significance. So if God answered our half-hearted prayer for a measly mower, and the prayer of a faith-filled group of believers asking for a mountain of dirt and rock to be moved, why would he not answer a mother's prayer for her dying child?

Since some mother's prayers for a dying baby have been answered, the question really should be, Why doesn't God answer all mother's prayers for their sick or dying babies? In fact, why doesn't God just answer all prayers?

Ultimately, we can only say that we do not know why God does or does not do a certain thing. But the question, or the charge of injustice implied within the question, betrays a perspective that if God does not do what we think he should, or what we would do if we had his power, then if he exists at all he is certainly not worthy of our devotion. It is really an argument against an imaginary God who is limited in his actions to what any human would do in a given situation. It implies that what we perceive is all there is and that God has no more information than we do about the circumstance. We expect an infinitely wise and just God to conform his decisions to our finite, selfish, and limited understanding.

This may sound like a cop-out to the non-believer. But the God we are talking about is the Christian God of the Bible. We have to allow him the attributes that he himself claims in his word or we are not even talking about the same God we are supposed to be questioning. If we are going to debate some action or inaction of God, we have to argue about the real thing, not an easily dismantled straw god that is no bigger than human perception.

So whatever God does is right, no matter how wrong it seems? The answer to that is yes! Everything God does is just because God is the author of justice. If he is not, who is? Mankind? Look around, every society on earth refutes that idea. Finiteness in understanding must always bow to infiniteness in wisdom. The God who decides to answer some prayers according to our will and not others is the God who created the universe.

The Bible is the only source we have for considering this God. We on the other hand, are mere mortals with minds easily confused, emotions that can lead us off in three directions at once, and a stubborn tendency to think we are the epitome of existence, knowledge, and understanding. We think an infinite God must be limited to our sense of justice. The story of Job in the Bible illustrates this perfectly. Even if you don't believe it is true, Christians do, and it paints a very human perspective on a man's sense of injustice and his problem with the God who allowed it.

As the story goes in the Bible, Job suffered unimaginably as God turned him over to Satan for testing. All his children died in a single day. All his livestock were stolen on the same day. He was afflicted with a horrible illness. His friends told him it was a punishment from God, no doubt because they believed that a loving God would not permit such suffering for a righteous man. Even his wife told him to *curse God and die.*

All the while Job believed he had done nothing to deserve such retribution from the God he served so faithfully. Just listen to how he felt. *God hath delivered me to the ungodly, and turned me over into the hands of the wicked. I was at ease, but he hath broken me asunder; he hath also taken me by the neck, and shaken me to pieces, and set me for a mark.* (Job 16:11-12) Job felt like a helpless puppy being shaken to death by an angry mongrel dog. That is a pretty strong indictment against God! His circumstances were tenfold worse than the woman whose baby is dying. Job was human and expressed his feelings honestly. They were not pretty or pious. That's one reason I believe the Bible. It reflects the full spectrum of human emotion, and in the case of Job, contrasts it with divine prerogative.

You have to read the entire book of Job to get the full measure of Job's journey with God through suffering and apparent injustice, to acceptance of his divine wisdom. But listen to how God responds to Job's complaints and questions. *Gird up now thy loins like a man, for I will demand of thee, and answer thou me. Where wast thou when I laid the foundations of the earth? Declare, if thou hast understanding. Who hath laid the measures thereof, if thou knowest? Or who hath stretched the line upon it? Whereupon are the foundations thereof fastened? Or who laid the corner stone thereof.* (Job 38:3-6)

Later in the same chapter, God continues. *Canst thou lift up thy voice to the clouds, that abundance of waters may cover thee? Canst thou send lightnings, that they may go, and say unto thee, Here we are? Who hath put wisdom in the inward parts? Or who hath given understanding to the heart?* This goes on for several chapters as God reminds Job of exactly who he is questioning. In pathetically inadequate human terms, it might be compared to a puny punk rocker criticizing the composing genius of a Beethoven or Mozart.

The point God was making to Job is the same one we make here for the question of why God would not answer the prayer of the dying baby's mother. If we are incapable of comprehending an eternal God and what he has done in the universe, then who are we to question his choices which may seem unjust from our finite perspective? In essence, God tells us what he was telling Job. "Do you know who you are questioning? Who do you think you are?"

No less profane a man than World War II general, George S. Patton, left posterity a model example of the superiority of God's wisdom. It was December 23, 1944. Patton was trying to advance his army to rescue the besieged city of Bastogne. The city was an American held garrison surrounded by Nazi forces. But his greatest enemy was the intolerable winter weather that was making it nearly impossible for him to advance, vanquish the Nazis, and rescue his countrymen. The general goes into a Catholic chapel, unfolds a written prayer and drops to his knees.

> Sir, this is Patton talking. The past fourteen days have been straight hell. Rain, snow, more rain, more snow — and I am beginning to wonder what's going on in your headquarters. Whose side are you on anyway. ...My army is neither trained nor equipped for winter warfare. And as you know, this weather is more suitable for Eskimos

than for southern cavalrymen. But now Sir, I can't help but feel that I have offended You in some way. That suddenly you have lost all sympathy for our cause. That you are throwing in with Runstedt and his paper-hanging god [Hitler]. You know that my 101st airborne is holding out against tremendous odds in Bastogne, and that this continual storm is making it impossible to supply them from the air. I've sent Hugh Gaffey, one of my ablest generals, with his Fourth Armored Division north toward that all-important road center to relieve the encircled garrison, and he's finding Your weather more difficult than he is the Krauts.[1]

Patton knew he was the only hope for the Americans trapped in Bastogne. The German general had already offered them terms of surrender rather than be slaughtered. It was refused. Patton continued.

Sir, I have never been an unreasonable man; I am not going to ask you to do the impossible. I do not even insist upon a miracle, for all I request is four days of clear weather. Give me four days so that my planes can fly, so that my fighter bombers can bomb and strafe, so that my reconnaissance may pick out targets for my magnificent artillery. Give me four days of sunshine to dry this blasted mud, so that my tanks can roll, so that ammunition and rations may be taken to my hungry, ill equipped infantry. I need these four days to send von Runstedt and his godless army to their Valhalla. I am sick of this unnecessary butchering of American youth, and in exchange for four days of fighting weather, I will deliver You enough Krauts to keep Your bookkeepers months behind in their work. Amen.[2]

But it was the same bad weather Patton cursed which kept the German army from advancing on Bastogne where it could easily have slaughtered the trapped 101st Airborne. The Germans delay allowed Colonel Creighton Abrams, commander of the 37th Tank Battalion of the Fourth Armored Division under Patton's command, to advance despite the despicable weather, punch through the German lines and relieve and reinforce Bastogne.

Patton, a military mastermind, "knew" he could not relieve Bastogne without good weather. His cause was just and the need urgent. Hundreds of lives were at stake. But his request, reasonable as it seemed, was denied. On December 27, 1944, after Bastogne had been rescued, Patton again enters a chapel and falls to his knees.

> Sir, this is Patton again, and I beg to report complete progress. Sir, it seems to me that You have been much better informed about the situation than I was, because it was that awful weather which I cursed so much which made it possible for the German army to commit suicide. That, Sir, was a brilliant military move, and I bow humbly to Your supreme genius.[3]

We would do well to remember when we consider prayer that by default it is to a being far superior in mind and reason than the mortal doing the praying. Otherwise, why pray at all? So it is contradictory to the very basis of prayer to suggest that we somehow have the more informed intellect and God should come around to our way of thinking.

In Romans 9:15 God says, *I will have mercy on whom I will have mercy, and I will have compassion on whom I will have compassion.* The person who has never had God answer a single prayer, no matter how sincerely it was prayed, or how deserving he or she seemed to be to have it answered according to their request, is still the recipient of his undeserved mercy. Just as we cannot escape the justice of God, we cannot live even a single day without his abundant and unmerited goodness, prayers answered or not.

Just for interest's sake, let's reverse the scenario of the Christian mother cradling her dying baby. A woman, who is a skeptic, cradles her dying baby. She does not believe there is a God and so does not pray. The doctors, who are her only source of hope and help, have done all they can and offered their professional prognosis. The baby is going to die.

The skeptic mother may cry, but she cannot pray. She cannot say, "Please" to anyone or anything because human intervention has been exhausted and there is no intelligent, sympathetic entity beyond the medical profession to whom she can appeal. She cannot blame or accuse some "being" that is responsible or could help if it really wanted to because there is none. She is a good and consistent skeptic and must simply accept that survival of the fittest is claiming the life of her baby.

It is not even unfair because fairness implies a standard by which a matter may be judged to be fair or unfair. And of course, if there is a standard, then someone or something that has a mind and a purpose had to set that standard. But she does not believe in any standard-setting entity. Her baby's imminent death is just an unfortunate natural event. I have to wonder, given such a scenario, just how consistent the skeptic mother would really be. God may be charged with injustice or not caring, survival of the fittest cannot.

One last point in this chapter should be addressed. People of other religions who believe in other gods also cite answers to prayer as evidence that their god is the true god. If worshippers of other gods testify to answered prayer, how can Christians say the God of the Bible is the only true God?

Doesn't the Muslim or Hindu who reports that their god answered prayer have just as valid a claim to the legitimacy of their religion as the Christian who reports the same? How does the Christian explain answers to prayer by what they would consider to be a false god? This is a reasonable question from a skeptic perspective and one to which I don't think Christians have given much thought.

The Bible teaches that God is not limited by the misdirected belief of individuals. Scripture records in Acts 10 how Cornelius, a centurion who feared God, was visited by an angel and instructed to send for the apostle Peter. According to this account, Cornelius was a devoutly religious man but had no knowledge of the salvation through Jesus Christ that Peter was preaching. In other words, he was not a Christian, just religious. When he and others heard the gospel message from Peter, the Bible says that the *Holy Ghost fell on all them which heard the word.* (Acts 10:44) That is New Testament vernacular for being "born again," or indwelled by the Holy Spirit, better known as becoming a Christian.

The point here is not whether you believe this story, but that the Bible itself relates how individuals who have some religious knowledge of God, incomplete or inaccurate as it may be, still receive his mercy, even to the point of God intervening on their behalf to make himself known to them. We know that Cornelius' religious devotion was misdirected because when he first meets Peter he falls down and worships him. Peter has to tell him, *Stand up; I myself also am a man.* (Acts 10:26) In this case, the religious man recognizes and accepts the truth when he hears it rather than persisting in his previous misguided devotion. God makes himself known. How that is interpreted, accepted, or rejected is up to the individual, which brings us to the second point.

If a Hindu's prayer to the god Ganesha is answered, and the Christian says that Hindu gods are false, then who answered the prayer? Either God answered the prayer, even though he is not the god to whom the Hindu was praying, or Satan deceived the Hindu into thinking Ganesha did. In the first case, would God really be fooling the poor Hindu who thinks that Ganesha is the one who answered his prayer? Skeptics of course, would say that it was coincidence, like all other prayers that appear to be answered.

Christianity teaches that everyone is without excuse when it comes to believing in God, not just any god they invented themselves, but the creator God, the one described in the Bible. Some may be confused as to the theological details, but according to the Bible no one can claim ignorance that this creator God exists because *that which may be known of God is manifest in them; for God hath shown it unto them. For the invisible things of him from the creation of the world are clearly seen, being understood by the things that are made, even his eternal power and Godhead, so that they are without excuse.* (Rom. 1:19-20)

Notice how this passage explains not only God's existence but even difficult concepts about him, like the Trinity (Godhead), which can be understood by looking at nature, or even ourselves, as we elaborated in chapter one. The praying Hindu is not being fooled by God. He is fooling himself, against all the natural evidence God has provided to lead him to the truth.

In the second and somewhat more questionable case, I don't think scripture allows for Satan to impersonate God by intercepting prayers and answering them. The Bible does teach however that Satan himself is *transformed into an angel of light.* (II Cor. 11:14) He can fool us. He is a deceiver. If a person rejects the true God, with all the evidence of his existence giving him no excuse, it may be that he opens himself to such deception.

So does Jesus answer prayer? Christianity says yes, and skepticism says we can't really know, but it is unlikely. The individual will form their view based on their own presuppositions, either biblical or skeptical, combined with personal experience. These arguments on answered prayer are, no doubt, not enough to convince the skeptic of Christianity's legitimacy, so let's move on to the next question.

FIVE

WHO IS A CHRISTIAN?

Twenty-first century Christianity has unquestionably splintered into such diversity of belief and practice that it is difficult to distinguish just who is a Christian. Anymore, you are as likely as not to find a professing Christian who drinks, smokes, cusses, watches sleazy movies, or supports the local casino. Evangelical Christians adopt the fads, dress, music, language, and habits of the unbelieving world, blending into their cultural surroundings like a chameleon, completely oblivious to how their actions contradict their confession. How can we blame the skeptic for wondering who is really a Christian? Interestingly, the skeptics observations on this point are related more to the theological than expectations of lifestyle.

How can any Christian blame skeptics for not embracing Christianity when the world's Christians can't even agree on precisely who Jesus is, what he wants us to do, how we are supposed to worship him, and how we get to heaven? (42) If I were a Christian, I would lose a lot of sleep worrying if I'd chosen the right version out of so many. (42) As for the simple question, "Who is a Christian," the only answer, the only fair and logical answer, is that those who say they are Christian are Christian. (43) Skeptics dismiss the Bible as being any sort of authoritative word on Christianity. **There is no hard evidence to rely on, no undeniable proof that transcends the words of men and women. (43)**

All of this confusion, and the confusion is very real, is not the fault of Christianity itself. The real culprit is the lack of understanding of what the Bible teaches or an unwillingness to accept it in areas of life where we are not living up to its standards. In Christianese, this is called "walking the talk," or "practicing what we preach."

If Christians expect to be taken seriously, at the very least we should make a daily effort to live up to the standards taught in the Bible we claim to believe. Jesus said, *And why call ye me, Lord, Lord, and do not the things which I say?* (Luke 6:46) Christians should live by the founding principles of their own faith. One of those principles is to be a distinct and peculiar people (I Peter 2:9).

An easy way to understand this is by looking at America and what it means to be an American. The founding fathers, and the first few generations of Americans, would likely say the same thing about America today as the skeptic says about Christianity if they could see what we have done to the nation they suffered and died to give us.

For example, according to an August 2014 Census Bureau report,

> 109,631,000 Americans lived in households that received benefits from one or more federally funded "means-tested programs" — also known as welfare — as of the fourth quarter of 2012.[1]

That's approximately one-third of the population that is either directly or indirectly dependent on taxpayer-funded assistance. While living in Europe in the 1760s, Benjamin Franklin wrote,

> in different countries ... the more public provisions were made for the poor, the less they provided for themselves, and of course became poorer. And, on the contrary, the less was done for them, the more they did for themselves, and became richer.[2]

Franklin would have thought that such dependence on government is in direct conflict with the fundamental American principle of independence.

The late Dr. Adrian Rogers said,

> You cannot legislate the poor into freedom by legislating the wealthy out of freedom. What one person receives without working for, another person must work for without receiving. The government cannot give to anybody anything that the government does not first take from somebody else. When half of the people get the idea that they do not have to work because the other half is

going to take care of them, and when the other half gets the idea that it does no good to work because somebody else is going to get what they work for, that my dear friend, is the end of any nation. You cannot multiply wealth by dividing it.[3]

This simply illustrates in just one area how far removed modern America is from the ideal that created it. A very similar thing has happened in Christianity, and the answer for the splintering of Christianity is the same as for what it means to be an American - get back to the original document. Look at the writings of the founders. For Christianity, that is Jesus Christ himself, the apostle Paul, Peter, and other inspired biblical writers. For America, it means getting back to the foundational principles upon which we were established. John Adams, George Washington's vice president, and our 2nd president said,

> Because we have no government, armed with power, capable of contending with human passions, unbridled by morality and religion. Avarice, ambition, revenge and licentiousness would break the strongest cords of our Constitution, as a whale goes through a net. Our Constitution was made only for a moral and religious people. It is wholly inadequate to the government of any other.[4]

One of the primary innovators of our very system of government said this nation cannot exist under our present Constitution without the restraining presence of religion and morality. Argue with that if you like, but it is like arguing with Michelangelo over the meaning of his painting on the ceiling of the Sistine Chapel.

The divergent path of Americanism and Christianity illustrates that the quality and integrity of the original should not be judged by a knockoff version. An "American" who does not believe in freedom of religion, freedom of the press, freedom of speech, the right to property, or the right to keep and bear arms, illustrates by his views that he does not understand basic American principles and therefore cannot legitimately be called an American. All ideas of what it means to be an American are not equal. They must be judged by the founding documents. Where they deviate or contradict, they are Un-American.

The same logic needs to be applied to evaluate Christians. Judge it by the founder's intent, by the original document from which the belief was birthed. If "believers" contradict the original, then despite what they claim their views are not Christian. Where they conform, or at least hold conformity to the original as the ideal to which they aspire, then you have the real thing.

When a skeptic says, **As for the simple question, "Who is a Christian," the only answer, the only fair and logical answer, is that those who say they are Christian are Christian,** (43) it is just as illogical as saying, those who say they are American are Americans, even if they want to impose sharia law. You are an American by virtue of birth or by adoption. That is, you go through the process of becoming an American and embrace uniquely American ideals as outlined in our constitution.

According to the Bible, no one is just born into being a Christian, so you must become one some other way. The Bible explains what that way is, and it isn't just because you say so. You can't invent your own way and call it the real thing any more than you can devise your own way to become an American. To become an American you follow the Constitution of the nation. To become a Christian, you follow the pattern God gives in his book, the Bible. It's as simple as that.

So what is that pattern? The simplest and most concise scripture on the topic is Romans 10:9 *That if thou shalt confess with thy mouth the Lord Jesus, and shalt believe in thine heart that God hath raised him from the dead, thou shalt be saved.* Notice how far removed this is from **those who say they are Christian are Christian.** (43)

Is there any evidence supporting the basics of what it means to be a Christian? Skeptics say no! **There is no hard evidence to rely on, no undeniable proof that transcends the words of men and women.** (43) In fact, there is. The Bible actually claims to transcend the words of men and women when it says, *All scripture is given by inspiration of God...* in II Tim. 3:16a. It is just that a skeptic does not believe it. He wants undeniable proof.

This book is not an attempt to provide undeniable proof that the Bible or Christianity is true. It is an attempt to do what is done in every courtroom in America. The standard that is given to every juror who must hear arguments and render a verdict is, "beyond reasonable doubt." Christianity does have hard evidence that transcends the words of men and women and proves beyond reasonable doubt that Jesus was and still is the Son of God, that while on earth he was who he claimed to be, that he came for the purpose he stated, and that he accomplished that purpose. Believing that, and living a life in conformity to that belief is called Christianity.

SIX

DOES CHRISTIANITY MAKE SOCIETIES BETTER?

I t would be expected that if Christianity is followed, then societies which embrace it should be among the best in the world. After all, Jesus himself said that the reason he came is so those who believe in him will have an abundant life. (John 10:9-10) The skeptic challenges this notion with statistics from the United Nations Human Development Index which appear to prove that Christianity, or any religion for that matter, does not make for a better society. Mississippi is specifically cited as evidence that its **high church attendance does little for the welfare of its babies. The state has the highest infant mortality rate in the country at 10.6 (deaths under one year old, per thousand live births).** (48) **In the United States, least religious Vermont has the forty-second-lowest infant mortality rate at 5.5.** (48)

Why infant mortality is an evidence that Christianity does not make for a better society is curious. Presumably, if a society is Christian, then it will also have low infant mortality rates. Why this should be true is unclear.

Another evidence suggesting religion does not make for a better society is an April, 2012 Wall St. article which names America's three least religious states - Maine, Vermont, and New Hampshire as the least violent. Louisiana, America's 4th most religious state, has the distinction of being the most dangerous with the highest murder and incarceration rates in the country.[1] (48)

Although Christianity does not solely get the blame for such incriminating statistics, skeptics look at them as evidence that the Christian faith does little to solve societies most pressing problems. In an interview with skeptic, Guy Harrison, on Sept. 6, 2012, Phil Zuckerman, professor

41

of sociology at Pitzer College in California offered conflicting reviews. **Extensive sociological research is clear on this front: Christian beliefs do not correlate with positive societal outcomes. ... Is Christianity bad for society? I wouldn't go that far. Is it good for society? Perhaps yes, in some instances. Maybe not in others. But is it necessary? No way?** (47)

Statistics and rankings do not prove that Christianity caused or exacerbates the challenges faced by the most religious states in America, of course. What is clear is that Christianity has not solved its most serious problems, despite repeated assurances from Christians that it can and does. (48) The conclusion is obvious. Religion, including Christianity, does not make for a better society. Statistically, one could even argue that less religion seems to make societies better. This black eye for Christianity's nebulous, or in some cases, perhaps negative impact on the culture is certainly worth examining.

If you are going to evaluate a society for the effect a given religion has upon it, the evaluation is immaterial unless the members of that society, who profess a particular set of guiding principles, actually live according to the dictates of those principles. Skeptics correctly point out that Christianity is a very splintered faith with wildly different practices. However, judging a belief system by those who may not even live according to the fundamental tenets of it can hardly lead to an accurate perspective. The only reasonable way to determine if Christianity makes for a better society is to consider what a truly Christian society would look like, not just a society where some significant percentage claimed Christianity as their religion, but where one-hundred percent actually lived according to Christian principles as outlined in the Bible.

There is no society like that. The Amish don't even qualify, as there are different groups with widely varying lifestyles and beliefs, some of which even contradict fundamental Christian doctrine. So using just a few biblical principles, let's create a uniquely Christian society to see if it would be better than any on earth today. Of course, this little exercise cannot be exhaustive, but here are several of the basic teachings of the Bible that should characterize Christianity.

Imagine a culture that lived by the following five Christian principles as found in the Bible.

1. In the Sermon on the Mount, found in Matthew 5-7, Jesus taught *Therefore all things whatsoever ye would that men should do to you, do ye even so to them: for this is the law and the prophets.* (7:12) The first characteristic

of our "Christian" society is everyone in it would treat others the way they want to be treated. This alone would solve ninety percent of problems confronting any society. Racism, ethnic cleansing, lying, robbery, rape, gang violence, drug peddling, murder, pornography, etc... could not exist when the golden rule was followed by all.

2. *And be ye kind one to another, tenderhearted, forgiving one another, even as God for Christ's sake hath forgiven you.* (Eph. 4:32) The apostle Paul, the primary author of the New Testament, wrote this to Christians in Ephesus. The second characteristic of our Christian society is that everyone would be kind and forgiving. That doesn't sound too bad either. Of course, if the golden rule taught by Jesus were followed there would be little to forgive anyway.

3. This society we are creating would also be characterized by husbands who sacrificially love their wives and wives who respect and submit to their husbands leadership. (Eph. 5:21-25) This is not the husband being authoritarian, but leadership where he loves and cares for his wife even to his own detriment, as the Bible teaches Christ did for us. I expect divorce rates would plummet in this society.

4. In Ephesians 6:1-4, we find another component of a Christian society. Children would obey their parents, honor their father and mother, and parents would not mistreat their children. This sounds like some kind of fantasy these days but is what a truly Christian family would be like according to our own book. Can you imagine the problems that would no longer exist if this were universally true?

5. There are some taboos in a Christian society as well. A few are listed in Romans 1. There would be no: fornication (sex before marriage), covetousness (wanting what belongs to someone else), maliciousness (a desire to injure others), murder, debate (from Greek word meaning intense arguing), deceitfulness, malignity (depravity), gossip, breaking verbal contracts, without natural affection. (This would include abortion and homosexuality.) It is unnatural for a mother to lack affection for her own baby. It is also not the natural course for a man to be physically intimate with another man.

This abbreviated list of negatives is mostly a moot point since they would not exist in a culture that is wholly living by the positive characteristics of items 1 through 4. Nevertheless, these five items provide an accurate, though not entirely complete picture of what a truly Christian society would be like.

Is this a fair snapshot of what the New Testament says about Christian behavior? Does this sound like a good society in which to live? If not, why not? Does it sound like a society free of the problems that plague American culture today? Is it not more accurate when considering whether Christianity would make for a better society, to evaluate a group of people that actually lived by Christian principles, instead of one in which many profess Christian ideals but do not live by them?

It is a logical flaw to imply that Christianity does not make for a better society by citing a state like Louisiana, which is ranked as a very religious state but also has a high percentage of crime. Are the religious people committing those crimes? Are those religious people Christians, or something else? If they claim Christianity, wouldn't such abominable behavior prove they don't really believe what they profess? Are most of the crimes being committed by the percentage of the population who do not profess a religious belief? If so, is it reasonable to infer that a state with a relatively high percentage of professing Christians, which also has high crime, is somehow a failure of Christianity?

There is another way for anyone to determine if he or she really believes that a Christian society is no better than a non-Christian one. Suppose you find yourself lost in the Amazon jungle. You were told the area you are going into is populated with scattered tribes that have had no influence from the outside world, except for one that was converted to Christianity through missionaries. The others follow whatever rituals and rites their tribal customs dictate.

Finding yourself at a fork in the jungle path, you notice that one is marked by a sign with this ⟨ΙΧΘΥΣ⟩ symbol on it. You don't know what the writing means but recognize the fish as a symbol of Christianity. The other path is marked with a symbol that means it leads to a village that has rejected all things Christian. The area is populated with natives practicing everything from Christianity to cannibalism.

Knowing only that one path leads to a village that identifies as Christian and the other leads to a village that rejects Christianity, which one would you choose? A true skeptic who doesn't believe in God, and finds that religious societies, even Christian ones, are no better than any other and perhaps worse, would now have to decide in which village he would be treated the best. His life may depend on this choice.

James Russell Lowell (1819-1891), the great literary genius who was one-time U.S. minister-ambassador to Great Britain, was once at a banquet where the Christian faith (the mission enterprise, in particular) was being attacked by scoffers. He spoke up and said, "I challenge any skeptic to find a ten square mile spot on this planet where they can live their lives in peace and safety and decency, where womanhood is honored, where infancy and old age are revered, where they can educate their children, where the Gospel of Jesus Christ has not gone first to prepare the way. If they find such a place, then I would encourage them to emigrate thither and there proclaim their unbelief."[2]

A critic of religion would have no basis to think the Christian village would be any better than the one that rejected Christianity and remained immersed in its own primitive practices. To a skeptic who finds that Christianity does not make for a better society, the path to the village that rejects Christianity should be more appealing, or at least just as good. However, given such a scenario, I doubt the unbeliever would act consistently with his lack of appreciation for a Christian culture, even a flawed one.

Christianity, if it is practiced according to biblical standards and patterns, would not only be a good society but the very best society in which to live. Look over items 1-4 again. What is it about these very biblically oriented standards that would make for an undesirable society? Even a skeptic would have to agree that the restrictions in item 5 would be intolerable if they were the norm among the majority in any culture. Conversely, the Christian norms of items 1-5 offer no unpleasant consequences, even to an unbeliever.

SEVEN

WHAT IS ATHEISM?

Skeptics often think that Christians don't have a very good understanding of what it means to be an atheist. To clear this up, a skeptic
defines atheism for us. **Atheism is the absence of belief in a god or gods.
That's it; there is nothing more to it.** (49) **To be an atheist is not to hate
a god or gods. How could it be? If one doesn't think any gods are real,
then one can't reject them, or hate them.** (49)

As far as atheism is concerned, **everyone is an atheist. It's just a
matter of degree.** (50) **The Christian and the atheist part ways only
on one specific god and one particular book.** (50) **So when a Christian
asks an atheist why she doesn't believe Jesus is a real god, her answer
might be, Probably for the very same reason you don't believe [insert
preferred god's name here] is a real god.** (50)

There has never been any question that atheists do not believe in God.
However, atheists have great difficulty living consistently according to this
lack of belief. It is similar to the charge against Christians in the chapter
on "Who is A Christian," in which Christianity was indicted for inconsistency and variability within its own professed belief system. Atheists
do the same. That is, they deny the existence of God but cannot consistently live that way.

An atheist likes to use logic and reason as the basis for his thinking,
nothing wrong with that. Without God however, he has no explanation
for the laws of logic as universal, immaterial, invariant, abstract entities.
These laws cannot be conventions of man developed over time because
then there could be different laws of logic for different cultures and they
could change with time and with cultural shifts, but they do not. They
remain the same as they have always been. Therefore, when the atheist

appeals to logic he is appealing to something for which he has no explanation. For those who may not be familiar with the laws of logic a brief summary might be helpful, though you may think them so obvious that they are hardly worth saying. There are three foundational laws of logic.

1. The law of identity says a thing is itself and cannot be anything else.
2. The law of noncontradiction says a statement cannot be true and false at the same time.
3. The law of the excluded middle says a statement may be either true or false, nothing else.

Aristotle first articulated these laws as necessary conditions for logical human thought. But who or what established them? How can they be universal, unchanging, and immaterial, yet be so binding on the very process of rational human thinking and communication?

In the Christian worldview, the laws of logic reflect the thinking of God and of his nature. Of course, we cannot prove it, but he also is immaterial, universal, and invariant. The laws of logic present no problem for the Christian, but the atheist, who insists on their use, cannot justify their existence. To an atheist, they are just another fluke that happened to turn out good for intelligent humans who are the only living things on earth that need or use them.

Why should an atheist reject an argument as illogical when the basis of his rejection are laws for which his worldview has no explanation? If he says the laws of logic are merely human conventions, then we can say they are his conventions, but that does not make them law. Consequently, he has no right to impose his conventions on my thinking, or anyone else's. If they are universal laws however, then all men everywhere must conform their thinking to them.

The laws of logic are just one example that where there are laws, there must be a lawgiver. The atheist, who appeals to such laws, is appealing to something that makes sense if Christianity is true but makes no sense at all if atheism is true. He must borrow from the Christian worldview to make sense of his own. Laws do not self-generate. According to the late Dr. Greg Bahnsen,

> No one is denying that atheists are able to reason and use laws of logic. The point is that if atheism were true, the atheist would not be able to reason or use laws of logic because such things would not be meaningful. The fact

that the atheist is able to reason demonstrates that he is wrong. By using that which makes no sense given his worldview, the atheist is being horribly inconsistent. He is using God's laws of logic while denying the biblical God that makes such laws possible.[1]

The end point is that Christians do not lack an understanding of atheism. We are just unable to comprehend the inconsistency of atheism's lack of belief in God as a universal, immaterial, and invariant entity, while at the same time resorting to a universal, immaterial, and invariant entity like the laws of logic to make atheism's arguments.

Another point which warrants closer consideration is the presumption that Christianity views atheism as arrogant. **Why would any Christian think atheists are smug know-it-alls who lack humility? (53) Ask a typical Christian how the universe began, and he or she is likely to give you a confident answer without hesitation. Ask me how the universe began, however, and I'll tell you a bit about the big bang theory followed by a long list of exciting mysteries and questions not yet answered by science. A Christian 'knows' how life began on earth. I do not. (53)**

What is remarkable here is the acknowledgment of a core belief in how the universe began but beyond that, only mysteries and questions not yet answered by science. Christians believe God created the universe out of nothing in six, literal, twenty-four hours days. Exactly how he did that is a mystery. We call that part of our belief faith. What do skeptics call their commitment to a theory that lacks the same kind of specific "how" details at the most foundational level? This sounds remarkably like faith as well.

Christians and atheists share this common ground. We both have a belief that is characterized by mysteries and questions not yet answered. The word "mystery" occurs 22 times in the King James version of the New Testament. We say it requires faith to believe despite unanswered mysteries. Atheists should be honest enough to say the same.

In Christianity, all roads eventually lead to the beginning — creation. With atheism, all roads lead to its beginning — evolution. So it is not surprising in a chapter on atheism that the *prima facie* evidence for human evolution is brought up. **I am up to speed on Homo erectus and Australopithecus afarensis and many other details of human evolution.** (53) But it is not clear just what is meant by "up to speed." Perhaps atheists are already aware that other leading anthropologists like Milford H. Wolpoff (University of Michigan), William S. Laughlin (U. of Connecticut), Gabriel Ward Lasker (Wayne State U.), Kenneth A. R. Kennedy (Cornell), Jerome

Cybulski (National Museum of Man, Ottawa), and Donald Johanson (Institute of Human Origins) have speculated in print that Homo erectus (supposedly 1.5 million years old) and Homo sapien (modern man) are one and the same.[2]

A. afarensis (a.k.a. Lucy) is exhibit A in the quest to unravel human evolution. But one has to wonder if "up to speed" means only having read a lot of the hype surrounding "Lucy" as an early hominid. Entire books have been written about this fossil as well as numerous articles by paleontologists who question its human connection. But perhaps the most indicting statements come from the discoverer himself, Donald Johanson. While on a fossil hunting trip in Ethiopia's Hadar region, on November 30, 1974, Johanson says,

> At midday, under a murderous sun and in temperatures topping 100 degrees, we reluctantly headed back toward camp. Along the way I glanced over my right shoulder. Light glinted off a bone. I knelt down for a closer look. This time I knew at once I was looking at a hominid elbow. I had to convince Tom, [colleague Tom Gray] whose first reaction was that it was a monkey's. But that wasn't hard to do. Everywhere we looked on the slope around us we saw more bones lying on the surface. Here was the hominid skeleton Owen (colleague Owen Lovejoy) wanted.[3]

The bones Johanson named "Lucy" and an imagined reconstruction
wikimedia commons, free content

There has since been much doubt about "Lucy" being anything other than a knuckle-walking primate, although such paleontological disputations do not have the wow factor of a "missing link" discovery. Consider these telling words from Johanson.

> There is no such thing as a total lack of bias. I have it; everybody has it. The fossil hunter in the field has it... In everybody who is looking for hominids, there is a strong urge to learn more about where the human line started. If you are working back at around three million, as I was, that is very seductive, because you begin to get an idea that that is where Homo did start. You begin straining your eyes to find Homo traits in fossils of that age... Logical, maybe, but also biased. I was trying to jam evidence of dates into a pattern that would support conclusions about fossils which, on closer inspection, the fossils themselves would not sustain.[4]

If Johanson was working "back at around three million" [years] how is it that the "Lucy" fossils he found were so close to the surface and in such pristine condition (Light glinted off a bone) that they could be immediately identified? In the same Hadar region, he recounts finding,

> a bone from the palm of the hand, a second metacarpal, looking more like a fresh twentieth-century bone than one that had been buried for 3 million years."[5]

Bias seems to have dictated how old the fossil was at first sight, despite appearances to the contrary. I don't want to get too hung up on "Lucy." For anyone interested, you can read tons of information pro and con about this "human ancestor" simply by googling, "Was Lucy human?" One excellent paper is, "Lucy Dethroned," ApologeticsPress.org.

This is only a very brief overview of one example offered by atheism of human evolution that at best is speculative. My father used to say, "The greatest friend of truth is time." Christian's, though they may be snickered at for not being "up to speed" on human evolution, can rest assured "Lucy" will eventually follow Nebraska Man, Piltdown Man, Java Man and all the other hoaxes and disappointments in the seemingly endless parade of now discredited exhibits for human evolution.

No one can blame a skeptic for his excitement over each fossil discovery touted as a new piece of the human evolution puzzle. Each one elicits euphoric waves of optimism that hard evidence for humans evolving from apes has finally been discovered. Evidence which appears for a time to support that view certainly would be exciting to the evolutionist, but paleontologists seeking evidence of a missing link between apes and man have a dismal batting average indeed. Even the apparent "home run," of *Australopithecus afarensis* eventually gets called back after numerous reviews by officials.

What is the Christian answer to the question, "What is an Atheist?" An atheist is one who does not believe in God. Therefore, he or she cannot objectively consider any evidence, statements, or suppositions which include reference to, dependence upon, or the possibility of God's existence, whether that be laws of logic, laws of morality, laws of nature, or the evidence of intricate and intelligent design in life itself.

One of the most influential atheists on the planet is Richard Dawkins. During a debate on BBC Radio with Giles Fraser, Former Canon Chancellor of St Paul's Cathedral, Dawkins criticized Christians because so many couldn't identify the first book in the New Testament. "But his claim that this indicated self-identified Christians were 'not really Christian at all' was challenged by Fraser, who said the poll asked 'silly little questions' to trip people up."[6]

Here is the transcript of the exchange that followed.

> **Giles Fraser:** Richard, if I said to you what is the full title of 'The Origin Of Species', I'm sure you could tell me that.

> **Richard Dawkins:** Yes I could

> **Giles Fraser:** Go on then.

> **Richard Dawkins:** On The Origin Of Species. Uh. With, Oh God. On The Origin Of Species. There is a subtitle with respect to the preservation of favoured races in the struggle for life.[7]

I am not sure what "God" Dawkins was invoking in this exchange, but he has acknowledged doing it frequently. Strange for an atheist though isn't it? He missed the part of the subtitle about natural selection. The full title is damningly racist. <u>On the Origin of Species By Means of Natural Selection or the Preservation of Favoured Races in the Struggle for Life</u>. Preservation of favoured races?

More than any other work, Darwin's "Origin of Species" spawned widespread acceptance of man's evolutionary development and the resulting notion that there may be subhumans among us. Ota Benga, a native of the Congo, was an unfortunate victim of Darwin's popular theory.

> Two years after an appearance at the 1904 St. Louis World Fair, he [Ota Benga] was brought to the New York Zoological Park (better known as the Bronx Zoo), where he was locked in a cage with an orangutan before a jeering throng. The display was more than mere entertainment; it was propaganda. The low evolutionary status of a monkey-man was supposed to persuade the masses who were resistant to Darwin and evolutionary theory.[8] At least part of the time, he was kept at the primate house.[9]

Ota Benga at the Bronx zoo, 1906
wikimedia commons, free content

The exhibit raised the ire of clergymen whose objections to zoo officials went unheeded. Almost 50 years of Darwinian indoctrination at the time prompted The New York Times to print the following in an unsigned editorial.

We do not quite understand all the emotion which others are expressing in the matter. Ota Benga, according to our information, is a normal specimen of his race or tribe, with a brain as much developed as are those of its other members. Whether they are held to be illustrations of arrested development, and really closer to the anthropoid apes than the other African savages, or whether they are viewed as the degenerate descendants of ordinary negroes, they are of equal interest to the student of ethnology, and can be studied with profit.

Pygmies, are very low in the human scale, and the suggestion that Benga should be in a school instead of a cage ignores the high probability that school would be a place of torture to him ... The idea that men are all much alike except as they have had or lacked opportunities for getting an education of books is now far out of date.[10]

In March of 1916, years after being freed from being a zoo exhibit, Ota Benga shot himself to death.[11] In this final desperate act, did Benga do the one thing only a human does, perhaps to prove to the world that he was human?

Thankfully, the mentality that made a man into a monkey exhibit is no longer tolerated even by atheists who, nonetheless, still revere the work of Darwin which exacerbated such human exploitation. However, if atheism is true, then evolution's premise that man emerged from the ape must also be true. While modern evolutionary anthropologists should rightfully recoil at tragedies like that of Ota Benga, the belief that made it possible remains. In a 2009 interview with Time magazine, Donald Johanson was asked where humans were headed as a species.

Where we are going as a species is a big question. Human evolution certainly hasn't stopped.[12]

Of course, if evolution hasn't stopped for humans, why should it have stopped for apes or other animals? Ponder the chilling repercussions of that philosophy!

Christians understand what atheism is, but that does not mean we understand atheism as a logically consistent worldview. Atheism relies on laws which it cannot explain and believes in occurrences which it describes as "mysteries not yet answered." It also believes that all life arose by fortunate accident, evolved upward until, once upon a time, something between apes and humans roamed the earth.

I once asked an atheist if he believed that life spontaneously generated. He knew where I was going. "Just because we don't know of any evidence it has occurred, does not mean that it could not have occurred. We don't know everything," he explained. "True," I replied. "But isn't believing in something for which you have no proof what you call faith?" His answer was predictable. "No, I wouldn't say so. It means that we believe that science will find an answer." Apparently, an atheist can define faith as believing in that for which there is no proof, so long as we are talking about religion. When atheism believes, despite the lack of proof, it is not faith, but confidence that the belief will be verified by some future event. Ironically, for all our other differences, Christianity and atheism share the common thread of walking by faith and not by sight (II Cor. 5:7).

EIGHT

WHAT ARE MIRACLES?

According to skeptics, a miracle may be defined as **any special occurrence performed by God, Jesus, the Holy Spirit, saints, or angels that does not conform to the normal workings of the natural world.** (57) Also considered miracles are, **Events that are too meaningful to have occurred by chance, such as when a person unintentionally misses a plane that later crashes.** (57) **The people who see miracles are almost always people who already believed in them, much like ghost believers are far more likely to think they have encountered ghosts than are people who do not believe in them.** (57)

Not surprisingly, skeptics do not believe in miracles, which are clearly outside the box of legitimate, scientifically verifiable occurrences. To illustrate how easily an extraordinary event could be viewed as a miracle, the skeptic relates a powerful, personal story of being lost and sickened while on a safari in Kenya. The incident demonstrates the difference of how an unbeliever and a Christian might view the same apparently miraculous event.

Unsure if he was suffering from malaria, food poisoning, or just the flu, and being miles from a hospital, **I had no choice but to ride it out and hope for the best.** (58) After walking a few yards from his tent to relieve himself in the night, and perhaps dazed from fever, he wandered even farther, finally collapsing in the tall grass. He awakened to the frightening sight of a spear-wielding Massai man standing over him. (58-59)

The skeptic explains how he learned later, from this same Massai native who turned out to be friendly, that lions were very near. **He believed that I had been in serious danger from the lions so he stood guard over me for a few hours.** (59) A skeptic views such an event through the lens of interpretation. **My conclusion about that night comes down to my prior attitude toward miracles. It is expected that unexpected things will happen over the course of a lifetime. There is little doubt, however, that if I were a Christian who believed in angels and miracles, I would have confidently concluded that my Massai encounter was proof that Jesus is real, that he cares about me, and that I had been in the presence of a miraculous guardian angel. (60) It was dramatic, weird, and wonderful, yes, but supernatural? Given the total absence of direct evidence for supernatural intervention, the only reasonable conclusion is that I benefited from a fortunate coincidence. (60)**

I have never had any experience remotely similar. However, if I did, I expect the skeptic's analysis would be correct. I would probably believe that God had sent a benevolent guardian at just the time I needed him most. Events that Christians often consider miracles are not really supernatural in the sense that natural laws were momentarily suspended, but that a beneficial circumstance occurs at precisely the time it is needed. To a Christian, such events are sometimes considered miracles. To a skeptic they are always coincidences. Since the skeptic shared his personal story that would be considered miraculous by a believer's standard, let me share two others that would fall in the miracle category by most anyone's standard.

It was September of 2014. I had spent the summer renovating a cabin on our property for my son, his wife, and their twenty-month-old daughter. Despite the fact there was no gas for the kitchen stove, they had already moved in. I decided to fix that temporarily until we got a commercial propane hook up. Using a small tank from our grill, I connected to the gas line from outside and opened the valve. I went inside through the sliding glass doors in the living room to the small kitchen, pulled the stove from the wall, and opened the shut-off valve.

I was not aware that as I was doing this, propane was pouring into the living room just around the corner. I had been working on a pipe the night before that was going to feed a small heater which was not yet installed. This was the main gas feed. The spur to the kitchen stove came off this main line so most of the gas was coming through the pipe in the living room. That line had a shut off on it too. But while I was changing the configuration of the line the night before, I must have inadvertently opened the valve. In my haste to get the kitchen stove lit, I failed to first check the valve in the living room.

Assuming all was normal, I lit the top burners on the stove to be sure everything worked all right. They did not come on as quickly as I thought they should. However, after a couple minutes they were all lit but not burning as high as normal. "Just a quirk of the stove," I guessed. I turned the burners off and attempted to light the oven, which uses an electric glow bar to ignite the gas once the heat from the glow bar opens the stove's gas valve. After about two minutes, the oven still had not lit. It had now been over five minutes since I turned on the gas from the outside tank. There was no smell of propane in the small cabin. I opened the oven door and saw that the glow bar was indeed bright red. We had bought the stove used. "Must be something wrong with the valve," I thought. The next few paragraphs happened in less than five-seconds.

There was a powerful explosion. The air in front of me instantly turned to fire. I jumped back and could then see directly into the living room. It looked like hell, literally! There was nothing but flames everywhere in front of me. Panicked, and fearing I would be on fire in seconds, I turned to go out the kitchen door just a few feet behind me. It was the only exit not consumed in fire, but it was blocked by the kitchen table!

A lot does go through your mind in a second or two in a life and death situation. The air in front of me was on fire. I truly thought I had only a couple seconds to get out. I feared in the time it would take me to clear the kitchen door I'd be on fire, or perhaps there would be another explosion. The quickest way out was through the living room! There was a water hydrant outside only twenty feet away. If I was on fire, I'd douse myself under the hydrant.

In that instant, probably two or three-seconds after the explosion, I prayed a line that came to me from the movie "Fireproof" when a fireman is trapped in a burning house. "God, get me out of here!" I turned to run through the living room, heading for the patio doors, uncertain how hot the air would be or how much it would burn me before I could get out.

I remembered that I had closed the heavy sliding glass doors behind me when I came in. "The time it takes to slide the door open is going to cost me," I thought. I remember too, wondering how fast you can run through intense heat before you feel pain. But by the time I committed to going through the inferno, it was gone.

The living room was filled with hazy smoke, but no longer on fire. The flash from the exploding gas had lasted only a couple seconds. I didn't need to worry about the sliding door either. It was laying intact on the patio. The force of the explosion had blown it out, frame and all. It landed on a plastic tub which kept the glass from shattering.

Once outside, I closed the valve on the propane tank then came back expecting to see the living room had caught fire, it hadn't. Only a few pieces of paper and some magazines were burning. I tossed them outside, made sure nothing else was on fire, and went up to our house to tell my wife what happened. No one had heard the blast.

On closer inspection, we found that the kitchen window, just a few feet to the right of where I was standing when the explosion occurred had blown out, spraying shards of glass thirty feet onto the neighbor's driveway. I was completely unaware of this when it happened. We also discovered that the flash of heat in the living room blistered the paint on the walls and turned the newly installed carpet into what felt like astroturf. Part of the sock on my left foot was melted to my shoe and the bottom half of my mostly polyester pants had melted. Aside from some singed hair, I was completely unharmed.

I had called 911 to send someone from the fire department to inspect the cabin because at this point I did not know what caused the explosion. That was when we discovered the open valve in the living room. I explained to the fire chief exactly what I was doing. He said, "And where were you when it blew up?" "Right here," I said, pointing to the spot in the kitchen where I was standing. His eyes got big. "And you didn't even get burned, nothing," he asked? I assured him I was perfectly fine.

So how could I walk away from something like this totally unscathed? Was it a miracle? My answer to that question may surprise the skeptic and disappoint the Christian. I do not think my escape was "supernatural." Nor do I believe God somehow made me temporarily fireproof. In fact, I have since learned just how I am able to be here to write about this instead of being badly burned or even killed. But that doesn't necessarily mean I do not think it was miraculous.

Propane is heavier than air. The pipe it was coming through into the living room was elbowed 90° and about six inches off the floor, so the gas remained low to the ground. As the living room filled with gas, it rose higher and higher. But in the kitchen where I was, it oozed around the corner remaining low, which is why I smelled nothing. When it made contact with the glow bar the explosion followed its fuel source up and in front of me, around the corner and erupted in full fury in the gas-filled living room. My sock and pants melted because the ignition point in the kitchen started very low to the ground. Had I gone into the living room a few seconds before the explosion, I might not have been killed instantly, but my skin would have looked like the paint on the wall, or worse.

With a blast powerful enough to blow a 200-pound door off the wall and spew broken glass 30 feet, why wasn't I at least knocked over? I learned from a fireman who heard my story that a flash gas explosion like this creates instant and equal pressure throughout the structure. The pressure blew out the weakest point — the patio doors and the kitchen window, but because the pressure was equal inside the cabin, I felt nothing.

While I am certainly thankful I experienced no pain or injury, there is another part to this which still makes me shiver when I think of it. My son, daughter-in-law, and granddaughter were not home when this happened. They came about a half-hour later.

For me this was a routine, do-it-yourself quick-fix to get them a working stove until we got a proper hookup. I would have had no reason to tell them to leave the cabin had they been home. I would have just done what I did. No one can say for sure what would have happened. Maybe they would have smelled the gas before it blew. But if my granddaughter, who wasn't much more than two-and-a-half feet tall, would have been in the living room... I'd rather not think about it.

So was it a miracle? If I were a skeptic, I would say that I benefited from a fortunate coincidence, so did my son, daughter-in-law, and granddaughter. The fact is, I understand the science of why I didn't get blown up or burned when I was in the epicenter of a fiery explosion. I also realize other people have survived even worse scenarios unscathed. A half-dozen factors came together that prevented me from dying a painful death that day, or living with the knowledge that my one oversight had caused unimaginable pain to my little granddaughter, my son, and daughter-in-law. I just don't have enough faith to chalk it up to "fortunate coincidence."

After we had surveyed the damage and the full scope of how bad it could have been, my wife and I and our children gathered in the yard of the cabin, bowed our heads and thanked God for keeping me and the rest of our family safe. Yes, I do believe God was watching over me, my son, daughter-in-law, and granddaughter. I do not believe we were the benefactors of an impersonal coincidence.

I have shared this experience several times and it always gives me goosebumps, but it pales in comparison to Dan's "miracle" story. I can write this just fine, but I have never told it to anyone without breaking down. You'll understand why.

Dan was 40 years old. Early one morning he woke feeling something was wrong. His wife Kim, who is a nurse, recognized signs of a stroke. They headed for the hospital. Within a couple days he could barely talk. When I went to see him he was in speech therapy. He struggled to speak. "It's we...i...r..d," he stammered. Eventually, he lost the ability to say any words at all except, "No," and "Umm," and something like "Uh...huh." His wife became his voice.

He went to all kinds of specialist's over the next couple years and had multiple neurological exams, MRI's, CAT scans, everything. The condition is called Aphasia. It may have different symptoms, but in Dan's case it was described as a disconnect between the speech center of the brain and the nerves and muscles that enabled him to talk. He was not paralyzed. He simply could not speak the words his mind knew how to say.

My own way of describing this is that when the mind initiates speech, the brain sends a message down the nerve pathway to the vocal chords, but somewhere along the way a bridge is out. The message can't get through. Dan was told that if his speech did not return within two years it probably would never come back. After that much time, the bridge simply can't repair itself. Two years came and went.

He carried a whiteboard with him so he could write what he needed to say when his wife was not with him. All this time he continued his job in web design. Dan had always been a talkative person, able to share deep thoughts and quick wit with equal effectiveness. He described this time as feeling the person he was had been taken over by someone he didn't know.

Dan and his wife are Christians. He had been a leader in his church's ministry to motorcycle gangs. Naturally, they prayed for healing — for years, but it did not come. He said once that while he had not given up, he did give in. If this was the way God wanted him to live, he would try to make the best of it. He was speechless.

Five years after his stroke, Dan and his wife were in church. The worship leader started the congregation singing with one of Dan's favorite songs, "How Great is our God." Dan stood beside his wife mentally wishing he could sing this song. He began mouthing the words, How-Great-is-our -God, and for the first time in five years, heard his own voice!

He described to us later that he had the feeling of a wave coming across him as he tried to sing. Not sure what was happening, but knowing he had sung words, he bolted from the sanctuary. Kim, who had not heard his voice, knew something was wrong and went out after him. She caught up to him in the church foyer. "Dan, what's wrong?" she asked. He looked into her face and spoke words he had not been able to say in five years, "Kim, I love you." They cried together and sang hymns to see if this was for real and going to stick.

At the close of the service, Dan went to the pulpit with his whiteboard. Everyone knew of his disability. Only a couple who were in the foyer with him knew about his speech returning. Why would this man who couldn't talk stand before the congregation as if he had something to say? What he said was not fluid, but it was clear. "This is Dan," he stuttered. "I'm back." He shared briefly what had just happened. "And I don't need this anymore," he said, breaking his whiteboard in half. It was no ordinary church service that Sunday at Glenview Christian Missionary Alliance.

That afternoon at our house, my wife was making dinner when the phone rang. It was Dan's wife, Kim. She was quite emotional. "Are you sitting down?" she asked. I assumed the worst. She explained what had happened. At first, Dan was too overwhelmed to talk, but he eventually took the phone. "Hi Dave, I can talk." I had not heard him speak for five years. I completely fell apart. Dan is my brother.

Dan's doctor said a miracle was the only explanation. His speech pathologist called the event "new territory," because stroke victims with aphasia do not regain the ability to speak after five years. If Dan were a skeptic, calling it "a fortunate coincidence" would be the only thing he could say. Please don't miss that point. It is the only thing a skeptic can say. There is no other possibility. A skeptic could be glad he recovered his speech, but he could not express thankfulness to anyone or anything. His doctors didn't do it. There is no deity who acted on his behalf. He just got lucky!

My own story of surviving the fire and Dan's story of having his speech restored would be considered miracles in anyone's book who believes in God. In my case, there were certain laws of physics that could explain why I wasn't burned, or even injured. Maybe there were other factors that kept my son and his family from getting home a half-hour earlier. There are lots of things we don't know. But chalking it all up to a series of mindless coincidences is very bizarre indeed.

In Dan's case, perhaps there was some unknown physical phenomenon that occurred in his nerve pathway that day which just happened at the instant he tried mouthing the words, "How Great is our God." If so, his doctors who specialize in neuroscience could not explain it, but a skeptic could. It was a coincidence. If you believe such events are just purposeless, random, unlikely occurrences, you are believing in something for which you have no explanation, nor evidence. It is simply an unexpected thing that happened. This is the default position of a skeptic.

A Christian has a broader view and is free to acknowledge that certain scientific principles may come together in a given situation that explains some of the "how" part of what happened, and yet still marvel at the goodness of God to let it happen at precisely the time it is needed. When all the necessary factors come together with precision timing, it renders the "coincidence" explanation more unbelievable than the miraculous.

Consider one of the more outrageous sounding miracles in the Old Testament, the parting of the Red Sea. In this account, the children of Israel had left Egypt where they had been enslaved for 400 years. Bible scholars say their numbers were probably close to a million. Pharaoh, who had given them permission to leave after a series of plagues, changed his mind and pursued them with his army. The Israelites eventually had the Red Sea before them and Pharaoh's army rapidly closing in.

With Moses leading them, God parts the waters of the Red Sea and the Israelites cross safely. Pharaoh's army drowns when they try to follow Israel through and the water returns upon them. Seawater parting so people could walk across on dry ground! Pretty crazy, huh?

In 2004, while vacationing in the Outer Banks of North Carolina, we went on a dolphin siting tour on Pamlico Sound. The guide told us that during Hurricane Isabel winds blew parts of Pamlico sound dry. The wind actually blew the water so far out that people could walk where there had been several feet of water a few hours before. You can see a video of this phenomenon during Hurricane Irene on YouTube. Search for "The Empty Sound."

No, I'm not suggesting that the Israelites crossed the Red Sea during a hurricane. The point is that miraculous events in the Bible often occurred by means of natural phenomenon: earthquakes, wind, hail, fire, and flood, precisely at the time they were needed to accomplish some purpose of God. The fact that there might have been some physical cause which contributed to the unlikely event, where all the necessary factors came together in a sort of "perfect storm," at just the right time, does not diminish its miraculous nature in the least. It is interesting to note that according to the account in Exodus 14:21 "...the Lord caused the sea to go back by a strong east wind all that night, and made the sea dry land, and the waters were divided." This is not exactly the same as what happened in Pamlico Sound but has very similar elements.

Another natural phenomenon occurring at precisely the time it was desperately needed happened during America's war for independence. George Washington's army had suffered defeat at the hands of the British on Long Island. He now had the East River at his back, British warships heading for the East River, and General Howe's army hemming him in on land. Washington's men were trapped and outnumbered more than 6 to 1. To fight or surrender would have meant the end of both Washington's army and freedom for America. For some reason still unknown, with all advantages in his favor, General Howe delayed an attack that would have ended the war.

While Howe delayed, Washington secured every available boat in the area and began floating his army across the river to the safety of Manhattan. A severe storm made the journey across the river treacherous. It seemed even God was against them, but it also discouraged the British navy from coming up the East River.

By just before dawn, most of Washington's army was safely across, except for a few regiments which would soon be exposed to the British army by morning's first light. Major Benjamin Talmage was one of those soldiers still on the island and he recorded what happened in his memoirs.

> As the dawn of the next day approached, those of us who remained in the trenches became very anxious for our own safety, and when the dawn appeared there were several regiments still on duty. At this time a very dense fog began to rise off the river, and it seemed to settle in a peculiar manner over both encampments. I recollect this peculiar providential occurrence perfectly well, and so very dense was the atmosphere that I could scarcely discern a man at six yards distance. ... We tarried until the sun had risen, but the fog remained as dense as ever.[1]

The fog remained until the last of the men left the island. About this and other seemingly providential events, George Washington wrote in his journal on Aug. 20, 1778.

> Undergoing the strangest vicissitudes that perhaps ever attended any one contest since the creation ... the Hand of Providence has been so conspicuous in all this — the course of the war — that he must be worse than an infidel that lacks faith. ... But it will be time enough for me to turn Preacher when my present appointment ceases.[2]

Fog is a natural phenomenon, like wind, rain, hail, and fire. Throughout the Bible, God used these natural events to "miraculously" deliver Israel from her enemies by causing them to occur at the exact time needed and in such a way as to spare Israel, but destroy or confound her enemies. During America's War for Independence, and wars since, many similar instances are recorded.

I don't argue that miracles prove God's existence, whether they are miracles of supernatural origin, like raising someone from the dead, or natural occurrences, like an earthquake or hail that destroys an enemy, or perfectly timed fog. What I believe proves the existence of a supernatural being interjecting himself into the lives of people, or at least argues strongly in favor of it, is that without it, events such as I have described, including the skeptic's Massai tribesman story, have no meaning. In a skeptic's world, there is no purpose behind anything that happens because there is no mind behind it.

When the skeptic denies the reality of miracles, he is denying meaningful existence. I do not say that to be antagonistic. For anything to be meaningful, there must be some purpose behind it, some kind of information or message which is being transmitted from an intelligent mind to an intelligent recipient. Let's illustrate it like this.

Suppose you are getting down to the last bite or two of your morning breakfast of Alpha-Bits. As you look down, you are startled to find the remaining pieces of cereal have formed the words "I LOVE YOU." Only a fool would assign meaning to such an event. Any thinking person would realize there is no intelligence behind the letters forming into a sequence that resembles words. These would not be real words in the sense that they have meaning. They would just be a coincidental arrangement of letters. The cereal is not telling you that it loves you, and no one at Post Cereals™ is trying to get a message to you. If it were ever to happen, and it certainly could, it would only be a coincidence precisely because there is no purpose involved. As miraculous as it might appear to be, it is not, because it has no meaning. No mind is behind it.

When the skeptic tells of the mysterious appearance of a Massai man that watched over his sickened body in the middle of the night protecting him from harm and attributes it to coincidence, he is assigning no more meaning or purpose to that event than breakfast cereal randomly forming the letters, I L-O-V-E Y-O-U. The Massai man himself may have had a purpose in what he was doing, but the skeptics "fortunate coincidence" explanation renders the timing of the man's presence meaningless.

This says nothing about the motives or benevolence of the Massai, but that his being at the right place, at the right time, with no prior knowledge of the skeptic's condition or location, was merely a purposeless, meaningless, random, event. Likewise, if my survival of the gas explosion was just a random sequence of events allowing me to walk away, with no one in my family who ordinarily would have been there being harmed, and without any mind behind the sequencing of those events, they have no more meaning than the breakfast cereal message. If you do not believe in miracles, then events that are precision timed, or that defy medical and scientific explanation, like my brother's speech returning at the moment he tried to sing, "How Great is Our God," share the same level of meaninglessness as that useless, purposeless, and mindless collection of letters in your cereal.

This is also what distinguishes miracles in the Bible from "miracles" of other religions, such as a statue of Mary weeping, or the Hindu god Ganesha drinking milk. Biblical miracles served a distinct purpose. The Red Sea parted so the Israelites could cross over to safety, and to demonstrate to the polytheistic Pharaoh the power of Israel's God. Water came from a rock to satisfy the thirsty Jews. The apostles were given the ability to heal the sick, and even raise the dead, to confirm the truth of their message in the early first century. These miracles served a specific purpose, at a given time, and were performed for an intelligent reason.

Taking the miracles in the Bible at face value, it is easy to see they were not performed as tricks or illusions to get people to worship the performer. The skeptic alludes to this possibility when he says, **Even if such events were accurately reported by people who saw them, we cannot possibly know if they were actually supernatural feats or nothing more than well-executed illusions. It is important to keep in mind the time period during which Jesus was supposed to have lived. It would not have been difficult to amaze and baffle most people back then. For example, any mediocre magician today could easily have his or her way with an Iron Age audience. (65) Imagine if Harry Houdini, David Copperfield, James Randi, or David Blaine were to walk the earth two thousand years ago. Do you think any of them would have any difficulty convincing virtually everyone they performed for that they were sorcerers or maybe even gods? (65)**

What the skeptic misses is that the apostles performed miracles, yet refused to be worshipped as gods. (Acts 10: 25-27 and Acts 14:12) Jesus performed miracles and accepted worship as a result because he is God. I mean, that is what the Bible tells us Jesus himself said. If New Testament miracles were illusions performed by crafty zealots seeking to be worshipped or to bilk the gullible out of money or into servitude, the skeptic needs to explain why they pursued this venture all the way to being crucified upside down (Peter), or beheaded (Paul). Most of the other apostles were cruelly executed as well. Is it rational to think it was all for the sake of perpetuating an illusion?

I seriously doubt that Penn and Teller, or David Copperfield, would maintain their "tricks" were actual miracles rather than illusions in the face of a tortured death. The skeptic argument here that New Testament miracles were possibly just illusions is a mind-bending stretch. To paraphrase Voddie Baucham, "The Bible is a reliable collection of historical documents written by eyewitnesses during the lifetime of other eyewitnesses. It relates supernatural events that took place in fulfillment of specific prophecies demonstrating that their writings are divine in origin." I know that doesn't prove the Bible or the fact of miracles, but once all realities are considered, it is more reasonable than believing that biblical miracles were illusions and their perpetrators martyrs for a cause they had faked.

To a skeptic anything can be explained as a fortunate coincidence, even humans. In the chapter on, "What is an Atheist," the skeptic refers to himself as **a fortunate collection of atoms.** (54) Please understand this kind of thinking puts a human being with a brilliant, highly educated mind into the same category as an unlikely collection of letters in his morning cereal. If it were true, the universe, and even human beings would have no purpose because there is no intelligence that produced the information which guides all the life we observe. Life itself, the greatest miracle of all, would have no meaning. To truly believe that requires an irrational act of faith of miraculous proportions.

NINE

DOES THE COMPLEXITY OF LIFE REVEAL AN INTELLIGENT DESIGNER?

E volution is to atheism what creationism is to Christianity. Without each of these foundations, the respective belief systems fall apart, leaving the other as the only alternative. Atheism must have evolution. Christianity must have Genesis 1 creation.

A key argument for special creation is intelligent design and the concept of irreducible complexity. Consequently, it is a prime target for the evolutionist. **No one, Christian or non-Christian, should allow themselves to be hoodwinked by intelligent design's central concept of "irreducible complexity."** (71) **The claim of irreducible complexity says there comes a point in our current scientific analysis of life when no more explanations are available.** (71) However, this significantly minimizes the point of intelligent design arguments regarding irreducible complexity.

Irreducible complexity is a term used to describe biologically complex systems which require all of their individual component parts to be in place at the same time in order for the organism which they compose to function. In other words, it is impossible to reduce the complexity of these systems without loss of function. Intelligent design says such organisms and biological systems could not gradually evolve the parts over time because they are all simultaneously necessary in their fully functioning form.

If evolution can be shown to be impossible at any point in the development of life, with all of its complex organisms and systems, it cannot be the explanation for life's origin. With the absence of any data documenting how it occurred in the simplest of organisms, it cannot be a belief rooted in scientific fact. Therefore, it would be a position of faith, just like creationism. The evolutionist must believe in something for which there is no scientific proof. Skeptics don't like to use the term "faith," but in the absence of answers and hard data, they still believe in evolution. **Sometimes we just have to accept that there are no available answers, at least not yet.** (68)

The problem is clear. Naturalistic science will not stop until it finds a materialistic explanation for everything. This is to be expected but is also futile if what is sought simply isn't there. So far, that has been the case in attempts to answer exactly how irreducibly complex structures formed. Hypotheses abound and concepts flourish, but since the structures they study do not cooperate by continuing to do what evolution says they must have done in the past to become what they are now, the best science can do is propose imagined possibilities.

Creationists and intelligent design advocates look at irreducibly complex structures as they exist now. Seeing no intermediate forms, and no logical pathway for the information necessary to produce new biological structures to self-generate, we conclude based upon observation that these structures exist in the same form they have always been. It is not that creation scientists think no further explanation is available, but the one that is scientifically observable and consistent with physical realities is adequate. That is, wherever we see intricate design there is always a designer.

The Bible says God created everything in six days, but we don't know the details of just how he did that. We can't prove it empirically with observable, repeatable testing. Ultimately, it is a position of faith, but as a college professor of mine liked to say, it is a reasonable faith that is consistent with scientific observation of natural realities.

Likewise, the skeptic says he knows that evolution is responsible for the development of life but cannot explain how it produced a structure like the bacterial flagellum, a favorite example of irreducible complexity. It is microscopic, requiring 50,000X magnification to observe, yet has numerous moving and interconnected parts all of which are simultaneously necessary for its function. Intelligent design argues that gradual change, such as is proposed by evolutionary theory, cannot explain the development of a structure that requires multiple components to be present simultaneously for it to be viable. If only one part is missing or incomplete in its development, the organism cannot operate. Under the doctrine of natural selection, such a useless organism would be eliminated.

In Origin of Species, Charles Darwin went so far as to say,

> If it could be demonstrated that any complex organ existed, which could not possibly have been formed by numerous, successive, slight modifications, my theory would absolutely break down. But I can find out no such case. No doubt many organs exist of which we do not know the transitional grades...[1]

There are innumerable examples of such organs, organisms, and systems which illustrate irreducible complexity and could not have been known in 1859, prior to the invention of electron microscopy in 1931, all of which fulfill Darwin's own criteria for the demise of his theory. It is interesting to consider that if Darwin had been born 100 years later, with the ability to see what we can see at the microscopic level, evolution would likely have no founding father.

The skeptic circumvents the problem by understating irreducible complexity, then wrongly presuming Christians use it as evidence for God. **This is the 'leaf argument' all over again, only this time believers are saying, Look at this cell. It's so complex and mysterious, but it works and it had to come from somewhere, right? What more evidence for God do you need? Just as it was with the leaf challenge, our current ignorance about every detail associated with the workings and origins of a cell do not prove the existence or involvement of a god.** (71)

Notice how the problem evolution faces here is minimized. This is not a matter of "every detail" of the workings of a cell. Science has learned how it works. It concerns how such a basic life form as bacteria could gradually evolve multiple interworking and interdependent components which must all exist instantly for the organism to function, hardly an obscure detail in the evolutionary process. It is foundational. Further, the creationist does not have to argue that the lack of evolutionary-based evidence for something as intricate as the bacterial flagellum is evidence of God. We only insist that belief in a process which is as yet unobserved and undocumented relegates evolution of complex organisms to the arena of faith and not science.

Just as creationists have no explanation for the particulars of "how" God created everything from nothing, science offers no explanation for "how" evolution, through a process of gradual change, produced intricately interconnected systems within organisms, much less the complexity within higher living organisms. To insist that it has, despite what skeptics refer to as **a big, fat blank in our scientific knowledge,** (68) is to believe in something for which no scientific documentation exists.

The origin of information at the microscopic level throughout all living organisms is one of those "big fat blanks." The deeper science probes into the complexity of life the more complex the problem of explaining how these systems could gradually evolve becomes. How can gradual evolutionary changes produce mechanisms that are self-generating, self-sustaining, and self-replicating? This could be compared to a computer not only coming into existence by random processes but also creating the software to run itself, as well as decoding that software and performing the programmed functions.

The "big fat blank" is because in every other occurrence of complex information systems which man has been able to examine, they are designed, not self-generating. For those who would like to read more deeply on the subject, Steve Laufmann wrote an insightful article titled, "Evolution's Grand Challenge." It is too lengthy to include here but may be viewed at https://evolutionnews.org/2015/07/evolutions_gran/.

Christians are not demanding documentation of the evolution of complex, information-saturated systems in the most basic of living organisms. We don't believe such details are forthcoming. We would propose the reasonable expectation that before evolution is offered up to school children as a fact of science, and before it is presented as an indisputable biological reality in natural museums all over the world, and before every secular institution of higher learning, and even some "Christian" ones, spoon feeds it to students, scientists either offer some rudimentary, scientifically obtained data for how random, undirected, and purposeless processes account for the production of complex, life-sustaining, biological information systems, or else acknowledge that belief in the chance development of this information, and the life-processes they guide, are really more like religious beliefs than they are scientific facts.

Instead, as quickly as intelligent design arguments are presented, they face a barrage of rebuttals. One effort to explain why irreducible complexity is not the problem for evolution that creationists think is entitled, "Irreducible Complexity Demystified," by Pete Dunkelberg.[2] Here is the summary of four possible explanations for the evolution of irreducibly complex (IC) structures. My observations are in italics.

1. Previously using more parts than necessary for the function.

This says that parts were lost to produce the function. Of course, this just begs the question of where the "lost parts" came from and why they would have evolved if they were of no use to the organism. And what would have been the function of the organism during the tens of thousands, or millions of years of the "losing" process? This "possibility" raises more questions than it answers.

2. The parts themselves evolve.

This is just kicking the can down the road. If the parts evolved, they still had to evolve simultaneously and assemble themselves perfectly. It does not address the question. It merely restates the problem.

3. Deployment of parts (gene regulation) evolves.

The deployment is described thus. "When a protein is deployed out of its usual context, it may be co-opted for a different function." *Notice "may be." This is blind speculation. It also presumes mutation, which is generally harmful to an organism. Deployment also implies intent, which requires instructions, arising from information, requiring intelligence.*

4. New parts are created (gene duplication) and may then evolve.

"Created?" Where did the information for gene duplication arise? More begging the question. Notice again the use of speculation, "may then evolve". In short, there are scientific-sounding guesses like these, but they are not provable and provide nothing beyond speculative verbiage and a determined effort to explain that which science has never observed.

Ken Miller, of Brown University, wrote an exhaustive paper entitled, "The Flagellum Unspun — The Collapse of Irreducible Complexity." He presents evidence of other bacteria, specifically the Type Three Secretory System (TTSS), which looks vaguely similar to the bacterial flagellum but with an entirely different function. He contends the TTSS and bacterial flagellum demonstrate a progression consistent with evolutionary development and therefore demolishes the notion that irreducible complexity is an evidence of intelligent design.

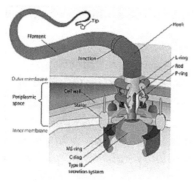

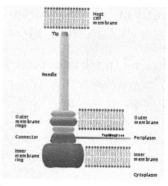

Bacterial Flagellum
commons.wikimedia.org

Type Three Secretory System
en.wikipedia.org

If we are able to search and find an example of a machine with fewer protein parts, contained within the flagellum, that serves a purpose distinct from motility, the claim of irreducible complexity is refuted.[3]

I'm not a molecular biologist, but anyone can read Miller's paper, examine drawings of the bacterial flagellum and the TTSS, and observe that they are two distinctly different structures with very different functions. The flagellum is used for locomotion. The TTSS is used to inject (secrete) toxin. Both have interdependent parts which are simultaneously necessary for function. In other words, they both exhibit the characteristics of irreducible complexity. Nevertheless, Miller reasons,

If the flagellum is indeed irreducibly complex, then removing just one part, let alone 10 or 15, should render what remains "by definition nonfunctional." Yet the TTSS is indeed fully-functional, even though it is missing most of the parts of the flagellum. The TTSS may be bad news for us, but for the bacteria that possess it, it is a truly valuable biochemical machine.

The existence of the TTSS in a wide variety of bacteria demonstrates that a small portion of the "irreducibly complex" flagellum can indeed carry out an important biological function. Since such a function is clearly favored by natural selection, the contention that the flagellum must be fully-assembled before any of its component parts can be useful is obviously incorrect. What this means is that the argument for intelligent design of the flagellum has failed.[4]

But this ignores the point. The bacterial flagellum uses all its interdependent components for locomotion. If any of those parts are missing, no locomotion is possible and the organism cannot function. The TTSS uses all its component parts, some of which are the same proteins found in the flagellum, for injecting toxin. Without those specific components being simultaneously available, it cannot function. To suggest that this variation of complexity within two somewhat similar looking but functionally different structures implies evolutionary adaptation because they share some common proteins, is like saying that an army tank and a bulldozer came off the same assembly line. Also, no documentation of the leap from one to the other is offered beyond imagined models which only predict possibility.

In addition, the fact that the flagellum and the TTSS share some common characteristics could just as legitimately point to a common designer. As pointed out in chapter one, the unique traits of a designer are often seen in very different examples of their work. Norman Rockwell paintings span the nostalgic diversity of Americana, yet share very common attributes. Variation in use of the same component for different applications is nothing unexpected. A screwdriver can turn a screw, open a paint can, pry open a latch, scrape paint, and scratch your back. But someone still invented it.

Miller further elaborates by using another favorite illustration of intelligent design proponents. The common mousetrap is an example of a simple, irreducibly complex machine. It has 5 parts which must all be present in order for the device to function efficiently. If one part is missing, the trap will not work.

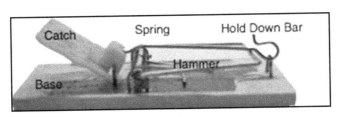

photo by the author

Miller has delighted audiences with his refutation of this as an example of irreducible complexity by removing the catch and the hold-down bar from a mousetrap, leaving only the platform, spring and hammer. He then opens the hammer slightly and clips it onto his tie to illustrate that, although the mousetrap is no longer good for catching mice, it makes a useful tie clasp.[5]

Creationists are mystified at how Miller gets away with such antics. It seems to completely escape him and his audiences that his "mousetrap tie clasp" illustrates the very thing he is attempting to refute. The mousetrap became a tie clasp because someone with intelligence removed some parts to adapt it for another specific pre-defined use. Not to be missed is the fact that even if its new use could have "evolved," it is substantially less functional than it was with all its component parts. In other words, it illustrates regression, not progression in function.

Skeptics say that creationists are obligated to present scientific evidence for their belief. **Intelligent design advocates ought to be arguing for acceptance in the places where science ideas win acceptance. But they don't. If intelligent design is real science, then the real scientific process will confirm it.** (70) But a skeptic cannot have it both ways. He cannot acknowledge **a big, fat blank in our scientific knowledge,** (68) plead for more time to unravel mysteries, all while affirming the fundamental "fact" of evolution. Science has so far failed to produce an observable and repeatable explanation for the evolution of the most basic structures of life on the planet. It is unreasonable to expect Christians to present a documented scientific process that confirms creation while being unable to present the same to confirm the evolution of irreducibly complex living structures.

Nevertheless, a peer-reviewed paper, "Information and Entropy — Top-Down or Bottom-Up Development in Living Systems?," by University of Leeds professor, Andy McIntosh, in the *International Journal of Design & Nature and Ecodynamics*, makes the scientific case for intelligent design. He writes, "The ultimate question in origins must be: Can information increase in a purely materialistic or naturalistic way?"[6] The 30-page research paper concludes:

> Of course, the implication of this paper is that it supports the so-called intelligent design thesis – that an intelligent designer is needed to put the information into the biological system. Even though many modern scientists find this conclusion unacceptable for philosophical reasons, it is, nevertheless, a logical outcome of the thermodynamic arguments as presented in this paper.[7]

Additionally, when skeptics criticize intelligent design advocates for not seeking acceptance for their ideas where scientific ideas win acceptance, primarily peer-reviewed scientific journals, he is overlooking the fact that intelligent design has historically not been accepted in scientific journals on philosophically biased grounds. The above-mentioned journal is a rare exception. Even then, McIntosh's paper was prefaced with the following disclaimer:

> Editor's Note: This paper presents a different paradigm than the traditional view. It is, in the view of the Journal, an exploratory paper that does not give a complete justification for the alternative view. The reader should not assume that the Journal or the reviewers agree with the conclusions of the paper. It is a valuable contribution that challenges the conventional vision that systems can design and organise [sic] themselves. The Journal hopes that the paper will promote the exchange of ideas in this important topic.[8]

Richard Sternberg, who has two PhDs in evolutionary biology and is not a creationist, was fired as editor of a Smithsonian science journal for publishing an article by Cambridge educated scientist, Stephen Meyer, that defended intelligent design. At the time, Sternberg was a Smithsonian research associate. An investigation by the Washington Post revealed that Sternberg was dismissed as a result of a coordinated campaign by the National Center for Science Education, a lobbying group that worked to keep criticism of evolution out of public schools.[9]

> In other words, the article Sternberg published was not attacked because of its arguments were poor [sic], but because it had already been decided by these elites that no questioning of naturalistic evolution was to be allowed.[10]

Skeptics who maintain that evolution is the means by which all of life has developed, despite the fact that it cannot offer a scientifically provable process for how a basic, yet highly complex living structure made of multiple interdependent parts could have gradually evolved, is like a creationist insisting that God created everything from nothing, without offering the first scientific documentation as to how he did it. But wait! That is exactly what creationists do. At the most foundational level, the specifics of "how" God created everything are not provided, and Christians have no answer other than he did it *ex nihilo*, out of nothing.

Evolutionists do not accept such an unscientific explanation but find themselves in the very same predicament, except they refuse to invoke faith as an element of their belief. I don't mean faith that science will find an answer, that is zealously acknowledged, but faith that believes in something for which there is no naturalistic proof. The unbeliever appeals for more time and research, but until concrete, repeatable, and observable evidence is discovered, as the scientific method requires, the unbeliever still "believes."

Apparently, skeptics are allowed to plead ignorance to this "how" question, while appealing to a future hope that science will discover the answer, without acknowledging that belief without proof is really faith. With such paradoxical reasoning skeptics make admissions that literally define the meaning of faith, all the while refusing to invoke terminology that is uniquely religious in nature.

Hebrews 11:1 says, *"Now faith is the substance of things hoped for, the evidence of things not seen."* That is a perfectly accurate description of belief in both creation and evolution as they relate to the process by which information-saturated, complex organisms came into existence. Both can point to a belief. Neither can produce the scientific evidence proving that belief because they lack the observable "how" details. Thus, they are both rooted in faith.

Let's expand Heb. 11:1 to illustrate how perfectly it defines the skeptic position. *"Now faith is the substance of things hoped for* (the hope that science will find an answer), *the evidence of things not seen* (the unshakable belief in that for which no scientific process has been observed). Notice how scripture refers to *the evidence of things not seen,* and the skeptic refers to **what science has produced with its evidence-based <u>ideas</u> about life's origin and evolution,** [emphasis mine] (69) which of course, have never been seen because no one was around when it is supposed to have occurred. When carefully examined the skeptic position literally animates the biblical definition of faith!

Is it reasonable then to presume that the complexity of living organisms and the information systems necessary for them to function originate from intelligence? Apparently. If investigators involved in SETI (Search for Extraterrestrial Intelligence) were to discover some ordered, complex, and most of all, useful information coming from somewhere in outer space, scientists would be scrambling like mad to find out where it was coming from, and who, or what was sending it.

Information, no matter how simple or complex, that is orderly, useful, and purposeful would be exactly what they are looking for — evidence of intelligence in the cosmos! The casual observer sees that evidence all around us in the natural world. The deeper we probe, the more microscopically we examine the tiniest particle of life, the more astounding and complex the information becomes. And yes, it has been sent by someone. Information doesn't self-generate, does it? Romans 1:19-20 says as much. *Because that which may be known of God is manifest in them; for God hath shewed it unto them. For the invisible things* [information] *of him from the creation of the world are clearly seen, being understood by the things that are made, even his eternal power and Godhead; so that they are without excuse.*

It should be acknowledged by both the Christian and the skeptic that arguments are always two-sided and both sides are espoused by men and women who are highly educated and have excelled in their field. There are volumes of articles in science journals and websites, as well as dozens of videos on YouTube, which appear to destroy intelligent design arguments along with irreducible complexity as its chief model. Likewise, there are many rebuttals to these arguments by creationists and intelligent design advocates which give perfectly valid, logical, and scientific answers to evolutionist's objections.

There is an obvious bottom line to this discussion. It is the word "believe." Evolutionists "believe" all things we now see came into existence by a series of chance, random processes, uninitiated and undirected by a purposeful intelligence. There is no observed occurrence of this happening, just a belief that it did happen. Creationists "believe" just the opposite, that God created the universe, information, and life itself, with design and intent. There is also no observed occurrence of this happening.

In the end, the individual must examine the rhetoric from both sides for objectivity, scientific validity, conformance to reality, and common sense. There is a lot of debate that degenerates into name-calling and joke-making which serves no purpose and should win no converts. But truth always sides with reality. Information systems and complexity in design of physical structures has never been observed to occur without intelligent input. That's reality!

TEN

HAVE YOU READ THE BIBLE?

Of all the questions skeptics could ask of Christians, this one is both the easiest and the hardest to answer. It is easy because the answer is painfully obvious, hard because it is not the answer I want to give. The skeptic contends that few Christians have ever read the Bible from cover to cover. I am afraid that is true. You don't need research or polls to find this out, just ask any professing Christian.

To be fair though, I think that many Christians have read the Bible, or at least most of it, just not from beginning to end. Many Bible studies go through a book at a time. Preachers preach through a book and many of the faithful read ahead. I do agree however, that to really understand the Bible you need to read it through. Even then, there are parts that are difficult to understand and correlate to each other unless a good teacher can provide explanation and commentary.

What I found particularly disturbing was this quote from the Barna Group, an evangelical Christian polling firm based in Ventura, CA. **American Christians are biblically illiterate. Although most of them contend that the Bible contains truth and is worth knowing, and most of them argue that they know all of the relevant truths and principles, our research shows otherwise. And the trend line is frightening: the younger a person is, the less they understand about their Christian faith. By and large, people parrot what their parents taught them.** (74-75) Incidentally, most Christians do not contend that the Bible "contains" truth, but that it is truth. Nevertheless, the skeptic point that many Christians are biblically illiterate is well taken.

From the book, "Religious Illiteracy: What Every American Needs To Know - and Doesn't," by Stephen Prothero, a professor at Boston University's Religion Department, come these remarkable citations:

1. **Only half of American adults can name at least one of the four gospels (Matthew, Mark, Luke and John).** (76)
2. **A majority of Americans can't identify the first book of the Bible (Genesis).**[1] (76)

Of course, this really says more about Americans in general than it does about Christians, but the statistics are deplorable nonetheless. In a nation that was established on many principles found in the Bible, most Americans, and too many Christians, know little of what this book is all about.

In the last few years of my ministry as a pastor, I initiated a study entitled, "Understanding the Bible." It was a basic overview of each book of the Bible, its primary contents, message, and characters, and where it fits in the timeline of events recorded in the Bible as well as the rest of world history. What was most surprising to me as I prepared this three-year study was how it illuminated and clarified the Bible for me.

I was raised in a preacher's home, grew up in Sunday school and church, attended private Christian schools, and a Christian University. Somehow, despite this saturation of biblical exposure, and knowing the Bible's primary theme, I had missed the continuity of its history and the correlation of each book to the others. I knew the trees pretty well but didn't know the forest.

When we finished, I could say that I now understood a vast amount more after three years of Sunday morning teaching than I had gotten in all the previous fifty-five years I had been attending church, including fifteen years of pastoring as well as many more years of preaching. Others involved in the study said the same.

In 2017, I challenged a youth Bible study group I was leading to read the entire Bible through in 90 days. About a dozen young people, age 11-16, and several adults, including me, took the challenge. Three months later, we had accomplished what many Christians never do in their lifetime. As helpful as this was however, the greater part of my understanding of the Bible came through the structured study I have described.

The difficulty many people have with the Bible is not because they have not read it all the way through, or because they do not understand it. Most of the Bible is not difficult to understand when taken as a complete story. Probably most Christians read the Bible in piecemeal fashion. Favorite books or passages get emphasized while lesser known books are almost completely unknown. This can leave the most devout believer with an impressive amount of Bible knowledge, but totally confused about how it all fits together.

I would not deny there are parts of the Bible that are perplexing and even disturbing, demanding scholarly, objective analysis. One of the mistakes skeptics often make is to latch onto anything in the Bible that seems particularly egregious and run with it, without checking first if their understanding of the passage is accurate, and if the biblical and historical context might clarify what appears on the surface to be objectionable. Confirmation bias is a powerfully persuading tool that allows both skeptic and Christian to embrace whatever interpretation suits their preconceived mindset.

Skeptics seem well aware of this and often reference matters in the Bible that some Christians don't know are there or don't take the time to investigate. This includes things like: the murder of babies, God approved kidnapping and rape of female virgins, the cooking, and eating of dung, execution of homosexuals, etc... To such charges the Christians respond, **No way. Impossible,** the skeptic says, **until I show it to them.** (74)

To the skeptic's credit, he acknowledges, **There may be reasonable arguments to be made for many of these excerpts regarding context or interpretation, but the fact remains that they are there and Christians should not be oblivious to them.** (74) But as any journalist could tell you, the headline is what gets the attention. The more provocative and shocking it is, the more easily people who are already biased can be persuaded merely by its "shock factor."

A few years ago our local paper ran a story with a headline that read, "Local dog breeder gassed 93 dogs." Far down in the detailed, graphic description of how this was done it was noted that the dogs had a disease considered incurable by many veterinarians. The breeder said, "he had been told by a veterinarian in a western state that there was a medication that could suppress the disease, though USDA inspectors overseeing his farm would not allow him to try treating the diseased dogs with that product."[2] Faced with almost 100 unsaleable dogs having an incurable disease, and a crippling cost to have them professionally euthanized, the man took matters into his own hands.

The point of this little sidebar is not to condone such action, but to illustrate how a shocking headline can carry the day and sway readers to form an opinion without caring about all the facts. While no one defended the breeder's conduct, those who learned a little more of the details through personal contact, beyond what was reported in the media, could maintain a more balanced perspective. Others ran with the sensationalized headline to the point of calling the man a murderer and demanding his prosecution. The story received national attention and spawned local outrage.

This is very similar to skeptic headlines that say, "God approves of rape in the Bible," or "The Bible calls for execution of homosexuals." The fact that such salacious statements are inaccurate and have been proven so by Bible teachers and scholars does nothing to limit their usefulness to those who want to implicate Christianity and the Bible in some negative way. The nineteenth-century English preacher Charles Spurgeon said, "A lie can travel half way around the world, while the truth is putting on its shoes." The truth is not always what is most easily apparent, which is why we have the American principle of being innocent until proven guilty. This would be wisely applied to critics of the Bible as well.

Additionally, skeptics and Christians should be aware that not all versions of the Bible are created equal. There has been an explosion of translations and paraphrases the past thirty years and many of them provide a modern interpretation that is inconsistent with the literal meaning of the original language. I prefer the time-tested King James version over other versions and translations. Some can serve a useful purpose for clarification, but I have found that a little study into some of the KJV's archaic language often results in greater clarity than another version's alternate word choices.

Mark Twain's famous quote sums up in one statement both the animosity and the ambiguity skeptic arguments demonstrate toward the Bible. "It ain't those parts of the Bible that I can't understand that bother me, it is the parts that I do understand." Perhaps he was referring to passages that skeptics like to cite where God instructs the Israelites to kill men, women, and children in their conquest of the promised land. That should bother anyone, but should also call for intense inspection of how a God who claims to be loving and forgiving could issue such a proclamation. The chapter on "Why is God so Violent?" addresses this question.

Maybe Twain was bothered by passages that demand repentance of sin and an eternal destination of separation from God in hell for those who reject his offer of forgiveness through Jesus Christ. Men abhor God's judgment against sin, whether it be the sexual perversion and human sacrifice of the ancient Canaanites, or the modern pornographer who profits without conscience from the demoralization of men and women, or the legalized wholesale slaughter of innocent developing human beings in the womb. Humans don't like accountability.

Modern "Christian" America is awash in the very same kinds of perversions and slaughters as the ancient world. I have to wonder how some unbelievers can demand and defend the right to kill unborn children, even at birth, and at the same time charge God with cruelty for commanding the murder of babies. Natural law, one of the guiding principles of America's founding fathers, as well as a full understanding of the nature of God, advocate against both.

When the skeptic says that Christians should not be oblivious to the difficult passages in the Bible he is quite right. But no one should be swayed by superficial arguments that broadside the Bible while neglecting the hard work of objective scholarship. The internet is saturated with answers to supposed biblical contradictions, alleged inconsistencies, and purported divine atrocities, but the charges persist. At the end of the day, all that can be done is to offer reasoned and rational responses. I hope this book is a constructive part of that effort and will serve as a catalyst for more Christians to read and understand their own book.

ELEVEN

WHY DO SOME CHRISTIANS DO BAD THINGS IN THE SIGHT OF JESUS?

The skeptic gives Christians too much credit. It is not just some Christians who do bad things in the sight of Jesus; it is all Christians. When Paul wrote to the Romans, *For all have sinned and come short of the glory of God,* (3:23) he was not just talking about unbelievers. Our pastor is fond of saying, "All means all and that's all all means." So to start with, all Christians do bad things knowing that Jesus is watching.

The Bible teaches that Jesus is God and is omniscient (all-knowing). He is also omnipresent (present everywhere), so when Christians sin, or anyone for that matter, Jesus is watching. Psalms 139 makes this doctrine clear.

> *O Lord, thou hast searched me, and known me. Thou knowest my downsitting and mine uprising, thou understandest my thought afar off. Thou compassest my path and my lying down, and art acquainted with all my ways. For there is not a word in my tongue, but, lo, O Lord, thou knowest it altogether. Thou hast beset me behind and before, and laid thine hand upon me. Such knowledge is too wonderful for me; it is high, I cannot attain unto it. Whither shall I go from thy spirit? or whither shall I flee from thy presence? If I ascend up into heaven, thou art there: if I make my bed in hell, behold, thou art there.*

But why is it that Christians still do wrong things if we really believe Jesus is with us and watching all the time? In order to understand the Christian response, and to put it in proper context, we have to consider a broader question first. Why does anyone, Christian or not, do things that are wrong when they know someone is watching? In the age of security cameras, cell phones, body cams, and street surveillance, why do people still commit crimes, or do stupid things, knowing they are likely on camera?

My daughter was working at a convenience store which had security cameras in plain view, including on the area behind the counter. Nonetheless, an assistant manager stole money from the cash register with a camera pointing right at her which she knew was there! She was promptly fired.

Most large stores have cameras recording every square inch of their merchandise to deter shoplifters. Yet, shoplifting remains an enormous and expensive problem. People steal while the cameras record pathetic attempts to conceal the crime. If it weren't so serious, it would be funny.

I hear first hand stories from personnel in law enforcement, street cops to corrections officers, who see every form of bad human behavior imaginable from people who know they are being recorded. The self-incriminating nature of this is staggering. Yet it happens every day all across the country.

Skeptics ask, **Are misbehaving Christians so impulsive that they just can't stop themselves — even though they know God is present and staring right at them?** (79) We might also ask if people who commit crimes, or just publicly do stupid things, are so impulsive they just can't help it, even though they know they are being watched and possibly recorded? Clearly humans, regardless of religious affiliation or none at all, impulsively do bad things in the sight of someone who could pass judgment on them.

And it is not just the criminal element that suffers from this self-incriminating behavior. Every year we hear of some new scandal involving prominent political figures. Some have even self-documented their own disgraceful and outrageous behavior! The most public of public people still do stupid, career-ending, and reputation-destroying things, despite the fact they are constantly being watched, monitored, followed, photographed, and examined for any inconsistency, infraction, or misdeed. Whether that is altogether fair is not relevant, it is a reality and they know it. But that does not produce good behavior from all politicians who know they live in a fishbowl.

Tabloids that line supermarket checkouts regularly feature celebrities caught in the act of lewd, embarrassing, or shameful conduct. Can they just not help themselves even though they know omnipresent paparazzi lurk behind every building and bush? Why is it that such public figures as movie stars are mean, thoughtless, indecent, or immoral when they know their behavior will be public knowledge in the next issue of, Stupid Things Celebrities Do For All The World To See, magazine?

The answer to these questions is the same for the bad behaving unbeliever as for the misbehaving Christian. All of us have a nature that gravitates to doing wrong things. Observing humans makes this obvious. You don't have to teach a child to lie or be selfish; it comes naturally. People don't need incentives persuading them to cuss at the person who just pulled out in front of them. Realities like this demonstrate the practical truth of the Bible. Romans 5:12 explains, *Wherefore, as by one man sin entered into the world, and death by sin; and so death passed upon all men, for that all have sinned.* Ecclesiastes 7:20 says, *For there is not a just man upon earth, that doeth good, and sinneth not.*

So why do Christians do bad things in the sight of Jesus? For the same reason anyone does bad things when others can see. It just comes natural. Undoubtedly, there are other factors too, like momentarily forgetting you are being watched, or just "heat of the moment" reactions when heightened emotions produce temporary amnesia regarding that security camera or the omnipresent eyes of Jesus. The Bible and Christianity call this the sin nature. It is impulsive and difficult to suppress. Scripture addresses this Christian dysfunction using one of the greatest examples of a Christ follower in history.

At least thirteen of the twenty-seven books in the New Testament were written by the apostle Paul. Eight of those were written to churches he established on his journeys spreading Christianity throughout Asia Minor. If you have any knowledge at all of Christianity's beginning, Paul would have to rank as a top contender for the supreme example of a Christian.

According to the Bible, he was once a persecutor of Christians, hunting them down and aiding in their execution before being converted on the road to Damascus (Acts Ch.9) and becoming Christianity's chief spokesman. Yet, this superstar of the faith acknowledged an inward battle between his right-loving conscience and his wrong-loving nature. *For that which I do I allow not: for what I would, that do I not, but what I hate, that do I, I find then a law, that when I would do good, evil is present with me. For I delight in the law of God after the inward man: But I see another law in my members, warring against the law of my mind and bringing me into captivity to the law of sin which is in my members.* (Rom. 7:15, 21-23)

The question before us is why Christians, who are supposed to believe God is always watching, still do bad things. If a Christian really believes God can see him and is actually right there with him, how could he allow himself to fudge on his income tax, be mean to his wife, short-tempered with his children, gossip, tell a lie, cuss, or treat someone unfairly? The skeptic says, **From the perspective of an outsider like me, this doesn't add up... could it be that they are less confident in the existence of an omniscient and omnipresent god than they let on?** (79)

A truly Christian answer to this question must originate from doctrine found in the Bible. Paul explains in Romans 7 that he had an inward struggle between what he called the *law of God,* which he delights in, and the *law of sin,* which sometimes made him feel like a captive. To the unbeliever, this sounds like the confessions of a weak man who cannot control his own actions. If you want to do what is right, then just do it. If you don't want to do things your belief tells you are wrong, then just don't do them.

The source of this apparent compulsion to violate our own beliefs by doing bad things is found in Galatians 5. Paul explains why Christians have this inner war between two competing factions. He writes, *For the flesh* (the part of us that has natural desires which if taken to excess are sinful) *lusteth against the Spirit* (the part of the Christian that delights in the law of God Paul had referred to in Romans 7) *and the Spirit against the flesh: and these are contrary the one to the other; so that ye cannot do the things that ye would.* (Gal. 5:17) It sounds like a hopeless situation for the Christian. But this description of an inner war between sin (the flesh) and righteousness (the Spirit) is sandwiched by a remedy. In verse 16 Paul says, *Walk in the Spirit, and ye shall not fulfill the lust of the flesh.* Then in verse 18, he adds, *But if ye be led of the Spirit, ye are not under the law* (law meaning the compulsion to sin).

So in a nutshell, here is the answer to the question of how Christians can do bad things if they really believe Jesus is watching. In contrast to an unbeliever, the Christian has two natures. The first we call the old nature, the one we are born with, and the second we call the new nature, the one received when we are born again, or when we accept Christ as our savior.

In Christian terms, it means that upon salvation we are indwelled by the Holy Spirit, the third person of the Trinity and promised by Jesus to his disciples in Acts chapter one. Christians also have the old sinful nature which is still alive and well and demanding to be satisfied. The Christian may be vigilant against satisfying this old nature but still fail at times to suppress it, which is done by what the Bible calls "walking in the Spirit."

So what does Paul mean when he says Christians should "walk in the Spirit" to avoid these wrong behaviors. It means that Christians must be conscious all the time of acting in such a way that would bring honor to Christ and be in obedience to the things he taught. The "bad things" a skeptic wonders how Christians can do if they really believe Jesus is watching, happen when we allow our minds to be guided by the old nature we still possess and act accordingly. It is a lifelong war, and for the true Christian, wrong deeds are followed by guilt which comes from the conviction of sin, then repentance, seeking forgiveness, making restitution where necessary, and purposing not to fall in that area again. We attempt to live in obedience to Christ out of love and honor for him.

I once heard a preacher tell of his teenage daughter being enticed by her classmates to do something wrong. They knew her Dad was a minister. She declined their invitation. "What's the matter," they teased, "afraid of what your Dad will do to you?" "No," she replied, "I'm afraid of what I would do to him." That is a pretty good example of what "walking in the spirit," is all about.

I fully understand that skeptics scoff at this explanation. I could offer a multitude of scripture references in support of this Christian concept, but I do not think their problem with it is that it is not biblical, but that it makes no sense, at least not to them. This is acknowledged in the Bible too. *But the natural man* (that's one who is not indwelled by the Holy Spirit) *receiveth not the things of the Spirit of God: for they are foolishness unto him: neither can he know them, because they are spiritually discerned.* (I Cor. 2:14) That is not a slam against skeptics. It simply means that a person who does not possess the "new nature" has no basis upon which to understand things related to it.

In reality, the real question the skeptic is asking the Christian is, "Why aren't you perfect?" For if Christians who do some bad thing are charged with being **less confident in the existence of an omniscient and omnipresent god than they let on?** (79) then any violation of Christian conduct, no matter how small, can become evidence he does not really believe God is watching.

But suppose someone was perfect, meaning they always acted as if God were right there watching them. Would that make any difference to the unbeliever who was observing? There was one person who actually did live this way - Jesus Christ. Even those who wanted him crucified could not state a single wrong thing for which he was guilty. In fact, Jesus himself said, *And he that sent me is with me: the Father hath not left me alone; for I do always those things that please him.* (John 8:29)

Skeptics may argue whether or not Jesus actually lived, (this is addressed in chapter 24) and those who say he probably did would put him in the category of a good teacher, like Buddha or Confucius, but they cannot point to any inconsistent aspect of his life between what he claimed and what he did. His earthly life was perfectly consistent. Yet that did not make him acceptable to the culture of his day, nor his teachings acceptable to our culture now. For his perfect life, he was and still is hated by many. Inconsistency in the life of the professing Christian as evidence he does not really believe what he says he does is a red herring, as the perfect life of Jesus still not making him or his teaching any more accepted testifies.

The skeptic also makes a notable error when he says, **Behavior does not define a Christian, only the professed belief in Jesus as a god does that.** (81) James 2:19 states, *Thou believest that there is one God; thou doest well: the devils also believe, and tremble.* To an unbeliever, **a basic secular description of who is a Christian is necessary: If one believes in Jesus and worships or follows him in some manner, then she or he is a Christian. It's as simple as that.** (82)

Here again is the construction of a straw man. The unbeliever who defines Christianity according to his own perception, contrary to what the Bible says, then produces evidence of how his defined Christian behaves contrary to his professed belief in God is only vindicating the truth of the Bible and of true Christian teaching. Notice how Matthew 7:21-23 illustrates this. *Not every one that saith unto me, Lord, Lord, shall enter into the kingdom of heaven; but he that doeth the will of my Father which is in heaven. Many will say to me in that day, Lord, Lord, have we not prophesied in thy name and in thy name have cast out devils? and in thy name done many wonderful works? And then will I profess unto them, I never knew you: depart from me, ye that work iniquity.*

Not everyone who claims to be a Christian is one. And according to the Bible, some who are preachers, or have performed healings, or who call Jesus "Lord" are not truly followers of Christ. In fact, God says some of them are workers of iniquity. We won't go into a theological discourse on why that is, but it should be sufficient to demonstrate the difference between what skeptics say a Christian is and what the book that Christianity is based on really says.

Jesus said, *Beware of false prophets, which come to you in sheep's clothing, but inwardly they are ravening wolves. Ye shall know them by their fruits. Do men gather grapes of thorns, or figs of thistles? Even so every good tree bringeth forth good fruit; but a corrupt tree bringeth forth evil fruit. A good tree cannot bring forth evil fruit, neither can a corrupt tree bring forth good fruit. Every tree that bringeth not forth good fruit is hewn down, and cast into the fire. Wherefore by their fruits ye shall know them.* (Matt. 7:15-20)

A follower of Christ is much more identifiable by his actions (fruits) than his words. Without the kind of guilt and repentance I mentioned earlier, I can agree with the skeptic's closing argument on this question, **actions speak louder than words.** (82) True Christians would do well to pay attention to this paraphrase of what Jesus actually said because Jesus, and skeptics, are watching.

TWELVE

HOW CAN WE BE SURE ABOUT THE RESURRECTION?

According to the Bible, all of Christianity hinges on the resurrection of Jesus Christ. Without the resurrection, Christianity falls flat. Even a skeptic realizes this when he says the resurrection **has to be true if Christianity is true. No less than the apostle Paul, probably the most influential architect of the Christian religion, wrote,** *And if Christ be not raised, your faith is vain; ye are yet in your sins.* **(I Cor. 15:17) The simple question that every skeptic asks is, How do we know that Jesus wasn't just a man who died like every other person has or will? Where's the proof for this extraordinary claim that he did not remain dead?** (83)

Throughout the ages Christ's resurrection has been questioned. Skeptics claim the upper hand in the argument. **The burden of proof lies with the Christians who make the claim. There is no burden of proof on the unbeliever's shoulders to disprove.** (83) But there is a caveat. How does one prove a single event that is supposed to have occurred in the distant past? There are skeptics today of the holocaust, despite eyewitness accounts, and there is still debate over details of the American Revolution, the assassination of JFK, and many other events in the more recent past. Time, prejudice, and confirmation bias all take their toll on what an individual believes about historical events. The best we can do is examine what is known, objectively consider facts and come to logical conclusions based on the preponderance of evidence. When all that is done, the Christian position on the resurrection is a strong one indeed.

It is fascinating to hear skeptics say, **for a big claim I need big proof.** (87) The resurrection of Jesus certainly is a big claim. But skeptics fully embrace and promote a claim that is just as big, if not bigger, when they accept the completely unproven notion that all life as we know it arose from non-living matter. Where is the proof this ever happened? Science has so far been unable to demonstrate a single occurrence of this supposed millions-of-years-old phenomenon, yet skeptics believe it virtually without question. Why does the doctrine of Jesus coming back to life after being dead cause such skepticism for the unbeliever who readily accepts that something which was never alive in the first place spontaneously came to life? Apparently, not all big claims require big proof.

While there is no proof of Christ's resurrection from the dead in the sense of modern empirical evidence, there are numerous arguments for it which are quite rational. None of them however, rise to the standard of an incontrovertible proof. You would be hard pressed to prove any ancient historical event without resorting to what was written about it at the time by those who were eyewitnesses. What we can do with evidence of the resurrection is see if it rises to the judicial standard of "beyond reasonable doubt." I would like to propose two arguments for the resurrection of Christ which meet this standard. First, the evidence from common sense.

In John 2:19-21 Jesus himself said, *Destroy this temple, and in three days I will raise it up. The Jews then said, It took forty-six years to build this temple, and will You raise it up in three days? But He was speaking of the temple of His body. So when He was raised from the dead, His disciples remembered that He said this; and they believed the Scripture and the word which Jesus had spoken.*

Jesus's ministry on earth lasted only three years. During that time, even his enemies did not take him for a fool or a lunatic. The Pharisees, his chief antagonists, argued that he blasphemed when he claimed equality with God and the authority to forgive sins, but they marveled at his wisdom nonetheless, wisdom which sometimes left them speechless. Neither they, nor later historians dismissed him as a madman.

Nothing of what we know about Jesus' life lends itself to conclude he was delusional or a fraud. The skeptic, even with his disbelief in the resurrection, does not go so far as to charge Jesus with being out of his mind for saying he would rise from the dead. While on earth, his teaching and his claims were taken seriously, even by those who did not believe that he was who he claimed to be. If you think objectively about this, it should make you wonder why someone could make such an outrageous claim and not be laughed out of town. Jesus enemies took him serious enough to both debate and attempt to silence him. A lunatic would simply be ignored or ostracized. You do not debate with someone who is delusional.

Additionally, if Jesus wanted to destroy his own reputation, sabotage the mission which he was supposed to have been sent to accomplish and prove to the world that, in fact, he was not who he claimed to be, not rising from the dead would seal his fate as the greatest fraud and biggest fool in history. Why would Jesus make such a claim if he knew he couldn't fulfill it, and in not doing so, invalidate everything he had said?

Once dead, the continuation of all he taught would be left in the hands of a ragtag bunch of followers who had so far proven themselves unworthy, unwilling, and unable to undertake such a task. He would be leaving it to them to somehow fabricate his resurrection. Such a strategy would ensure that history would discard him as nothing more than another religious charlatan. In the case of Jesus Christ, it appears that common sense says there is substantial need for proof that he did not rise from the dead, or else some reasonable explanation for how the teachings of a lunatic have impacted the entire world even though he said he would come back to life after being dead for three days but never did.

If the Bible relates the words of Christ, it defies common sense to believe that Jesus would have made this audacious claim knowing when it did not happen it would prove he was a fraud. Perhaps he hoped his disciples, who up to this point were often confused by his teaching, frightened by their enemies, and in Peter's case at the time of Jesus' crucifixion, afraid to even admit knowing him, would overpower Roman guards, steal his body, and perpetuate the masquerade until they were tortured and killed for it themselves. Is there any common sense to that? What could explain the transformation of these timid, often confused, and at times even unbelieving men, into bold preachers if it was not the fact that Christ's resurrection cemented the reality of his identity as the Son of God he claimed to be?

In light of what Jesus said about his coming resurrection, and his reputation among non-Christians for the 2000 years since as being, at the very least, a good teacher, is it reasonable to insist that his most spectacular claim was an empty boast he knew would never come to pass? Wouldn't that make him not just a bad teacher, but a horrendous liar? And wouldn't the proof that is all he was be as simple as producing his dead body? Wouldn't those who worked so tirelessly to discredit him simply display his body three days later as evidence that he was the fraud they knew he was all along? This would be such a simple way to expose a religious hoax, eviscerate his message, and put an end to the fledgling Christian religion.

This may have been exactly what the Pharisees had in mind after Jesus' crucifixion when they came to the Roman governor Pilate to remind him that, *the deceiver said, while he was yet alive, After three days I will rise again. Command therefore that the sepulchre be made sure until the third day, lest his disciples come by night and steal him away, and say unto the people, He is risen from the dead.* Pilate agreed. *Ye have a watch: go your way, make it as sure as ye can.* (Matt. 27: 63-65)

Extraordinary measures were taken to make certain that Jesus Christ's body remained in the tomb. Clearly this was not because his enemies thought he might rise again, even Jesus own followers were not expecting that, but because they feared some last-ditch effort by his disciples to fabricate his resurrection and perpetuate his teachings. Jesus was dead. It was his message they wanted silenced. Despite the efforts of the Jewish religious leaders and the most powerful army on earth at the time, three days later, Jesus' tomb was empty and the news was circulating that he was alive! Jesus' death and burial were public events. Were his resurrection not a reality, this would have been the simplest of rumors to expose.

The second evidence that is compelling for the resurrection is complementary to the common sense argument. The very existence of Christianity is powerful confirmation of the resurrection. The reality of Christianity cannot be rationally accounted for apart from the resurrection of Jesus Christ. We have already observed that Jesus not rising from the dead after saying that he would seals his fate as a liar and a fraud.

If Jesus did not rise from the dead, his disciples knew after three days that he was not the Son of God he claimed to be. They knew that his teaching, though profound, was no different from the proclamations of Caesar, or self-proclaimed prophets of the day whose predictions did not come true. If Jesus remaining dead was a fact of history, no one would have known that better than his closest followers who had been told this incredible lie.

The very existence of the Christian faith, from the first century to the present, argues strongly in favor of the resurrection of Christ as a real event that occurred just as it is described in the New Testament. Of course, this is not a "proof." However, trying to explain Christianity rationally without it results in purely speculative arguments that his disciples simply perpetuated and died for what they knew to be false.

Which brings us to some of the other arguments for Jesus' resurrection which skeptics challenge. While I do not think these are as strong as the common sense argument and the argument from the existence of Christianity, they are often used, so let's examine the skeptic's refutation of them.

1. People died for Jesus

Why would anyone die for Jesus if he wasn't who the Bible says he was? Christians point to the apostles who were martyred and the early Christians who were tortured and executed for their religion, and they ask, who would die for a lie or a hoax? Maybe it's a case of pride or the hope that projecting confidence will somehow win out in the end. More likely however, early Christians stuck to their beliefs in the face of death because they sincerely believed. It's not rare for people to believe something that is certainly or probably not true and be willing to die for it. Christians are pretty sure that Islam is an inaccurate belief system, but some Muslims trust it enough to fly planes into buildings and strap bombs to their bodies. (84)

There is a big difference between dying for something you believe is true, and something you know to be false because you perpetrated the falsehood yourself. Besides, the first mention of Jesus' resurrection came from several women who told the disciples the news, which when they heard it, the Bible says, *And their words seemed to them as idle tales, and they believed them not.* (Luke 24:11) So according to the book which tells us of Jesus' resurrection, even his followers were skeptics until they actually saw him for themselves.

There is nothing in the biblical account to suggest that Jesus' disciples were projecting confidence or too proud to admit Jesus was gone. Their belief was not based on something they hoped for or wished was true. They had already accepted the fact that he was dead. The transformation in their thinking was based on the very thing skeptics require, big proof. They saw him themselves. Their belief was based on eyewitness observation, the kind of evidence used in a court of law to establish fact. Moreover, the accounting of it was written during the lifetime of other eyewitnesses who, if the account was false, could have easily proven it so.

2. Paul's conversion

The premise is that the change in Paul from being a persecutor of Christianity to being its chief spokesman, after seeing Christ, must mean the resurrection is true. **Paul had been persecuting Christians until he "saw" the resurrected Jesus on his way from Jerusalem to Damascus. Something caused a radical change in his way of thinking, no doubt. But skeptics see no proof or good evidence of a resurrected god in this story.** (85)

The problem is that Paul's conversion in Acts 9 occurred quite some time after Jesus had ascended into heaven (Acts 1). Additionally, the biblical account says that Paul saw a *light that shined round about him,* and heard a voice saying, *Saul, Saul, why persecutest thou me?* (Acts 9: 3&5) Remember, Paul's name was Saul prior to his conversion. It was the voice within the light that said, *I am Jesus whom thou persecutest.* (Acts 9:5) The passage also states that the men traveling with Paul were *speechless, hearing a voice but seeing no man.* (v.7)

The skeptic seems to recognize that Paul was a real historical figure and a primary factor in the spread of Christianity, and that this is a stark contrast to his previous life as a persecutor of Christians. In other words, something happened to change Paul's life, skeptics just doesn't believe it was what the Bible says. This approach means that Paul, the primary author of the New Testament, either suffered from some kind of hallucination, was deluded, or perhaps just didn't remember the event accurately. **It's fine to trust Paul's word that he believed he saw Jesus that night, but we can't be sure that he did not hallucinate, misperceive, or misremember events.** (85)

There are two observations to be made about this point. First, Luke, who later traveled with Paul, is the author of Acts. So in the Acts 9 account, it is Luke who is relating the event, not Paul. However, Luke undoubtedly got this account from Paul, since he was not traveling with him at the time of his conversion. Years later, in Acts 22, Luke tells of Paul's recounting of his conversion in an oral address to an angry mob in Jerusalem which is almost word for word to Acts 9. This argues favorably for the accuracy of the event since it would be highly unlikely that Paul could recall a hallucination or retell a misremembered event so consistently years later.

Second, when the skeptic says we can't be sure that Paul wasn't hallucinating, or just did not remember it right, we should acknowledge that the same can be said of any unusual event. For example, when the skeptic tells his story of being watched over by a mysterious Massai tribesman during the night while he lay unconscious in the brush, we might also say, "We can't be sure that he did not hallucinate, misperceive, or misremember the event." This is why skepticism is too easy. Anything can be doubted, eyewitness account, first-person narrative, a corroborated story by multiple witnesses, such as Paul's conversion, or one man's account of a perfectly timed, chance, nighttime encounter with a benevolent Massai tribesman.

Pauls' life and ministry as recorded in Acts, and corroborated by historical and archaeological evidence of real people and actual places, is not at all conducive to a man who underwent such a radical change in his life as the result of a hallucination or an event he remembered wrong. There is far better reason to believe the truthfulness of events in Paul's ministry as recorded in the Bible than to chalk it up to misperception or hallucination, ideas for which there can be no evidence at all.

3. The tomb was empty

The best one can do is tell people who make this claim that the limited collection of sources that say Jesus' tomb was empty are the same limited collection of sources that say he was resurrected. These are hardly objective sources. Even if we allow ourselves to accept the Bible's account of what happened to Jesus' body as accurate reporting of what people really said at the time, the empty tomb claim is still based on hearsay about eyewitness accounts. How can we accept that? It's too important to accept on the word of fallible human beings alone. They could have lied or been honestly mistaken. (85)

If Jesus did not rise from the dead, then his body was stolen. Unless you resort to entirely imagined tales of going to the wrong tomb, or that Jesus wasn't really dead in the first place, there are no other options. All that needed to be done to stop the hearsay that he was alive was to check his tomb. The Jewish leaders could easily have requested this of the Roman government to squelch the troublesome rumor. The fact that Jesus' enemies took such elaborate measures to prevent his body from being stolen places a skeptic in the precarious position of believing something extraordinary, no matter which side of the resurrection story he comes down on.

Jesus' tomb, which belonged to a man named Joseph of Arimathea, was typical of tombs of the day. The stone used to seal such a tomb weighed 1-1/2 to 2 tons.[1] If the disciples stole the body, they would have had to either sneak past or overpower a guard of professional Roman soldiers, move a stone that weighed as much as a mid size car, and haul Jesus' body to some secret location all completely undetected. According to the Bible, the disciples went into hiding following the crucifixion. Such a covert operation, executed flawlessly by frightened fisherman and peasants, who by now realized they had been duped by a clever preacher who said he would rise from the dead but didn't, is an incomprehensible stretch and argues for the possibility of the preposterous for which there is only imagination for evidence.

4. Five hundred witnesses

Much is made by some Christians about the number of people who Paul says saw the resurrected Jesus after his death. But no one knows who these people were or where they saw Jesus. Hundreds of witnesses may sound impressive until you consider that many more than that have "seen" UFO's and Bigfoot. Anonymous witnesses from ancient times, no matter how many, are just not sufficient to confirm something so important. Remember, for good skeptics, the quality and quantity of evidence needs to at least balance the weight of the claim. (85-86)

I hope you notice something in the skeptic's arguments on these last two points. In the case of the disciples, who were eyewitnesses to the resurrected Christ, their testimony is discounted because they **are hardly objective sources.** (85) In the case of the 500 witnesses referred to by Paul in I Cor. 15:6, their testimony is discounted because **Anonymous witnesses from ancient times, no matter how many, are just not sufficient to confirm something so important.** (85) So we have criteria which excludes witnesses that were close to Jesus as not objective, and those who were not close to Jesus as anonymous and not sufficient. In other words, the testimony of all eyewitnesses is excluded.

If five-hundred witnesses each testified for five minutes in a court of law, you would have over 42 hours of corroborative, first-hand, eyewitness testimony. This would be enough to make for a lop-sided trial with opposing attorneys left to only argue that such a magnitude of testimony must be dismissed because we don't know who these people are, or they were too close to either of the parties in the case. The Christian is well within reason to ask, "If 500 eyewitnesses plus a few close associates saw Jesus Christ resurrected, and his tomb was never shown to contain his body, and the theft of his body was logistically impossible, and the lives of his frightened disciples radically changed into bold preachers of his divinity, what other explanation is rationally plausible?"

5. Roman guards don't sleep on duty.

Are we to believe that no soldier in the history of the Roman Empire ever stole a quick nap on duty, were corruptible, or were incompetent? This argument seems totally implausible. If the guard detachment fell asleep, all of them, surely it is reasonable to presume that the movement of a nearly two-ton stone just a few feet from where they slept would wake them up. Furthermore, as Josh McDowell points out:

> The fear of their superiors' wrath and the possibility of death meant that they paid close attention to the minutest details of their jobs. One way a guard was put to death was by being stripped of his clothes and then burned alive in a fire started with his garments. If it was not apparent which soldier had failed in his duty, then lots were drawn to see which one would be punished with death for the guard unit's failure. Certainly the entire unit would not have fallen asleep with that kind of threat over their heads. Dr. George Currie, a student of Roman military discipline, wrote that fear of punishment "produced flawless attention to duty, especially in the night watches."[2]

The notion that perhaps Jesus body was removed from the tomb by some of his faithful followers while a whole detachment of Roman guards snoozed is laughably unrealistic.

Even the most hardened skeptic must acknowledge, like it or not, that Jesus is the most significant person in history. What is it about him that warrants such hatred and devotion for two-thousand years? Why does his teaching compel commitment by some and animosity by others not seen in that of a Confucius, or Buddha? All of human history pivots on the birth of Jesus Christ. No one, ancient or modern has been more venerated and vilified. Why? Is it not his resurrection?

THIRTEEN

HOW DO WE KNOW THAT HEAVEN IS REAL?

There is a pretty simple and logical answer to this question, but skeptics will not accept it. We know that heaven is real because Jesus said it is. *In my Father's house are many mansions: if it were not so, I would have told you. I go to prepare a place for you. And if I go and prepare a place for you, I will come again, and receive you unto myself; that where I am, there ye may be also.* (John 14:2-3) We don't even have to guess at the response. **Without evidence and testing, it is just a story and nothing more.** (93) Skeptics would certainly disallow what Jesus said as evidence for anything because it is not subject to scientific verification. Again, this is much too simplistic. We have already seen that skeptics accept extraordinary claims without proof, so physical evidence cannot be the only standard by which we accept something as true.

You cannot prove that your spouse is being faithful to you. You trust his or her integrity and the promise they made to be faithful to you till death. All you have to base this extraordinary promise on is the word of someone you trust. You can't really prove it, but you believe it nonetheless. The question here is, can we trust the word of Jesus Christ that he is preparing a place called heaven for those who follow him? Let's explore if it is logical to answer yes to that question.

First, was Jesus existence on earth a real historical event? Only a relatively small handful of skeptics deny that Jesus actually existed. We will examine this in detail in chapter 24. But to justify the belief that heaven is real because Jesus said it is, let's first look at just one evidence for his existence, then consider if belief in his claims about heaven is rational.

Pliny the Younger, a Roman lawyer, author, and magistrate, in a letter to the Roman emperor Trajan, refers to Christ, and explained his methods of punishing Christians:

> Meanwhile, in the case of those who were denounced to me as Christians, I have observed the following procedure: I interrogated these as to whether they were Christians; those who confessed I interrogated a second and a third time, threatening them with punishment; those who persisted I ordered executed. Those who denied that they were or had been Christians, when they invoked the gods in words dictated by me, offered prayer with incense and wine to your image, which I had ordered to be brought for this purpose together with statues of the gods, and moreover cursed Christ--none of which those who are really Christians, it is said, can be forced to do--these I thought should be discharged. Others named by the informer declared that they were Christians, but then denied it, asserting that they had been but had ceased to be, some three years before, others many years, some as much as twenty-five years. They all worshipped your image and the statues of the gods, and cursed Christ.[1]

The most thorough picture we have of the character of this Christ comes from the four gospels in the New Testament: Matthew, Mark, Luke, and John. Skeptics should not object to this as reasonable and historical biographical information. Far from being mythological, or allegorical, the New Testament refers to real places like: Jerusalem, Damascus, the Sea of Galilee, Capernaum, Bethlehem, and an obscure little city called Nain. It also references actual people, including world leaders of the time including, Herod, Caesar, and Pilate.

The New Testament cannot be reasonably perceived as a book of fables and legends for which there is no evidence. Many of the places mentioned go by the same names today. If you do not believe the message of the New Testament, you should at least acknowledge that it speaks accurately about geographical places, rulers, empires, and even structures like the Coliseum at Ephesus or the temple in Jerusalem, the ruins of which are still popular tourist attractions.

So that brings us to Jesus himself. Even many unbelievers will at least regard Jesus as a decent man. And most would acknowledge that he was known for teaching things that are noble and good: honesty, fairness, forgiveness, mercy, generosity, humility, trust, patience, charity etc. Such things have earned Jesus the title of a "good teacher" among those who discount his deity. The point is, during his earthly life, Jesus was not dismissed as a madman, a braggart, or a revolutionary. He threatened the beliefs of some, but raised no army, incited no riot, and advocated the overthrow of no government. His words, including those about the resurrection and heaven were taken seriously, even by those who did not like what he had to say.

Jesus talked about a place called heaven. *Verily I say unto you, Except ye be converted, and become as little children, ye shall not enter into the kingdom of heaven.* (Matt. 18:3) He refers to heaven sixteen times in the Sermon on the Mount alone. Jesus promised his disciples he was going to make a place for them and would take them there. If none of this were true, if all his talk about heaven was just a big fat lie, then not only was Jesus not a good teacher, he wasn't even a good person. If all his teachings were rooted in a promise he knew very well he wasn't going to keep, if heaven isn't real, Jesus was either a pathological liar or a delusional fool.

The greatest proof of heaven is in the historical character and reputation of Jesus Christ himself. As we learned regarding his resurrection, if he did not rise from the dead, then he lied, and his disciples would have been the first to recognize that fact. Nothing he said would have been trusted, much less followed. Wouldn't his other pronouncements have been considered just as suspect, like this outlandish tale of a place called heaven? Consider if someone accused your wife of having an affair despite her lifelong reputation of being devoted, chaste, honest, and faithful. Would you believe the word of strange accusers or the word of your wife whose reputation and character you have known for decades?

During Jesus earthly ministry, he was observed healing people and showing compassion for the sick and suffering. His reputation was so stellar that the only accusation made against him was that he blasphemed by saying he was God and could forgive sins. He was not accused of being a liar. He was called a deceiver, but not because he had been caught deceiving anyone. It was because the Pharisees who accused him disapproved of his claims. Jesus spoke of heaven as a real place. He was a real historical earthly figure known at least for being good, honest, and true. How could he have this reputation while also being guilty of repeatedly lying? Heaven is real because Jesus said so.

There are many stories from people who say they died, went to heaven, then came back to tell about it. I have read some of these accounts. Though interesting, I share the skepticism of the unbeliever of these being "proofs" of heaven primarily because most of the ones I have read do not harmonize with what the Bible says. If someone really went to heaven and came back to tell about it, I'd expect what they describe to sound a lot like Revelation 4, which was written by John but inspired by Jesus Christ. God gave John the opportunity to get a glimpse of heaven. I would be skeptical of any descriptions that enhance, conflict with, or contradict that one.

FOURTEEN

WHY IS GOD SO VIOLENT?

The charge that God is violent is a staple among critics of the Bible. Old Testament passages where God authorizes the killing of entire groups of people, including men, women, and children seem to confirm this as fact. Skeptics, and frankly many Christians, are troubled by this apparent ruthlessness. God's alleged cruelty is often cited as evidence that he is not loving and if he exists, should not be followed.

This is a hard question, not because it is hard to answer, but because it requires a somewhat detailed explanation of the Bible and its revelation of God's dealings with man historically throughout the Old Testament, all the way through the prophetic passages in the New Testament. It also requires exploring a difficult to comprehend aspect of God's nature - that he exists outside of time. However, it is a frequently asked and fair question. Answering every charge the skeptic makes regarding this matter is not practical, but let's deal with the most severe.

The skeptic cites various examples of God's violence.

1.   God afflicts all of mankind with the curse of death for eating the forbidden fruit. (98) Genesis 3
2.   God destroys all life on earth, including babies, except for Noah's family and an ark full of animals. (98) Genesis 7
3.   God even destroys livestock when he executes the tenth plague on Egypt that kills all firstborn. (98) Exodus 12:29
4.   God says you can beat your slaves as long as you do not kill them. (98) Exodus 21:20-21
5.   God tells Israel they will eat the flesh of their sons and daughters. (98) Lev. 26:29

6. Ps. 137:9 says, *Happy shall he be that taketh and dasheth thy little ones against the stones.*

There are a few more, but these are pretty representative examples of a skeptic's assertion that God is violent. Furthermore, **God is not only violent himself but condones and requires violence from his followers.** (99) **Christians don't think those laws** (referring to OT instances of violence) **apply to them or to our time. However, that attitude might oppose what Jesus wanted, according to the New Testament.** (99) To prove this, skeptics quote New Testament passages where Jesus said things like, *Till heaven and earth pass, one jot or one tittle shall in no wise pass from the law, till all be fulfilled.* (Matt. 5:18) We'll come back to this point. For now, let's address the examples of God's violence.

Although many skeptics have an admirable grasp of some aspects of Christianity, most do not understand the Bible story as a cohesive whole. They do not know what the Old Testament is all about, nor how it illustrates and prepares the way for God's redemptive plan. This lack of understanding is seen in point one above in the analysis of Adam and Eve eating the forbidden fruit. **This single act, eating a piece of fruit, is, according to many Christians, the reason for all the suffering and death in the world due to disease, old age, and even the gruesome predator-prey dynamic in the animal kingdom.** (98) To a skeptic, a small infraction like eating a piece of fruit hardly justifies God cursing the whole earth and taking away man's immortality while imposing disease and death on all living things.

What skeptics do not accept is that Adam and Eve's actions were direct disobedience to a command of God. It means they decided, using the free will God allowed them, that they knew better than God. Simple as it seems, it was an act of defiance and rebellion that introduced sin and its consequences into a previously perfect world. It turned them and everything with which God had surrounded them from holy to sinful.

It is my personal belief that disease, death, and even the predator/prey dynamic were not inflicted by God as punishment, but were inevitable consequences which accompany sin. It's like jumping into the Niagara River a few hundred yards above the falls. You are going over. It's not a punishment for jumping in, it's a consequence that could have been avoided by staying safely where you belonged. God wanted Adam and Eve to enjoy the safety and pleasure of holiness, but he made that a voluntary possibility, not an inescapable divine mandate. They could choose to trust

God or decide to indulge in what was forbidden. Without the forbidden, there could be no free will.

This is not to say however, that God never punishes sin. Sin is simply disobeying God. It is the antithesis of holiness. Just as we punish crime because it is disobedience to civil law, there are consequences for sin because it is disobedience to God's law. Since Adam and Eve were the mother and father of all mankind, the nature to sin was passed on to all of us. As stated earlier, you do not need to teach a child how to lie or be selfish. It comes naturally. We are born with a nature to do what is wrong. God's actions regarding sin is mirrored in real life. Wrong actions always have consequences.

A skeptic does not believe in sin as any kind of real thing. Of course, if you do not believe in God, it follows that you would not believe in violations of his commands he calls sin. Nor is the word "holiness" part of the conversation. Yet these two concepts, sin and holiness, are central to the message of the Bible and Christianity. That is why despite some knowledge of the Bible and Christian doctrine skeptics often criticize a self-made caricature of Christianity, not the real thing.

God created man, set the rules, and gave fair and advanced warning of the consequences awaiting if the rules were broken. In an immeasurably smaller scale, every parent, business, and organization does the same thing. Rules and consequences are part of life. In the case of God, some simply do not like or agree with the rules and the consequences of their violation, thus declaring them to be unfair or unloving.

What about the contention that God is violent because he destroyed all living things on earth, including babies and children, except for Noah, his family, and the animals on the ark? To a skeptic, **this would have to be considered the greatest mass murder in history.** (98) If we are going to question an act of God, we have to examine the whole story surrounding the act. Genesis 6:5 describes the conditions on earth before God destroyed it with a worldwide flood. *And God saw that the wickedness of man was great in the earth, and that every imagination of the thoughts of his heart was only evil continually.*

Critiquing God's act of destroying the earth means we must do it on the basis of the reasons given for it, not just how we feel. According to the account in the Bible, except for Noah and his family, all of mankind had deteriorated into the epitome of evil. We get a small picture of this in our modern culture when terrorists armed with automatic rifles unleashed a massacre in Paris on Nov. 13th, 2015, killing over 100 people. While weapons and capabilities were different, this kind of barbaric mentality was the norm in Noah's world. Keep in mind that the Bible says even the thoughts of man were *only evil continually*. The culture was rife with every imaginable form of violence, hatred, vice, greed, and moral perversion. Kindness, generosity, mercy, thoughtfulness, patience, honesty, wholesomeness and everything else good and pleasant were nonexistent except in Noah and his family. So if we are going to question God's actions, we must do it on the basis of what the Bible says the conditions were that warranted those actions. That is only fair and reasonable.

But what about the children? Surely little children and innocent babies could not be considered evil. Admittedly, this is a difficult question. I believe the answer lies in a seldom considered aspect of God's nature — that he exists outside of time. Genesis 1:1 says, *In the beginning, God...* This means that according to the Bible, time had a beginning point. But at the beginning of time itself, God was already there. He existed before time began and is unbound by this dimension which defines our existence. Simply put, it means that God exists in and sees the past, present, and the future simultaneously.

Besides Gen.1:1, there are several other scriptures that corroborate God's timeless nature. In Rev. 10:6 it says, *...that there should be time no longer.* The Bible teaches that time had a beginning and it will have an end. II Peter 3:8 says, *But, beloved, be not ignorant of this one thing, that one day is with the Lord as a thousand years, and a thousand years as one day.* At the very least, all of human history since the birth of Christ is like yesterday and today to God.

I am not going to try to explain how this is possible. I do not think human beings are capable of comprehending something like existence outside of time. But it is a Christian concept and part of the nature of the Christian God according to the Bible. The fact that we cannot comprehend it does not mean that it cannot be. This is similar to the atheist who says that just because he cannot explain the beginning of life, does not mean he cannot believe it's naturalistic origin.

Ironically, there has been a surge of interest recently in speculations about time travel. Movies like "Interstellar" bend the mind to think about what could happen if a man were to experience some form of an alternate dimension where time was different. Of course, these are merely theoretical and theatrical projections, but in the case of "Interstellar," there was serious and significant consultation with astrophysicists to produce a story that had some elements of scientific legitimacy. This is discussed in The Daily Galaxy.com, "The Science Behind "Interstellar's" Stunning Wormhole Voyage," November 24, 2014.[1]

So what does this have to do with the flood in Noah's day and the drowning of innocent babies? It means that God could see those babies as grown adults. What they would become in earthly time is what they already were to God, and that was thoroughly and completely evil. God did not destroy the innocent, he destroyed the wicked. The fact that we cannot see that guilt does not mean it wasn't there for God to see. In Interstellar, "Cooper" returns unaged after traveling through a wormhole to find the 13-year-old daughter he left just days before in earth time now on her deathbed as an old woman. I don't mean to compare God to a movie character, but only to illustrate in some way how the human imagination might try to comprehend what timelessness could be like.

The problem skeptics have with what they see as the injustice of the flood is one of perspective. In fact, it is a problem we all have. I don't like the image of drowning babies either, but if I were to draw a picture of the flood, there would be no other way to draw it. God's picture, if we could see it, would look quite different.

It is something like parents who can see the inevitable consequences of their older children's bad decisions. Not that they literally can "see" the result, but they know based on their own life experience and ability to discern things their children have not yet seen. Wise children will listen to their parent's counsel because they realize parents know things and have experienced life, (or time if you will) in a way they have not. It is based solely on trust, not a present understanding.

It is similar with God when he does something that to our limited experience and finite perspective seems unjust. He sees what we cannot and knows what we do not. We have to believe that he is just. Mark Twain expressed this on a purely human level. "When I was a boy of 14, my father was so ignorant I could hardly stand to have the old man around. But when I got to be 21, I was astonished at how much the old man had learned in seven years."

Children can trust their parents and avoid many of life's pitfalls, or they can presume they know better and make their own mistakes. Often, later in life and from a more mature perspective, they finally see the wisdom and reality of what they did not trust in their parent's advice years earlier. Likewise, we can trust that God is not a vicious killer but had good reason and just cause for his actions, even though from our time-limited perspective we cannot see it.

Alternatively, refusing to trust beyond what we can see and understand at the moment, we can charge God with cruelty, reject the love he offers through his son Jesus Christ and suffer the inevitable consequence. At the end of the day, we trust God, science, political leaders, teachers, or ourselves. All of life, theistic or atheistic, is based on trust.

We should also acknowledge that, according to the Bible, it took 120 years for Noah to build the ark. It is certainly reasonable to presume that building a vessel of this size would have attracted significant attention, skepticism, and probably no small amount of ridicule. All of this would have offered Noah the opportunity to warn the people of impending doom. The warnings would have come from at least three sources:

1. from the fact that Noah was actually building an ark
2. from the conscience of man which inherently knows when he has done wrong
3. quite likely from the words of Noah himself

It is not much different from the situation in the world today. Preachers who actually preach about God's judgment for sin are ignored, criticized, or ridiculed. I am not referring to a judgment like a flood, but an eternal judgment of separation from God in hell. Just like many refuse to listen, consigning themselves to a judgment from which God offers to spare them, so it was in the days of Noah. Noah is described as *a preacher of righteousness,* in II Peter 2:5. Escape was possible. No one listened.

Another objection is the 10th plague on Egypt, which included the death of all the firstborn, including cattle. This is another evidence to a skeptic of God's violent nature. **God even killed livestock when he went after the firstborn children of Egypt.** (98) One might conclude that God was just itching to get at the nation's firstborn children and any other firstborn that got in his way. But let's think about this from the standpoint of what the Bible actually says about this particular part of Jewish history.

The Jews had spent the last four-hundred years as slaves in Egypt. Remember, in the Bible, the Jews are God's chosen people. From God's promise to Abraham, to their eventual acceptance of Christ as the Messiah in Revelation, God has a specific plan for the Jews which includes preserving them as a people. This can be seen in everything from the plagues on Egypt, to the Balfour Declaration of 1917 which paved the way for the Jews to resettle their homeland in 1948 and once again become a nation.

God raised up Moses to be the one who would lead Israel out of slavery in Egypt to the land he had given to the descendants of Isaac, Abraham's promised son. Nine times Pharaoh refused to let the people go after God had plagued the country. Skeptics should be interested to learn that there is extra-biblical evidence for these plagues. A document called the Ipuwer Papyrus, dating to around 1400 BC, describes great disasters that took place in Egypt.

- the Nile turning to blood. (Ex. 7) "Plague is throughout the land. Blood is everywhere. The river is blood, men shrink from tasting... and thirst for water."
- death of livestock (Ex.9) "All animals, their hearts weep. Cattle moan. Behold, cattle are left to stray, and there is none to gather them together."
- Hail and fire (Ex. 9) "forsooth, gates, columns and walls are consumed by fire. Grain has perished on every side. Forsooth, that has perished which was yesterday seen."
- Three days of darkness (Ex. 10) "The land is without light."
- Death of firstborn (Ex. 11) "Forsooth, the children of princes are dashed against the walls. He who places his brother in the ground is everywhere."[2] (The Ipuwer Papyrus is housed in Leiden, the Netherlands, at the Dutch National Museum of Antiquities, the Rijksmuseum van Oudheden.)

God had allowed his people to grow up in Egypt. They were hardened from centuries of labor and steeled by the harsh treatment of their captors. It was time now for Egypt to bow to the true God. Each of the ten plagues was an assault on one of Egypt's many deities. The last plague, death of the firstborn, humbled the ultimate power in Egypt, the Pharaoh.

God warned Egypt through Moses of the coming plagues and offered a way of escaping their destruction - letting the Israelites go free. Pharaoh refused. After nine devastating plagues, which by now had destroyed the economy of Egypt, Pharaoh threatened Moses with death if he showed his face again.

He could have let the people go, but he would not, thus welcoming another judgment from a God whose power over his own gods he had already seen with devastating results. God's intent with all the plagues, including the 10th, was to humble the proud Pharaoh to the point of obedience to his command, *Let my people go.* It took the death of all first-born for him to bow to the will of Israel's God.

Even as we shudder at the horrific nature of the 10th plague, we should be honest enough to acknowledge that, according to the Bible, it was Pharaoh that extended the contest with God and refused his offer nine times. God offered mercy. In this case, he was emancipating slaves. Pharaoh would have none of it. To charge God with unnecessary cruelty, without considering the entire picture, is like accusing someone of being a bully just because you saw them hit someone.

When I was a young teenage boy delivering newspapers, there was a local kid who decided to make me the target of his mud balls. As I pulled up on my bike to the next customer's house, several of his mud grenades splattered on the driveway. I decided I would do nothing unless one actually hit me. About the time I returned to my bike, 'splat!' I took a mud ball to the neck! I was off my bike in a flash and the bully started to run. I chased him several hundred yards through woods and briers before knocking him down on a patch of grass and cuffing him several times across his face. He was soon heading for home telling me how I was in big trouble with his Mom, who was one of my customers!

It is hardly on a comparable scale, but chastising God for his "cuffing" of Pharaoh through the 10th plague, when all Pharaoh had to do was let slaves go free, is a bit like someone seeing me beat up the bully, then accusing me of cruelty. We have to look at the entire picture in historical context and in the scope of four-hundred years of brutal slavery, along with the nine previous plagues Pharaoh welcomed by his refusal of God's offer. He had multiple opportunities to retain his dignity, the pride of his country, and give a million plus people their freedom. Critics may say God was the bully in this story, but the slaves would tell you different.

God says it is okay to beat your slaves so long as you don't kill them. (98) The passage referred to is in Ex. 21:20-21 and is directed to the Jews who had just left Egypt. *And if a man smite his servant, or his maid, with a rod, and he die under his hand; he shall be surely punished. Notwithstanding, if he continue a day or two, he shall not be punished, for he is his money.* A careful reading of this passage reveals that God is not authorizing anything like beating your slave. It is premised on a condition, which if it happens, then there is a protocol to follow. It was a judicial edict. If a man injures his slave to the point of death, the master is to be punished. If the slave does not die, but recovers, the punishment for killing your slave is not to be administered.

Reading the verses before and after this passage helps to get a more accurate perspective than the knee-jerk reaction that God is okay with beating slaves as long as they don't die. Two verses prior (Ex. 21:18-19) God said that if two men are fighting and one hits the other with a stone, or even his fist, and he does not die, the assailant is not to be punished but must pay the man for any lost time he suffered and for his healing. This is the principle of restitution. I think it might be a good idea for our time. How do you think it would affect crime rates if anyone who purposely injured another would have to pay the man's wages for lost time due to his injury, and pay for the cost of treating his injuries?

In Ex. 21:22-23, God said that if men hurt a pregnant woman so that her baby is born prematurely, (*her fruit departs from her*) yet no other harm follows, they are to be punished according to what the husband decides and pay what judges determine. If the baby dies, then the law is *life for life.* Some think that *her fruit departs from her* means the baby dies, but the Hebrew word for "depart" literally means, "to exit," or "to come out." God is saying here that if a man hurts a pregnant woman, causing a premature birth, the woman's husband becomes the judge and decides how much restitution must be made. If the child dies as a result of the assailant's actions, he is to be treated as a murderer.

These passages provide context and perspective to the passage in question (Ex. 21:20-21). God is seeking fairness and justice in the laws for his people, not justice in one case, and thoughtlessly looking the other way in another. Passages in the Bible that seem difficult to understand should always be interpreted in light of the ones that are easier to understand. God's Word, when taken as a whole, casts light not shadows.

Now we come to the charge of **threats from god for disobedience**. (99) The most severe example the skeptic offers is Lev. 26:29. *And ye shall eat the flesh of your sons, and the flesh of your daughters shall ye eat.* This is taken as a threat from God rather than a prophetic word of how desperate the nation of Israel would become as a result of their idolatry and turning away from the God who brought them out of bondage in Egypt.

The fact is, the people of Israel did exactly what God said they would. We read about it in II Kings 6:24-29. It is about 640 years later. Benhadad, the King of Syria, had sent his army to lay siege to Samaria, the capital of the northern kingdom of Israel. The result was a devastating famine. Things got so bad that two women agreed to eat their sons. But after one allowed her son to be eaten, the other woman backed out on the agreement.

Throughout much of Israel's history, which is what most of the Old Testament is about, God allowed foreign nations to overrun the Jews in order to bring them to repentance for their idolatry. In this case, a Syrian siege reduced Israel to cannibalism, just as God had told them would happen in Lev. 26:29. The case here is not one of a violent threat on the part of God, but a warning to his people of where their rebellion would lead them.

Ps. 137:9 is a favorite Bible passage to prove the point that God is violent. *Happy shall he be that taketh and dasheth thy little ones against the stones.* What kind of loving God equates brutality against children with happiness? Regarding verses like this, and others already cited, the skeptic says, **There are many Christians who are simply unaware of or have somehow not fully absorbed intellectually and emotionally the depth and fury of God's wrath.** (98) On the surface, this is clear evidence right from the Bible that God is not loving. Few Christians know this verse is in the Bible. The image it projects is disconcerting but should be understood in its proper historical and biblical context.

Psalm 137 is a lament over Jerusalem's fall to Babylon which occurred around 586 BC. This is a documented historical event. Though David wrote many of the Psalms, he is likely not the author of this one since Babylon overran Jerusalem long after his death. It expresses the anger and desire for revenge that was typical following a national defeat. It is also a song of mourning by Jews who saw their own children battered in a manner they now wish upon their conquerors. Many ancient empires were especially brutal toward their enemies and Babylon was no different.

> The judges of ancient Babylon were particularly enthusiastic. The cutting off of feet, lips and noses, blinding, gutting and the tearing out of the heart were all standard punishments in this corner of the ancient world.[3]

We also understand from the context that when Babylon overthrew Jerusalem, parents watched helplessly as their own children were battered in this way. When the Psalmist writes in verse 8, *happy shall he be, that rewardeth thee as thou hast served us,* then follows with, *Happy shall he be that taketh and dasheth thy little ones against the stones,* he is writing about a reality of the warring culture of the time and recalling what happened to them when they were overthrown. He is basically saying, "Babylon is going to get what it has coming to them, and the nation that is on the giving end of that retribution is going to be happy about it and so will we."

The writer here is expressing a sentiment not unlike what many Americans felt on September 11, 2001. While the World Trade Center towers burned and collapsed to the ground, killing thousands in a hellish inferno, people in nations that descended from the Babylonians, including children, cheered and celebrated. Americans were infuriated.

As Christians, we believe *All scripture is given by the inspiration of God.* (II Tim 3:16) But that does not mean that everything in scripture is endorsed by God. The Bible says that David was a man after God's own heart. It also tells of David's adulterous affair with Bathsheba. It is telling the truth about the sinful act of a man, not equating adultery with reflecting the heart of God. It is the same with this verse. Ps. 137:9 tells about the vengeful feelings of defeated Jews toward their conquerors, not that God endorses and is happy about the human slaughter of children.

Let's go back to the statement that **Christians don't think those laws** (referring to OT violence) **apply to them or to our time. However, that attitude might oppose what Jesus wanted, according to the New Testament.** (99) To support this, Matt. 5:18 is cited. *Till heaven and earth pass, one jot or one tittle shall in no wise pass from the law, till all be fulfilled.*

The problem comes from confusing Old Testament history with prophecy. When the skeptic says **God is not only violent but also condones and requires violence from his followers,** (99) he is suggesting that Jesus is teaching in Matthew 5, that Christians are required to repeat everything that ever happened in the history of the Old Testament! This is an absurd line of thought devoid of reason and scholarship. It is like the old preacher's joke where a man is trying to get advice from the Bible. His Bible falls open to Matthew 27:5 and he reads, *And he cast down the pieces of silver in the temple, and departed, and went and hanged himself.* Thinking this to be bad advice, he tries again. This time it is Luke 10:37. *Then Jesus said to him, Go and do thou likewise.*

Knowledgeable Christians recognize that the Bible is a chronicle of Israel's history. It is also a narrative of the teachings of Jesus Christ, a record of the beginnings of Christianity, and prophecies of events that are yet to occur. It is not a book of teachings that can be randomly mixed and matched and called Christian doctrine because it all came from the Christian's book. No book is read and understood that way.

The final skeptic blow on this subject relates to hell. **Then there is popular belief among Christians that God sends billions of people to**

hell where they will suffer unimaginable torture for eternity. From the viewpoint of a typical non-Christian, this is the ultimate in hate and violence and cannot be reconciled with the image of a loving god. (100)

It is a common misconception among those antagonistic toward Christianity that God sends people to hell. According to what the Bible says, hell is a place for the devil and his angels. *Then shall he say also unto them on the left hand, Depart from me, ye cursed, into everlasting fire, prepared for the devil and his angels.* (Matt. 25:41) But this verse seems to say that God is the one sending people to hell. However, if you read the context, you discover that this verse is part of a continuum of verses describing the final judgment. Those whose actions reflect their acceptance and love for Christ are told, *Come ye blessed of my Father, inherit the kingdom prepared for you from the foundation of the world.* (Matt. 25: 34) Those whose actions reflect their unbelief and rejection of Christ are told to *depart.* In verse 46 we are told, *And these shall go away into everlasting punishment...* Notice they *go away.*

Rev. 20:15 says, *And whosoever was not found written in the book of life was cast into the lake of fire.* Now that sounds for sure like God is literally throwing people into hell! But the sentence cannot be divorced from the crime. Rejecting God, and in particular the salvation offered through Jesus Christ, is a decision people make in this life which determines their eternal fate. When God casts them into hell, he is giving them for eternity what they wanted their whole life, separation from him, his holiness, and everything he instituted for man's benefit. That is what hell really is, eternal separation from God. The unbeliever is given his earthly preference of a life without God for all eternity.

If an atheist finds this objectionable, he must ask himself why he finds a doctrine of separation from God forever so terrible if he has voluntarily tried to live his entire life this way. Unbelievers who, despite considerable knowledge of the Bible reject the existence of God, the deity of Christ, and his offer of salvation from the eternal consequence of sin, still take offense at the concept of God providing a place where they can exist forever as they have lived on earth. "But hell is supposed to be a place of torture!" you may protest. That is true. And that is what total separation from God and all he has given man would be like.

Where did man get the ideas of justice, mercy, compassion, forgiveness, reward, fairness, morality, restitution, punishment, compensation, advocacy, charity, sacrifice, incentive, and on we could go. None of these things are inventions of man, but they do exist and are unique to humans.

We all benefit from their practice, but an atheist cannot explain their existence. They are all introduced in the Bible. Christians believe they were instituted by God and reflect his nature and goodness. Atheists live on these borrowed blessings. Hell will be their absence. You might even say that hell is the atheist's heaven — a place without God, but also without all he provides.

If all this violence and misery are somehow necessary, why wouldn't a loving god have made his story and claims convincing enough to all so that every sensible person could be exempt from destruction on doomsday? (101) This is a curious question indeed. Skeptics today are not much different than they were in Jesus' day. These people, many of whom were quite religious, saw blind people made to see, those who were lame made to walk, and even some who had died brought back to life. I know the skeptic finds these stories outrageous, but they are central to what is being questioned as part of recorded Christian history. So we have to ask, If these miracles were not convincing, then what would be? What would it take to convince a skeptic?

The late Dr. Gordon Stein, a prominent atheist, said that a miracle in his very presence would be one evidence he would accept as proof of God's existence.[4] But if this is the skeptic standard, then we must ask two questions.

1. Why doesn't the Bible record that miracles were convincing enough to persuade those who saw them in the first century? Many believed when they saw Jesus' miracles, but many others did not find them to be convincing evidence.
2. If Dr. Stein, or any atheist, were an eyewitness to a miracle, it might have made a believer out of him, but how would he convince another who did not see it? The standard of proof skeptics require would mean his wife and children would think him either a liar or a fool because no proof is offered other than his eyewitness testimony to an unnatural event.

This also reveals a problem with the skeptic standard of "convincing evidence." It has to be seen by every individual throughout time, or everyone who did not see it is going to have to take the word of another who did. Most of the Bible is a first-hand account of God's dealing with mankind. If it is unconvincing, it is because the skeptic demands proof which he can see for himself, not an eyewitness testimony from someone else. The truth is, if skeptics could be transported back to the time of Jesus and see the miracles first hand, some of them would believe and others would dismiss what they had seen the same as many did in Jesus' day.

This book is an analysis of sincere questions and concerns about Christianity and the core message of the Bible. That message is clear enough for anyone to understand who tries to be objective. It explains the message of salvation, "so that every sensible person could be exempt from destruction on doomsday." Hopefully, some will be convinced, repent, and accept Christ, but many will reject the reasoning presented here the same as they do the Bible. I remember my Dad saying in one of his sermons, "A man persuaded against his will, is of the same opinion still."

When a skeptic charges God with violence and insists that because it is in the Bible Christians are obligated to emulate it, he mistakes the recording of historical events for current commands. He also mistakes God's wrath for his own personal preference to live apart from him. Interestingly, skeptics seldom consider the teaching of Christ in the New Testament about things like grace, mercy, charity, forgiveness, sacrifice, compassion, and redemption. You will not hear an even mildly informed unbeliever accuse Jesus of violence or hatred. Nor is there much criticism of Jesus' teachings throughout the four gospels. It is very curious to notice the emphasis on what could be perceived as God's violence, yet completely passing over that part of the Christian story that tells of God's sacrificial love and offer of salvation from the eternal consequence of sin through Jesus Christ.

FIFTEEN

WHAT DO PROPHECIES PROVE?

I was working at an Ivy League university doing food research. "Jake," who worked as a janitor in our complex, began circulating a prediction that our facility was going to be shut down. No one took him seriously. Like many others, I was a skeptic. He wouldn't tell anyone what he based this "prophecy" on, he just knew. As proof, he cited other occurrences involving administrative decisions which he claimed to have predicted before they happened. The accuracy of his statements were self-verifying.

Many years came and went. Eventually, though the department did not shut down entirely, most of the food research work was shifted to the main campus fifty miles away. "Jake" could certainly claim his prediction came true. Today, the facility is but a shadow of what it was when a lowly janitor prophesied its demise.

Many people view Bible prophesies like the janitor's predictions, general statements, not so specific that they could not be considered fulfilled by the normal ebb and flow of events, and self-verifying because the same source that cites them also records their fulfillment. For Christians, fulfilled prophecies confirm the trustworthiness of scripture and demonstrate its supernatural nature. But how are they any different from "Jake's" prophetic pronouncements?

The skeptic is correct when he insists, **Predictions are meaningless when they are so vague that they can be interpreted in many ways.** But is he correct when he states, **This is a key problem with biblical prophecies?** (104)

Before examining criticism of Bible prophesies, we should establish what Christians mean when they speak of prophecy. The late Dr. Tim LaHaye, General Editor of the Prophecy Study Bible, keeps it simple.

"Prophecy is history written in advance." He went on to state, "It is God's way of telling us what will happen in the future. It involves the prediction of specific events before they actually happen."[1]

The Bible contains over a thousand predictions, many of which were made hundreds or even thousands of years before they happened. Some speak of events still to come. The most intriguing prophecies involve foretelling of very specific incidents that would have seemed preposterous at the time they were given. Before looking at several of these, we must get a better understanding of the skeptic view on Bible prophecy.

Despite what many people say, none of the prophecies [in the Bible] are so straightforward that anyone could read them and conclude that they came true as predicted and that they could only have been brought about by supernatural means. Not one. It's not that skeptics are being stubborn. No doubt they would be taken aback if the Old Testament contained very specific predictions of unique and important things or events that ancient people could not possibly have known about. But we don't find anything like this. (104)

There are numerous problems with this analysis of Bible prophecies.

1. Most Bible prophecies are very straightforward (i.e. "a virgin shall conceive" Isa. 7:14, Daniel's interpretation of the writing on the wall, "Thy kingdom is divided, and given to the Medes and the Persians." (Dan. 5:28) Jeremiah's prediction of 70 years of desolation for Israel is recorded in Jer. 25. The list could go on and on.

2. Most Bible prophecies did not come to pass by "supernatural means," nor do Christians need to claim that they did. Daniels interpretation and prediction that Babylon would fall to the Medes and Persians came to pass by military stealth and strategy, not a supernatural act. Yet, at the time it was given, it was unthinkable that the mighty Babylonian empire would fall. Supernatural fulfillment is not a prerequisite for Bible prophecies. Of course there are some, like the virgin birth and the resurrection of Christ which are supernatural.

3. The Old Testament does contain specific prophetic statements of important events that ancient people could not possibly have known about and which have occurred just as they were foretold. An entire book could be written about just one such prophecy, let alone the over 1000 prophecies in the Bible. Let's look at four that defy the skeptic's analysis.

Ezekiel's prophecy against Tyre - Ezekiel 26

In 332 BC, Alexander the Great built a half-mile long, two-hundred feet wide causeway into the Mediterranean Sea using the rubble of previously destroyed mainland Tyre to reach and conquer the city's impregnable island fortress. It was an amazing and unlikely military and engineering feat. What is truly astounding however, is that what Alexander did was predicted in exacting detail by the prophet Ezekiel 240 years earlier. Here is the text of the main part of this prophecy in Ezekiel 26.

3 Therefore thus saith the Lord God; Behold, I am against thee, O Tyrus, and will cause many nations to come up against thee, as the sea causeth his waves to come up. 4 And they shall destroy the walls of Tyrus, and break down her towers: I will also scrape her dust from her, and make her like the top of a rock. 5 It shall be a place for the spreading of nets in the midst of the sea: for I have spoken it, saith the Lord God: and it shall become a spoil to the nations. 6 And her daughters which are in the field shall be slain by the sword; and they shall know that I am the Lord. 7 For thus saith the Lord God; Behold, I will bring upon Tyrus Nebuchadnezzar king of Babylon, a king of kings, from the north, with horses, and with chariots, and with horsemen, and companies, and much people. 8 He shall slay with the sword thy daughters in the field: and he shall make a fort against thee, and cast a mount against thee, and lift up the buckler against thee.

9 And he shall set engines of war against thy walls, and with his axes he shall break down thy towers. 10 By reason of the abundance of his horses their dust shall cover thee: thy walls shall shake at the noise of the horsemen, and of the wheels, and of the chariots, when he shall enter into thy gates, as men enter into a city wherein is made a breach. 11 With the hoofs of his horses shall he tread down all thy streets: he shall slay thy people by the sword, and thy strong garrisons shall go down to the ground. 12 And they shall make a spoil of thy riches, and make a prey of thy merchandise: and they shall break down thy walls, and destroy thy pleasant houses: and they shall lay thy stones and thy timber and thy dust in the midst of the water. 13 And I will cause the noise of thy songs to cease; and the sound of thy harps shall be no more heard. 14 And I will make thee like the top of a rock: thou shalt be a place to spread nets upon; thou shalt be built no more: for I the Lord have spoken it, saith the Lord God.

We can better understand this prophecy by breaking it down into three parts. Verses 3-6 are general statements of what will happen to Tyre. Verses 7-11 refer to Babylon's conquest of the city of Tyre under Nebuchadnezzar and the siege on the island fortress. *And he shall set engines of war against thy walls...* Verses 12-14 refer to Alexander the Great's final annihilation of the island fortress of Tyre and his use of the ruins left by Babylon to, *lay thy stones and thy timber and thy dust in the midst of the water.*

In this prophecy, there are at least seven specific statements regarding Tyre, both the mainland city and the island fortress, none of which could be construed as vague, not straightforward, or able to be interpreted in many ways, and all of which the ancients could not possibly have known about.

1. Nebuchadnezzar shall take the city of Tyre. 26:7
2. Other nations are to participate in Tyre's destruction. 26:3
3. The city is to be made flat like the top of a rock. 26:4,14
4. It is to become a place for spreading of nets. 26:5,14
5. Its stones and timber are to be laid in the sea. 26:12
6. Other cities are to fear greatly at the fall of Tyre. 26:16,17
7. The old city of Tyre shall never be rebuilt. 26:14

All of these predictions came true precisely as they were prophesied. For those unfamiliar with this biblical prophecy, or the historical events fulfilling it, here is some background.

"Ezekiel was a priest who was called to the prophetic ministry at age thirty, some five years after being carried away captive in the second deportation to Babylon in 597 B.C."[2] Tyre was a prosperous Phoenician city on the coast of what is today, Lebanon. Economically, Tyre was like the New York City of the ancient world. Aside from the massive wealth and prosperity of the city, which is documented by both secular historians and the Bible, it consisted of a mainland city and an impregnable island fortress about one-half mile off the coast in the Mediterranean Sea. When Babylon finally destroyed Jerusalem in 586 BC the people of Tyre celebrated, unaware that they were also on Nebuchadnezzar's hit list.

Many Bible scholars believe that Ezekiel wrote this prophecy not long after being deported to Babylon. Some argue that it could have been written after Nebuchadnezzar had already begun his assault on Tyre. That would make point one simply an observation of current events, except for one thing. Nebuchadnezzar only succeeded in conquering the mainland part of the city. After a 13 year siege on the island fortress, and well after dates given for the writing of Ezekiel, he gave up. Tyre had not been totally annihilated as this prophecy predicts, but the mainland city had been destroyed. However, Nebuchadnezzar did fulfill the part of the prophecy in verses 7-11 that appears to pertain to Babylon alone.

It should be noted that Tyre, particularly the island fortress, was so impregnable that no one would have predicted its total destruction. The entire island fortress was protected by a wall 150 feet above the sea. Whether you are a skeptic or a believer, a brief study of this astounding fortress is fascinating.

> The ancient historian Quintus Curtius Rufus (most likely writing in approximately AD 50), listed several of these defensive traits that had remained intact as late as the siege by Alexander in 332 BC. The force of the water and the wind that prevailed on the side of the city closest to the land was said to have produced a "corrosive force of waves" that would hinder the construction of any type of bridge or causeway from the mainland (4.2.8). Furthermore, the water nearest to the walls of the city was "especially deep" and would force any would-be attackers to position any type of siege mechanisms in the unstable foundation of a ship, and the wall "dropped sheer into the sea," which prevented the use of ladders or approach by foot.[3]

So was the prophecy that Nebuchadnezzar would take the city not fulfilled? In verses 7-11 of Ezekiel 26, the personal pronoun "he" is used, indicating this part of the prophecy relates to Nebuchadnezzar as the leader of the Babylonian army. All that is said in this portion of the prophecy was fulfilled when he destroyed what was known as "Old Tyre," the mainland city. Then in verse 12, the pronoun switches to "they."

> Regarding the prediction that "many nations" would come against Tyre, the historical records surrounding the illustrious city report such turmoil and war that Ezekiel's prophecy looks like a mild understatement of the facts.

After Nebuchadnezzar's attack of the city "a period of great depression" plagued the city which was assimilated into the Persian Empire around 538 BC. (Fleming, p. 47). In 392 BC, "Tyre was involved in the war which arose between the Persians and Evagorus of Cyprus" in which the king of Egypt "took Tyre by assault" (p. 52). Sixty years later, in 332, Alexander the Great besieged Tyre and crushed it. Soon after this defeat, Ptolemy of Egypt conquered and subjugated Tyre until about 315 BC when Atigonus of Syria besieged Tyre for 15 months and captured it (Fleming, p. 65). In fact, Tyre was contested by so many foreign forces that Fleming wrote: "It seemed ever the fate of the Phoenician cities to be between an upper and a nether millstone" (p. 66). Babylon, Syria, Egypt, Rome, Greece, Armenia, and Persia are but a sampling of the "many nations" that had a part in the ultimate destruction of Tyre. Thus, Ezekiel's prophecy about "many nations" remains as a historical reality that cannot be successfully gainsaid.[4]

Two-hundred and forty years after Ezekiel's prophecy was written, Alexander the Great used the ruins of mainland Tyre to construct his causeway to the island fortress. *...and they shall lay thy stones and thy timber and thy dust in the midst of the water.* When Tyre destroyed part of the causeway using its navy, Alexander used the ships from other nations to protect the causeway and assist in the assault. *I am against thee, O Tyrus, and will cause many nations to come up against thee, as the sea causeth his waves to come up.* A visual representation of this can be seen on YouTube - "The Biblical Prophecy about Tyre." Other video's from secular sources are more dramatic but tell essentially the same story. Not only did Alexander make use of other nations to assist him in his conquest of Tyre, but historically, Tyre was assaulted on numerous occasions by various nations as Ezekiel said would happen.

"Today, Tyre (Sour or Sur)) is a depressed city that suffered greatly during Lebanon's civil war and Israel's subsequent occupation of southern Lebanon. The modern isthmus that joins the island to the mainland holds streets of houses and shops. There is a picturesque fishing harbor on the north side of the isthmus, adjoining a lively souq."

"And I will make thee like the top of a rock: thou shalt be a place to spread nets upon; thou shalt be built no more." Tyre has a number of unplanned squatter settlements. As important as any industry to modern Tyre are the Greek and Roman archaeological remains which cover the ancient mainland city of Palaetyrus, the accumulated isthmus and the island city."[5]

All seven parts of Ezekiel's prophecy against Tyre were fulfilled to the letter. The fact that Tyre still exists today in no way contradicts the prophecy. Present day Tyre is hardly a rebuilt version of the ancient wonder. It would be the same as if New York City had been totally flattened and its debris dumped in the Atlantic, then over two-thousand years later, calling a small village whose main commerce is fishing and tourism, a rebuilt New York City.

The Prophecy of Jesus Isaiah 7:14, Isaiah 53, Micah 5:1-2 (all around 700 BC)

There are many other prophecies relating to the birth of Jesus, but these few are sufficient for our purpose.

Isaiah 7:14
Therefore the Lord himself shall give you a sign; Behold, a virgin shall conceive, and bear a son, and shall call his name Immanuel.

Seven-hundred years before Christ was born, a man walking the streets of Jerusalem said that a virgin would become pregnant and have a son whom she would name Immanuel. Of all the prophecies in the Bible, this one probably sounds the most outrageous. But even a skeptic should ask a fundamental question. Why would anyone who wants to be taken seriously say such a thing? Wouldn't a man who had a message he thought people needed to hear limit his words to things that were at least believable? Would he not be concerned about his credibility? Was Isaiah some kind of lunatic? Apparently not, his prediction of the destruction of Jerusalem came true, although he did not live to see it.

Incidentally, there are many names given to Jesus that were descriptive of his nature and character but that he was not specifically called by name. Immanuel means "God with us." Jesus' name was not Immanuel, but he was the meaning of the name Immanuel.

Isaiah prophesied over 100 years before Jerusalem fell to Babylon in 586 BC. In fact, much of Isaiah is warning the nation of Judah, Israel's southern kingdom, of God's coming judgment for their wickedness and idolatry. Those prophecies came true with detailed precision.

Despite the biological impossibility of a virgin conceiving, Isaiah still said it would happen. According to New Testament scripture, this was fulfilled in Luke 1:30-31 *And the angel said unto her, Fear not, Mary: for thou hast found favour with God. And, behold, thou shalt conceive in thy womb, and bring forth a son, and shalt call his name Jesus.* Mary's response was skeptical at first. *How shall this be, seeing I know not a man?* (Luke 1:34) It kind of reminds you of the self-verifying nature of the janitor's prophecies. The Bible records a prediction that a virgin would conceive. Seven-hundred years later, the same Bible tells of it happening. On the surface, this is hardly convincing.

Remember, from a skeptic perspective **none of the prophecies are so straightforward that anyone could read them and conclude that they came true as predicted and that they could only have been brought about by supernatural means. Not one.** (104) So the Christian has a legitimate question. If the virgin birth of Christ was not supernatural, what do you call it? The obvious answer, and the only answer an unbeliever can give is that either Jesus never existed, or if he did, his birth was natural just like everyone else's. It is a closed system of skeptic thought regarding fulfilled biblical prophecy. There is no evidence of supernatural fulfillment because supernatural events do not occur — another tautology — a logical statement in which the conclusion is equivalent to the premise.

This places the skeptic at a loss to provide a rational explanation for the life of Christ and the development of Christianity. The simplistic answer is that Jesus was just a charismatic individual who was persuasive and gathered a following, just like Muhammed or Buddha. But fulfilled prophecy renders the claims of other faiths impotent, particularly when it comes to the resurrection of Christ which we have discussed already in chapter 12.

Some skeptics claim that Christianity's virgin birth claim was copied from earlier religions who also said their gods were virgin born. In fact, such claims were made about Buddha and Hindu's, Krishna. However, neither these nor others resemble in any way the virgin birth of Christ, particularly in the fact that they were not prophesied 700 years before the event. They also lack historical context. A close inspection of these stories reveal that they are not even virgin births at all, but tales of some other kind of mythical conception. Buddha's mother for example, was said to be impregnated during a dream by a white elephant which pierced her side with one of its six tusks.[6]

Only the virgin birth of Christ is really taken seriously, even by those who are not Christians. Entire books are written to discredit the claim of Jesus Christ's virgin birth. However, little attention is given to the virgin birth claims of other religious figures of history. They are just not taken seriously enough to warrant scholarly analysis. Jesus' birth is different. Why?

Isaiah 53

Who hath believed our report? and to whom is the arm of the Lord revealed? 2 For he shall grow up before him as a tender plant, and as a root out of a dry ground: he hath no form nor comeliness; and when we shall see him, there is no beauty that we should desire him. 3 He is despised and rejected of men; a man of sorrows, and acquainted with grief: and we hid as it were our faces from him; he was despised, and we esteemed him not. 4 Surely he hath borne our griefs, and carried our sorrows: yet we did esteem him stricken, smitten of God, and afflicted. 5 But he was wounded for our transgressions, he was bruised for our iniquities: the chastisement of our peace was upon him; and with his stripes we are healed. 6 All we like sheep have gone astray; we have turned every one to his own way; and the Lord hath laid on him the iniquity of us all. 7 He was oppressed, and he was afflicted, yet he opened not his mouth: he is brought as a lamb to the slaughter, and as a sheep before her shearers is dumb, so he openeth not his mouth. 8 He was taken from prison and from judgment: and who shall declare his generation? for he was cut off out of the land of the living: for the transgression of my people was he stricken. 9 And he made his grave with the wicked, and with the rich in his death; because he had done no violence, neither was any deceit in his mouth. 10 Yet it pleased the Lord to bruise him; he hath put him to grief: when thou shalt make his soul an offering for sin, he shall see his seed, he shall prolong his days, and the pleasure of the Lord shall prosper in his hand. 11 He shall see of the travail of his soul, and shall be satisfied: by his knowledge shall my righteous servant justify many; for he shall bear their iniquities. 12 Therefore will I divide him a portion with the great, and he shall divide the spoil with the strong; because he hath poured out his soul unto death: and he was numbered with the transgressors; and he bare the sin of many, and made intercession for the transgressors.

For anyone who knows something about the life and death of Christ, the specificity of this prophecy written 700 years before Christ was born, and the precise fulfillment of each aspect of it should be immediately clear. Even many non-religious people who have some idea about Jesus Christ would probably recognize him in these words of Isaiah. Some argue that parts of this passage could have been added after the life and death of Christ to make it appear prophetic. However, the Great Isaiah Scroll,

> ...is written in Hebrew and contains the entire Book of Isaiah from beginning to end, apart from a few small damaged portions. It is the oldest complete copy of the Book of Isaiah known. Pieces of the Isaiah Scroll have been carbon-14 dated at least four times, giving calibrated date ranges between 335-324 BC and 202-107 BC.[7]

Those who argue that the original text could have been corrupted by later authors still have to explain why manuscripts dated from 100 to 300 years before Christ, and 400 to 600 years after the book of Isaiah was written, contain the exact same prophecy! In fact, the entire Isaiah scroll is nearly identical to the text in the King James Bible translated in 1611. With traceability like that, when did the corruption take place and where is its documentation?

Imagine a settler of the Jamestown colony in 1607 publicly predicting that one day a man of African descent, who claimed to be born on a remote island, educated in prestigious universities that had not yet been thought of, in a country that would not be established for another 169 years, would become the President of a land called the United States of America, and whose name would be Barack Hussein Obama. Had such a prediction been made in Jamestown, and were the one who made it known, he would today be considered to have uttered the most incredible prophecy in the history of the world! And that is just six prophetic statements. There are more than 300 in the Bible which were all fulfilled to the letter in Jesus Christ.

Prophecies in the Bible about the birth, life, death, and resurrection of Christ have been subjected to mathematical probability analysis. Professor Emeritus of Science at Westmont College, Peter Stoner, has calculated the probability of one man fulfilling the major prophecies made concerning the Messiah. Twelve different classes representing some 600-university students worked out the estimates. The chances that one man could fulfill just 48 of the 300 prophecies concerning Jesus are 1 in 10 to the 157th power. If only 8 prophecies are considered, the probability of one man fulfilling them is equal to covering the entire state of Texas with silver dollars two feet deep, marking one of them, then stirring the entire pile thoroughly and picking the marked one on the first try while blindfolded.[8] I have no clue how statisticians figure out such probabilities.

Extrapolate that probability to three-hundred prophecies and, if it is not already there, it stretches into the astronomically absurd. There is nothing in any other religious figure that can even be in the same universe as the prophecies fulfilled by Jesus Christ. No doubt this is why skeptics, believers, and the just plain curious, take the birth of Christ and the prophecies it fulfilled seriously enough to subject them to painstaking analysis, while leaving the virgin birth claims of other religious figures to folklore and myth.

The Prophecy of Israel

The fact that a skeptic refers to the creation of the modern state of Israel as a prophecy Christians claim has been fulfilled indicates some knowledge and exposure to Christian teaching. Indeed, many Christians view the creation of Israel in 1948, and its survival as an infant nation against aggressors that had a thousand-year head start militarily, as a significant sign that God still has his hand on this tiny nation. It is also fascinating to see skeptics sidestep the prophetic nature of this event.

When Israel was in captivity in Babylon, after the 586 BC destruction of Jerusalem, Ezekiel said, *Then they will know that I am the LORD their God, for though I sent them into exile among the nations, I will gather them to their own land, not leaving any behind.* Ezek. 39:28. This was partly fulfilled after Persia (modern Iran) overthrew Babylon and Persian king Artaxerxes allowed the Jews to return to their homeland, although they were still under Persian rule. Note however, that it was by decree of a man that the people of Israel could return. The Bible says in Proverbs 22:1 *The king's heart is in the hand of the Lord, as the rivers of water: he turneth it whithersoever he will.*

When the skeptic says, **But skeptics don't agree that it proves anything about God because all the evidence points to people, not God, creating the modern state of Israel,** (105) he is saying that if God is going to fulfill prophecy to his satisfaction, it has to be by some obviously supernatural means. The skeptic simply disallows God from employing human beings in working out his ultimate will. Conveniently, this eliminates nearly all events in the Bible involving nations, empires, rulers, armies, kings, prophets, preachers, and ordinary people who were part of fulfilled prophecy. Apparently, what would convince the skeptic is for there to have been a historically documented event in which suddenly hundreds of thousands of Jews were teleported to the biblical land of their forefathers where they immediately set up a government and became a nation. But then, who would believe that and how would it be proven generations later?

However, truth is even stranger than fiction. How did this infant nation, in a matter of just nineteen years, come to be such a military powerhouse that it repelled the invasion of Egyptian, Syrian and Jordanian forces, all of which had centuries to develop weapons, military might, and strategic defenses. In the 1967 six day war, history records the reasons for Arab losses: the element of surprise attack, Israel's superior strategy, and poor leadership of Arab forces,[9] all of which have parallels in military victories by Israel recorded in the Old Testament.

However skeptics want to spin it, the reality is that the Old Testament is not just a collection of ancient legends, fables, and vague prophecies. It is about real people in actual historical places, real rulers, and real empires. Daniel prophesied the fall of the Babylonian empire to the Persians, and Persia's fall at the hands of the Greeks, and the rise of the Roman empire hundreds of years before these things happened. Most of all, the Old Testament is the story of God's hand in the development of the nation of Israel and his redemptive plan through Jesus Christ, who is pictured throughout. The Old Testament is Israel's biographical history.

Ironically, or providentially, depending on your point of view, Israel today is still the epicenter of world events. Unless you understand the Bible, you will never understand the Arab-Israel conflict that began in Genesis 16.

If I were a skeptic looking at the world today, biblical prophecies would both intrigue and bother me. Why is Israel the centerpiece nation in the Bible, and in current world events? Why is there such hatred of the Jews by Arab nations? Where did that animosity begin? The Bible has the answer. I would be bothered by the statement written almost two-thousand years ago referring to the two witnesses in Rev. 11 which says, *And their dead bodies shall lie in the street of the great city, which spiritually is called Sodom and Egypt, where also our Lord was crucified. And they of the people and kindreds and tongues and nations shall see their dead bodies three days and a half, and shall not suffer their dead bodies to be put in graves.*

Just one-hundred years ago, it could have been said that this passage proves the Bible is not accurate. It was not possible for people of all nations to see something as it was happening. Today, anyone with a cell phone can pull up live feeds to view events currently happening on the other side of the world. How could a man named John, in AD 90, have even guessed that a single event could be seen simultaneously as it was happening from anywhere in the world? If I were an honest skeptic, that would trouble me.

In conclusion, the skeptic wrongly says **And then there is also that apparent problem of the most important Bible prophecy of all failing to come true. Jesus said he would return and assume power over the world before his disciples died. But as we all know, he did not.** (108) The passage referred to here is Matthew 24:34. *Truly I tell you, this generation will certainly not pass away until all these things have happened.* Once again, you cannot divorce a verse from its context then make bold claims about the error of that isolated statement. Reading all of Matthew 24 clears this up easily. Jesus even told his disciples in this same conversation that they would be killed, so what sense does it make to claim Jesus said he would return before his disciples died? He spoke of *nation rising against nation and kingdom against kingdom.* He said all this would happen before his coming.

When Jesus refers to *"this generation,"* he is not talking about the generation of those to whom he was speaking at the moment, but the generation that would see the things he had predicted would happen earlier in the passage. Many Bible scholars believe this refers to a future period known as the Great Tribulation. We again have to consider if Jesus expected others to follow his teaching after he was gone, why would he make statements that he knew would be proven false when he died and that was the end? Jesus would have become human history's greatest fool, not its focal point.

What do prophecies prove? Nothing. However, fulfilled prophecies are an entirely different matter. Biblical prophecies which foretell specific events, in specific places, involving real people, and which come true one-hundred percent of the time exactly as they are predicted, prove that the Bible is no ordinary book, Jesus is no ordinary person, and that God has communicated truth to us in an unmistakable way. Trying to find a way around that is an exercise in futility.

SIXTEEN

HOW IMPORTANT ARE THE TEN COMMANDMENTS?

Atheists really don't like the Ten Commandments. Recent years have seen a plethora of court cases involving the removal of displays of the Ten Commandments from public places, usually on the grounds that it violates the separation of church and state. Interestingly, the Bible explains why these ten commands from God, sometimes referred to in the New Testament as "the law," are so offensive to some. *Wherefore the law was our schoolmaster to bring us unto Christ, that we might be justified by faith.* (Gal. 3:24)

The Ten Commandments work like a teacher who uses what is right to reveal to students why their answers are wrong. The reason a good teacher will do that is to bring the student to a point of understanding, acceptance, and conformity to what is true and correct. God gave the Ten Commandments to do the same. They reveal where our thinking and actions are wrong. Of course, we don't like that. No one likes to be shown where they are wrong, but that is part of real life.

Before analyzing some objections to the Ten Commandments, we must acknowledge a sad but true statement **...many smart and relatively informed Christians know surprisingly little about the Ten Commandments beyond what is taught in Sunday School. For example, a 2007 survey found that most Americans can name more Big Mac® hamburger ingredients and *The Brady Bunch* children than laws of the Ten Commandments.**[1](110)

While this statement makes me cringe, I do not doubt its truthfulness. Although the survey cites lack of knowledge of the Ten Commandments by Americans, it is probably just as true of many believers. Most professing Christians could tell you who directed which movie, which songs are in the top ten, or the starting lineup of their favorite baseball team before they could recite the Ten Commandments.

To help with that, I've developed a simple memory cue that anyone can learn in five minutes so they will never forget the Ten Commandments and could recite them in order upon request. I've used this with youth in camp and found that in the following year, with no reminders in between, the same young people could recite them in order after just a moment of thought. I'll give it to you at the end of this chapter. From then on you will always know the ten laws God gave to Moses.

Despite the fact that the Ten Commandments figure prominently in our American system of government and are central to civil, social mores skeptics find fault with all of them. Not one is considered appropriate for modern society.

Thou shalt have no other gods before me.
This commandment blatantly conflicts with the concept of religious freedom. It couldn't possibly be a real law in any country that respects the rights of its citizens to worship or not worship as they please. (110)

What skeptics don't seem to understand is that religious freedom, that is the freedom to worship or not worship whoever or whatever you want, is man's idea, not God's. God never authorized such "freedom." Most of the Old Testament is the history of God's dealing with the nation of Israel. When they rejected the worship of God and chose idolatry he brought punishment upon them in the form of pestilence, warfare, and slavery. That was not to infringe upon their freedom. That kind of freedom actually enslaved them in the very worst forms of idolatry, including child sacrifice. God's chastisement on them was to lead them out of bondage to such perversions.

If the Bible and Christianity are true, then all other religions are false. It is senseless to think that God does, or should, view them all equally. That has never been the case! It is logically incoherent to think otherwise, the same as it would be for a husband to allow his wife the freedom of intimacy with other men. She belongs to him alone and he belongs to her alone. I think everyone gets that.

Throughout the Old Testament, God's relationship with Israel was the same. They were his chosen people and he did not want them cavorting with other gods. This becomes more clear as we look at other objections to the Ten Commandments.

Thou shalt not make unto thee any graven image

The complaint against this command is similar to the first; it violates freedom. The prohibition against graven images is intended to prevent idolatry - Israel's chief sin. Skeptics complain, **If someone wants to make a "graven image" of a dolphin or a tree and then bow down before it, shouldn't they be free to do so? If so, this law has no place in a free society.** (111)

While I believe the Ten Commandments are relevant to modern life and would make for a much better society if they were followed, we must remember that they were written to the Israelites shortly after they left Egypt. As all of the Old Testament documents, Israel had a serious problem with idolatry for hundreds of years, graven images and all.

God looked at their idolatry the same way a man would look at his wife committing adultery. This is very apparent throughout the Old Testament and becomes crystal clear in the New Testament where God always speaks about the wife being the one who commits adultery. I don't know the statistics, but no doubt many more men are guilty of this than women. You would think God would have known that and spoken more strongly to men on the subject. The reason he didn't is not because men are less guilty, or because God is a chauvinist, but because the wife committing adultery pictures the Christian forsaking his relationship with God and becoming "intimate" with worldly (sinful) pleasures. Christians call this "spiritual adultery" or "spiritual idolatry." It comes right from the first and second commandments. When the skeptic says it seems odd to him that God would say, *for I the Lord thy God am a jealous God,* he fails to recognize that the idolatry of worshipping graven images results in the same violation of trust and relationship to God as adultery does in human marriage.

Thou shalt not take the name of the Lord thy God in vain

To a preacher, it is troubling when a skeptic shows more insight into proper Christian conduct than many believers. **Profanity that includes "God" is common. Less offensive phrases, such as "oh my god," and "God darn it," are even more common. Furthermore, everyone who has ever said "gosh," "golly," or "gee," might be in trouble too because these are nothing more than euphemisms for "God."** (112) I'm not sure about "golly," but I agree about the others and have been guilty of letting this slip from my own lips on occasion. Many Christians however, are not as honest as the skeptic when it comes to "replacement cursing" violating the third commandment.

I once preached about the inappropriateness of such "Christian swearing" and the using of God's name in an irreverent way. One man challenged me that looking into the heavens and saying, "Oh my God," could be a reverent use of the otherwise offensive phrase. Some Christians will defend in minutiae what every atheist knows is irreverent, even though an atheist has no reason to concern himself with irreverence. This highlights the accuracy of Luke 16:8b "...for the children of this world are in their generation wiser than the children of light."

I have often wondered why it is that the name of God, or Jesus Christ, is so frequently used as an expletive while other deities or prophets get a pass. Do Hindus say, "Oh my Krishna!" I can hardly imagine a Muslim using the name of Allah or Mohammed lightly, but do atheists? Why is it that the name of Christ is commonly used profanely but not other professed deities? There must be something unique about the name of God, and Jesus Christ, to warrant this distinction, unbecoming as it is.

A skeptic says, **Restricting the use of the word or name "God" violates free speech.** (112) However, many of our laws violate free speech. Slander (spoken defamation) and libel (written defamation) are both punishable under civil law. Civil societies demand language that is respectful. We all want to live in a society where this is the norm. A person who shows disrespect for a court, its officers, or its authority, can be held in contempt, fined, or even jailed.

Free speech does not mean we can talk disrespectfully or defiantly toward authorities. According to First Amendment Center,

> ...you may have a right to curse on the street, don't assume you have a right to curse at your public employer or at your public school. Context — as well as content — is important in First Amendment law. The government has greater power to regulate speech when it acts as employer or educator than it does when it acts as sovereign.[2]

All but the most belligerent citizens understand and accept this. For some reason, when the authority of the universe expects the same, skeptics cry foul. Of course, a skeptic doesn't acknowledge God, so not wishing to submit to his commands is pretty much a given. The "violation of free speech" criticism of this commandment apparently only holds true for God's commands. Man's laws that restrict disrespectful or contemptible speech are part of decent social behavior. The hypocrisy of the double standard is glaring but understandable since, in the one case, the prohibition originates from an authority the skeptic does not believe exists.

Remember the Sabbath to keep it holy

Skeptics cite Old Testament passages that call for the death penalty for doing work on the Sabbath as an indicator of just how serious God is about reverencing the seventh day and why it is not a good idea to live by the Ten Commandments today. **And I sure wouldn't want anyone to be executed if they did some work on the Sabbath, as God calls for in Exodus 31.** (112)

I grew up in a very Christian world, preacher's kid, Sunday School and church, youth group, Christian schools, Christian University, the whole shebang. However, I have never heard of an evangelical Christian church, or any church for that matter, calling for capital punishment or even excommunication for "violating the Sabbath." Is it reasonable to suppose that virtually one-hundred percent of evangelical Christians simply choose to defy God and ignore this command? Is it possible they know something skeptics do not? Is it possible that preachers across America are not just glossing over such an obvious and serious command of God because it infringes on modern life? Let's see if we can understand this commandment a little more thoroughly before jumping to the conclusion that God wants any and all violators stoned to death.

Prior to God giving this command the Israelites had spent the last 400 years as slaves in Egypt. It is obvious by their actions at Mt. Sinai, where they fashioned the likeness of an Egyptian god to worship because they thought Moses was not coming back, that they knew how to worship idols and would resort to it without hesitation. From Egypt to Canaan, God was teaching Israel who he is and instructing them in how to worship him.

This commandment reminded the Israelites each week that the God who brought them out of Egypt is the God who created the universe and everything in it in six days and then rested on the seventh. It reminded them of the impotency of pagan gods by which they were so heavily influenced. It also drew a line in the sand for those who were defiant toward God.

At the time God gave this command to Israel, they were a theocracy. They had no king and no governmental structure. God spoke to the people through a leader of his choosing. In this case, it was Moses. Violating this command was a rejection of God himself. It was a statement that man does not need to follow his commands or patterns, nor obey what he says. It is understandable that skeptics would criticize the severe punishment for breaking this commandment because they look at it as an arbitrary rule of a celestial dictator who does not respect freedom of choice when it comes to worship, rather than as an instrument to purge the defiant and rebellious from his chosen people. Here is a way to look at it that is similar, though not a perfect parallel.

In the early days of our nation's colonies, there were those who wanted to remain under British rule. They were called Tories or Loyalists. They were the opponents of becoming a free and sovereign country. Very soon we would declare our independence as a nation and pass a Constitution that gave citizens the right to freedom of speech. But it was not like that when the United States was in its formative years. There was no tolerance by patriots for loyalists to the King of England. Once the United States was free of British rule, many of these loyalists, half-a-million by some estimates, fled to remote parts of the country, into Quebec, and the Caribbean. It was a painful and sometimes ugly process, but those who desired to be shackled to the King of England were purged.

The fourth commandment, and the severe penalties for its violation worked similarly for Israel. God was forging a nation that had to be purged of pagan influence and outright defiance of God as their authority. Interestingly, this command has no corollary in the New Testament, so skeptics and Christians alike can rest easy.

In the gospels, which document the life of Christ, Pharisees were waiting to see if Jesus would heal a man on the Sabbath so they could accuse him. Jesus healed the man with a withered hand. (Mark 3) By the time we get to the book of Acts, Christians are treating the Sabbath like any other day and meeting for worship on the first day of the week, in complete contrast to the Old Testament regulation.

Paul, the primary author of the New Testament, never corrects this practice nor even advises against it. Jesus never taught that the Old Testament prohibition was still intact. Apparently, something changed and God is fine with worship on the first day of the week and work on the seventh. In fact, Colossians 2:16 says, *Let no man therefore judge you in meat, or in drink, or in respect of an holy day, or of the new moon, or of the sabbath days:* Paul wrote to the Roman Christians, *One man esteemeth one day above another: another esteemeth every day alike. Let every man be fully persuaded in his own mind.* (Romans 14:5)

Entire books have been written on the subject of this commandment alone. For now, let it suffice to say that either the incarnation of Jesus Christ wrought significant changes in Old Testament laws for Israel, as well as the New Testament Christian church, or the Bible is a hodgepodge of jumbled up laws that make absolutely no sense. Even Jesus himself would have broken the commandment without conscience or consequence. Skeptics may default to the hodgepodge option, but it behooves them to consider the former if they are going to critique Christianity, because within it is the entire foundation of the Christian faith.

Surely Christian philosophers like Irenaeus (AD 160), Origen (AD 200), Athansius (AD 367) and many others, were not just misguided ignoramuses, nor are modern-day scholars. If the Bible were no more sensible in terms of historical context and theological consistency than what many unbelievers claim, it is not reasonable that brilliant men only one or two centuries removed from much of its writing would have been so easily duped by what naysayers call obvious nonsense. Just maybe there is something more involved.

Honor thy father and mother

Objections to this commandment focus on abused and neglected children. **I worked as a live-in supervisor at a residential facility for abused and neglected children, so I know better than most how badly some parents treat their children. This commandment is wrong to suggest that all parents deserve to be honored by their children.** (114) Are there exceptions to this command in cases of abused children? Must an undeserving parent still be shown honor?

A wife and mother leaves her husband and two children to carouse with other men. She is unrepentant and offers no substantive care for her abandon children. Even their birthdays go by unacknowledged. Should her children still show her honor? Are they obligated to do so by this command? Their mother deserves no honor whatsoever, but that does not mean she should not have it, at least to some degree.

Christianity is all about two things, what we deserve from God, and what he offers us instead. At best, we are all sinners who have violated his law and are deserving of his righteous sentence, but he offers us grace, forgiveness, and mercy. Jesus taught us not to respond in kind to mistreatment from others. He taught us to go the extra mile, to do the extraordinary thing. He taught us that forgiveness is superior to vengeance, or a lifetime of holding a bitter grudge. Linda White, a woman who suffered the rape and murder of her daughter said, "Unforgiveness is a poison you drink, hoping someone else will die."[3]

For children to show some form of honor to a mother who abandoned them for a life of carnal pleasure doesn't mean they dismiss past wrongs as okay or of no consequence, or that their mother deserves the same degree of honor as she would have if she had cared for, nurtured, and sacrificed for them like good mothers do. It means that they can still choose to forgive and act in an honorable way toward their birth mother. That could be wishing her well with a Mother's Day card, or a call on her birthday. There are degrees of honor and it can take many forms. In the case of abusive situations, this commandment affords the opportunity to exchange hate, bitterness, anger, vengeance, and self-pity, for mercy, grace, forgiveness, peace, and yes, even honor.

I knew a pastor whose father-in-law was a Satan worshipper. He felt convicted that this verse included showing honor to him too. But how could he show honor to a man whose beliefs and practices were the polar opposite of his own without compromising his own convictions? One day he hit upon an idea. The next time he was at his in-laws he asked his father-in-law if it would be all right if he called him Dad. The man was surprised and pleased because his preacher son-in-law had never called him Dad. It was a small thing, but it showed honor without condoning or excusing objectionable beliefs or conduct.

Thou shalt not kill.

I have to wonder just how far skeptics are willing to stretch to avoid acknowledging that even one of the Ten Commandments is worthwhile. Skeptics find fault with this commandment because it is not clear enough. **Many Christians seem to be of the opinion that this commandment is conditional because some support wars and some support capital punishment. Many Christians also feel it is okay to kill someone in certain cases of self-defense or to protect another person. Some Christians prefer "Thou shalt not murder." But it's not clear at all. (114)**

Many versions do translate this commandment, *Thou shalt not murder.* It is not merely something that some Christians prefer. The Hebrew word translated "kill" reflects a killing by malicious, premeditated intent. Some translators used the word "kill" instead of "murder," never imagining that critics would conclude that this prohibits someone from defending themselves or their children from attack, or from accepting a call to serve their country in time of war. No matter how simple something is worded, there will always be those who try to confuse what is plain by interjecting some unintended technicality.

When I was teaching junior high science, I gave a homework assignment. "Read the rest of chapter 6 and answer the questions at the end." Pretty plain right? The next day one girl had not completed all the questions. When I asked her why, she said, "You only told us to answer the questions. I answered some of them, but you did not say we had to answer all of them." To her adolescent mind, the assignment was not clear at all. In reality, she was trying to avoid the obvious on a conjured up technicality.

God said we are not to kill people. All the little technicalities are just smokescreens to avoid what is plain. There should be little question as to what is really meant by this command.

An easy way to see this is to look at another command from the New Testament. Ephesians 6:1 says, *Children obey your parents in the Lord for this is right.* That is easy to understand and good advice, but it does not cover every conceivable situation that may arise. It does not need to. Suppose a parent tells a child to go rob someone. We could imagine hundreds of scenarios that might make this simple little rule sound not so wise. Inventing ethical dilemmas only introduces confusion to what is obviously clear in the normal ebb and flow of life.

Thou shalt not commit adultery

This commandment is not appropriate in any society that places a high value on freedom and privacy. (114) I do not expect unbelievers to agree with or support many biblical commands, but I have to say that the above quote is over the top, even for a skeptic. Adultery has catastrophic emotional consequences for those who are betrayed, as well as the adulterer. A betrayed husband or wife has their entire world shattered. If children are part of the betrayal, the far-reaching effects of adultery can scar them for life. The skeptic objects to this command because it infringes on freedom and privacy, but I wonder if a skeptic grants such freedom and privacy to his or her spouse?

The central focus of this commandment is trust. Without that, human relationships disintegrate. Such a cavalier attitude toward adultery would undoubtedly disintegrate as well if the critic were the victim of such betrayal. I can hardly imagine a skeptic who discovers his wife has been having an affair saying, "It's okay dear, I place a high value on your freedom and privacy, so you are under no obligation to be faithful to me!" Objecting to this commandment seems horribly forced just to avoid agreeing with even one moral law given in the Bible.

There is also a theological element to the commandment against adultery. God uses the marriage relationship to illustrate how he views the relationship between himself and the church, that is, the worldwide body of Christians. Eph. 5: 22-27 says,

> *Wives, submit yourselves unto your own husbands, as unto the Lord. For the husband is the head of the wife, even as Christ is the head of the church: and he is the savior of the body. Therefore as the church is subject unto Christ, so let the wives be to their own husbands in every thing. Husbands, love your wives, even as Christ also loved the church, and gave himself for it; That he might sanctify and cleanse it with the washing of water by the word, That he might present it to himself a glorious church, not having spot, or wrinkle, or any such thing; but that it should be holy and without blemish.*

We have already observed that God referred to Israel's idolatry in the Old Testament as "adultery." It was a violation of a trust, a promise they had made after leaving Egypt. *And the people said unto Joshua, Nay; but we will serve the LORD. And Joshua said unto the people, Ye are witnesses against yourselves that ye have chosen you the LORD, to serve him. And they said, We are witnesses.* (Joshua 24:21-22) Notice what God said to Israel in Jeremiah 3:9 *And it came to pass through the lightness of her whoredom, that she defiled the land, and committed adultery with stones and with stocks.*

When Israel reverted to idolatry over worship of God, he viewed it the same way a husband would view his wife having intercourse with another man. God knows that when trust is shattered relationships are broken and the very fabric of civilization falls apart. Despite the skeptic objections, a command against adultery is foundational to the core elements of a healthy and civil society.

This commandment places the skeptic in a precarious situation. If he is true to his ideals that freedom and privacy supersede this commandment, he has no claims on his own wife and no gripe with another man courting her affections. She is free. If he objects, he is in agreement with this command.

I think the real opposition to this command is that acceptance of it as a moral code implies it was given by some authority. If that authority was man, then it is not universally binding. If it is universally binding, meaning everyone should live by it, then the one who gave it has the authority to make such a universally binding law. That prospect is unacceptable to a skeptic, so he cannot endorse this commandment. But he still hopes his wife will keep it.

Thou shalt not steal

Skeptics generally like this commandment, except for the exceptions. **If one of my daughters is starving and the only immediately available solution is to swipe a loaf of bread from the supermarket, I'm breaking this commandment.** (115) This is a false dilemma, providing only two possible solutions, steal or starve.

When I was a young boy growing up in a small town, we had neighbors who were twin brothers. Their family was quite poor. One day they did just what the skeptic advocates in his exception to this commandment; they swiped a loaf of bread from the local market. The owner saw them take something but didn't know what it was and ran after them. He caught them a hundred yards up the road as they were running home. When he discovered they had stolen a loaf of bread, he told them that if they were that hungry, all they had to do was ask and he would have given them bread. They did not need to steal.

This commandment addresses a universal truth. It is wrong to take something that does not belong to you. It is a moral law written in the hearts of human beings regardless of culture, Christian or not. Creating an ethical dilemma to argue for exceptions is nothing more than being argumentative in order to avoid agreeing that God had even one good idea in the Ten Commandments.

Thou shalt not bear false witness against your neighbor

There is a barrage of questions to highlight the uncertain nature of this commandment. **Does this commandment forbid me from lying to anyone about anything? Is it some kind of legal-speak for not misrepresenting the truth in court or in formal business dealings? Does it mean that I can lie to everyone except those people who are my** neighbors? **What if my overweight friend asks me how she looks in her new, tight dress? Can I lie just a little bit in order to be kind?** (115)

This commandment says that we should not speak things about others that are not true. The word "false" literally means, "lie or deception." The word witness means "testimony or evidence." While we can look to other scripture to gain guidance about everyday situations, this commandment, once understood, is quite straightforward. Do you want someone saying untrue things about you or presenting faulty, contrived evidence in order to defame your character? Would you do that to someone else? If not, then you are on board with this commandment.

Thou shalt not covet

The worst part of this commandment is the fact that wives and servants/slaves are listed along with oxen, asses, and whatever else one's neighbor may own. This may have been sensible and acceptable in cultures thousands of years ago, and sadly, it still holds up today, but hopefully you live in a society that is advanced enough to recognize that women should not be the property of men. This commandment shows how blatantly sexist and outdated parts of the Bible are. (116)

So I have a simple question for the person who thinks this way. Who does your wife belong to? Is she yours? Do you introduce her as "my wife." Does another man have just as much right to claim her as you have? If he decides he likes "your" wife better than his own, would you be at all bothered if you knew he wanted "your" wife for himself and was devising ways to lure her away from you? To be consistent and logical, the skeptic who objects to this commandment on sexist grounds must acknowledge that his wife is not really his, and is fair game for any man who wants her and who cares nothing for that other outdated commandment against adultery.

The language of this commandment is no different than everyday use when we refer to things that belong to us: my car, my house, my dog, my husband, my wife, my children etc... The fact that I refer to "my wife" in the same type of language as I do "my dog" is never rationally interpreted as equating my wife to my dog, or that they are both, in the same way, my property.

Once again, when this commandment is examined in very practical terms, even in modern society, we all identify with the fairness and reasonableness it presents. Even those who don't like its language still want others to live by its principle. I would not like it if I knew some other man wanted my wife and imagined ways he might get her. I would not like it if he thought that way of my dog either. To say that I am therefore considering both my wife and my dog as equally my property is just plain silly.

In closing out the objections to the Ten Commandments, the skeptic hopes we **can at least now better understand why many people don't think the Ten Commandments are appropriate, logical, or relevant today and why they don't want to see them displayed in public school classrooms or inserted into government. It's not about trying to insult God, oppressing anyone's religion, or refusing to acknowledge the significant role of Christianity in society. It is about recognizing that seeking to impose the very specific religious laws of some undermines fairness for all.** (116)

But there is a glaring flaw in this conclusion. Posting the Ten Commandments in schools, or having our government honor them as guideposts for society, is not the same as imposing them on anyone. It does not force people to live by them. Our government hoists the American flag over the capitol as the symbol of our nation, our freedom, and our guiding principles. But there are lots of citizens of this country who do not agree with American principles or what the flag stands for. There are some who favor communism. A few hate our flag and burn it in protest to what it represents. Others refuse to show respect when the Star spangled Banner is played at sporting events.

Millions of immigrants live in this country while still keeping customs of their own. Are we imposing our American values on them simply by displaying the American flag? We do have laws that impose certain American principles on citizens, or others who just live here, but we have no laws against adultery, not taking the Lord's name in vain, or coveting your neighbor's possessions. Public display of the Ten Commandments may make them more visible, but that does make their violation criminal.

Overlooking our American Congress are numerous sculptures of individuals who influenced the creation of America.

> The 23 marble relief portraits over the gallery doors of the House Chamber in the U.S. Capitol depict historical figures noted for their work in establishing the principles that underlie American law. They were installed when the chamber was remodeled in 1949-1950. Created in Bas relief of white Vermont marble by seven different sculptors, the plaques each measure 28 inches in diameter. The

11 profiles in the eastern half of the chamber face left and the eleven in the western half face right, so that all look towards the full-face relief of Moses in the center of the north wall.[4]

When skeptics say that the Ten Commandments are irrelevant, inappropriate, and illogical for our modern American culture, they are attempting to overrule the views and convictions of the very ones who established America in the first place and what is memorialized all over our nation's Capital. They do not like it if government makes them visible to society, but when it becomes personal, they kind of like them and want others to live by them, at least some of them.

Now, about that memory cue for the Ten Commandments I promised. If you are a skeptic and do not want the Ten Commandments permanently etched into your mind, you might consider skipping this because it really works. The secret to remembering the Ten Commandments in order is to break them down into three sections using one key word for each commandment. Here they are.

HAVE - MAKE and TAKE HOLY - HONOR KILL - A - STEEL - BEAR - CUB

The first three are four letter words and make a little rhyme. They also point to the central theme of the first three commandments.

Thou shalt **HAVE** no other gods before me.

Thou shalt not **MAKE** unto thee any graven image.

Thou shalt not **TAKE** the name of the Lord thy God in vain.

The next two words both start with 'H' and are high and majestic sounding, which are good clues to the next two commandments.

Remember the Sabbath to keep it **HOLY**.

HONOR your father and mother.

Now the last five come all at once. The memory clue for this is really stupid, which makes it harder to forget, but the key words, or first letters of the key words are all there.

Thou shalt not **KILL**.

Thou shalt not commit **ADULTERY**.

Thou shalt not **STEAL**.

Thou shalt not **BEAR** false witness.
Thou shalt not **COVET**

Of course, the 'C' in cub stands for COVET. This is the hardest of the clues to remember, but it's the last one, so even if you forget it, which isn't likely, you still know nine of the ten. So one more time:

Have, Make, and **Take - Holy, Honor - Kill, A, Steel, Bear, <u>C</u>ub.**

Review that in your mind a couple times, along with the commands they represent, and the Ten Commandments are yours forever.

SEVENTEEN

DO YOU KNOW THE REAL TEN COMMANDMENTS?

I was in my second year coaching varsity basketball. During one practice, the father of two of my players walked in and asked if he could talk to the team. I was apprehensive, but assuming he was going to give them a pep talk, I consented. He proceeded to instruct them in some basics of the game where he apparently thought their present coaching left them deficient. He thought he knew a lot more than his short coaching session revealed. His sons were embarrassed. He soon left, I guess feeling like his "coaching" had enlightened the team.

The skeptic's enlightening of Christians on the real Ten Commandments reminded me of the basketball Dad's few minutes of coaching glory. In only a minute, he demonstrated that his knowledge of the game's fundamentals was seriously flawed. It was embarrassing for everyone but him. It is much the same when a skeptic claims the real Ten Commandments are buried in an obscure chapter of Exodus, unknown to centuries of Bible scholars, teachers, preachers, and ordinary Christians.

The Bible gives just enough rope for those seeking alternatives to its laws and principles to hang themselves. I think that is what happens when a Bible critic insists that Christianity has somehow missed the real Ten Commandments. I must admit though, a casual reading of the passage could lead someone who already thinks the Bible is fraught with inconsistencies to the conclusion that he has found one more.

For those unfamiliar with the common skeptic assertion that Exodus 20 is not the home of the real Ten Commandments, here is a brief explanation. In Exodus 34, Moses goes back up Mount Sinai with two freshly carved stone tablets for God to write on again. Moses broke the original set in his anger at the children of Israel's abrupt return to idolatry while he was on the mount receiving those first tablets. However, it appears that the commandments given in Exodus 34 are quite different from those in Exodus 20. Here are the skeptic's "real ten commandments" as they appear in Exodus 34.

1. verse 14 For thou shalt worship no other god.
2. verse 17 Thou shalt make thee no molten gods.
3. verse 18 The feast of unleavened bread shalt thou keep.
4. verse 21 Six days thou shalt work, but on the seventh day thou shalt rest.
5. verse 22 And thou shalt observe the feast of weeks, of the first fruits of wheat harvest, and the feast of ingathering at the year's end.
6. verse 23 Thrice in the year shall all your men children appear before the Lord God, the God of Israel.
7. verse 25 Thou shalt not offer the blood of my sacrifice with leaven.
8. verse 25 Neither shall the sacrifice of the feast of the passover be left unto the morning.
9. verse 26 The first of the first fruits of thy land thou shalt bring unto the house of the Lord thy God.
10. verse 26 Thou shalt not seethe a kid in his mother's milk.

Most Christian's immediate reaction to this list is doubt and skepticism. They feel that it can't possibly be the real Ten Commandments because many of the laws are just too weird and they can't understand why they wouldn't have heard of them before. But they are the real Ten Commandments, as the lines immediately following these laws in Exodus 34:27-28 indicate. (118)

Sure enough, following this list God tells Moses in verse 27, *Write thou these words; for after the tenor of these words I have made a covenant with thee and with Israel.* Then in verse 28, *he [Moses] was there with the Lord forty days and forty nights; he did neither eat bread, nor drink water. And he wrote upon the tables the words of the covenant, the ten commandments.*

It sounds pretty open and shut. So how did Bible scholars for centuries miss such an obvious irregularity regarding the most basic set of laws in the Bible? Furthermore, why are the commands in Exodus 20 called the Ten Commandments when they are not even referred to as such in the chapter where they are cited while these apparently are?

Jason S. DeRouchie, associate professor of Old Testament at Bethlehem College and Seminary, has provided a scholarly analysis of this passage and notes the following observation.

> Yahweh (the Hebrew name for God) announced in 34:1 that he, not Moses, would write the same Words on the new tablets that he had written before with his own finger: "Yahweh said to Moses, 'Cut for yourself two tablets of stone like the first, and I will write on the tablets the words that were on the first tablets, which you broke.'" Yahweh, not Moses, is the antecedent to the third masculine singular verb phrase "and he wrote" in v. 28, which means that "these words" that Moses is charged to write in v. 27 (i.e., 34:11-26) are not the actual Ten Words of the covenant.[1]

What this means is that in Exodus 34:27 when God tells Moses, *Write thou these words...* he is referring to the instructions given in verses 11-26, which includes these not so famous ten commands. Moses wrote those down. Then in verse 28, when it says, *and he wrote upon the tables the words of the covenant, the ten commandments,* it is referring to God writing again the commandments given in Exodus 20. This makes sense when Exodus 34 is taken as a whole because the chapter begins with God saying that it was he who was going to write again what had been written on the first stone tables.

Additionally, in Deuteronomy 4:13 we read, *And he declared unto you his covenant, which he commanded you to perform, even ten commandments; and he wrote them upon two tables of stone.* This verse alone removes any doubt that the real Ten Commandments are the ones God gave in Exodus 20 and later rewrote in Exodus 34. Exodus 32:16 also is unmistakable, *And the tables were the work of God, and the writing was the writing of God, graven upon the tables.* So we can conclude that, as far as what the Bible says in multiple passages, it was God who wrote on the stone tablets the first time, in Exodus 20, and the same commandments a second time in Ex.34.

Not yet finished with objections to the ten commandments the skeptic says, **If God wanted us all to be aware of, comprehend, and obey a short, ten-item list of laws, wouldn't he have thought to make them a little less mysterious and a lot more relevant? Why do many**

of them seem hopelessly outdated and have no place in free and democratic societies? (120)

It's not clear whether the skeptic is referring to the Ten commandments in Exodus 20, or his "real ten commandments," in Exodus 34. It probably doesn't matter though, because the attitude is the same for both. So let's ask a few simple questions.

1. What is mysterious or irrelevant about a command that marriage partners should not cheat on each other? Isn't that kind of commitment pretty fundamental to the concept of marriage? Do you want your spouse to follow this commandment?
2. Is a command to not kill (murder) other people really mysterious? What would make this commandment more relevant? Isn't this pretty foundational to all free and civil societies?
3. Does the skeptic want to be honored by his children? I don't mean worshipped or idolized, just treated honorably? Would a society be better off if this were the norm? If all parents and children lived by the Ten Commandments, wouldn't this honor be virtually inherent and inevitable? Would that be so bad?
4. What is difficult to comprehend about, "Thou shalt not steal?" Sure, we can invent a thousand ethical dilemmas, but isn't this commandment pretty relevant just as it is? Who wants to live in a society where a law against stealing is too mysterious to understand, or considered not relevant because there might be some situation come up where someone feels they need to steal something? If this commandment is just taken at face value, every reasonable person understands and agrees with it.
5. Are you okay with someone lying about you? A commandment against bearing false witness seems like something everybody would want to be applied in a courtroom, a board room, or on a job reference. A law against bearing false witness is mysterious? Really?

Some of the commands should actually seem relevant to a skeptic, albeit in a facetious sort of way, like having no other gods, or not taking the name of the Lord thy God in vain. Skeptics don't believe in God, or gods, so not having any other gods isn't really a problem. And not taking God's name in vain isn't a problem for a skeptic either. Why would someone invoke the name of a deity they don't even believe exists?

Yes, according to the Bible, once it is properly understood, the real Ten Commandments were written, and rewritten a second time, by God himself. By the way, if you read from Exodus 20 to Exodus 34 you will find a whole bunch of other commandments too. God gave these to Israel for the purpose of government, worship, and human relations. Some of the principles found in these laws were used as a model to create a free and representative republic called the United States of America.

In fact, many of the founders of America had a high regard for the Ten Commandments as foundational to a free and civilized society.

- "The Ten Commandments and the Sermon on the Mount contain my religion" John Adams, November 4, 1816, letter to Thomas Jefferson

- "The moment the idea is admitted into society that property is not as sacred as the laws of God, and that there is not a force of law and public justice to protect it, anarchy and tyranny commence. If 'Thou shalt not covet,' and 'Thou shalt not steal,' were not commandments of Heaven, they must be made inviolable precepts in every society, before it can be civilized or made free." John Adams, Defence [sic] of the Constitutions of Government of the United States, 1787

- "The law given from Sinai was a civil and municipal as well as a moral and religious code...laws essential to the existence of men in society and most of which have been enacted by every nation which ever professed any code of laws." John Quincy Adams, Letters of John Quincy Adams to his son on the Bible and its teachings, 1850

- "It pleased God to deliver, on Mount Sinai, a compendium of this holy law and to write it with His own hand on durable tables of stone. This law, which is commonly called the Ten Commandments or Decalogue...was incorporated in the judicial law." William Findley, Revolutionary Soldier, U.S. Congressman, 1812

- "The opinion that human reason left without the constant control of Divine laws and commands will give duration to a popular government is as chimerical [unlikely] as the most extravagant ideas that enter the head of a maniac...Where will you find any code of laws among civilized men in which the commands and prohibitions are not founded on Christian principles? I need not specify the prohibition of murder, robbery, theft, [and] trespass."

Noah Webster, Letters of Noah Webster to David McClure on October 25, 1836

- "The Ten Commandments are the sum of the moral law." John Witherspoon, Signer of the Declaration of Independence, February 21, 1762

It seems a bit presumptuous, does it not, for any twenty-first century American to insist that the very founders of America, whose knowledge of the Ten Commandments far exceeded his own, were simply mistaken about those Commandments? Skeptics would also have us believe that America's progressive moral decay is preferable to the commands God gave Moses, commands that America's founders enshrined into the very fabric of our national structure. Like the father who walked triumphantly out of basketball practice believing he had set something right that needed fixing, unaware he had just demonstrated his own lack of understanding, skeptics flaunt their lack of knowledge when they insist that generations of Christians, from scholars to Sunday school students, have completely missed the real Ten Commandments.

EIGHTEEN

IS CHRISTIANITY GOOD FOR WOMEN?

I t wasn't until the presidential campaign of 1992 that I finally understood how the strategy of political accusation operates. It occurred to me while listening to the debates, news reporting, scandals, and mudslinging that particularly characterized this election cycle. Accuse your opponent of the very thing you are guilty of yourself. Do it first. Do it often. Do it with passion. Criticize your opponent for waging a war on women, then assassinate the character of women who dare to come forward about sexual harassment suffered at the hands of the very same candidate who is making the accusations. Just keep your opposition on the ropes in constant defense.

In a similar way, Christianity gets hammered hard and often for treating women poorly, but as we shall see, it is really the secular culture that demeans and exploits women. In 2017, Hollywood moguls and Washington politicians, many of whom professed to champion women's rights, received a well-deserved, yet self-inflicted pummeling as news of sexual harassment buried the nation in an avalanche of scandalous reports detailing salacious treatment of women. Professing Christians have not been untarnished, so a fair analysis of the skeptic charge against Christianity, and an equally objective evaluation of the guiltiness of the secular culture making the charge is certainly warranted.

First, let's examine the suggestion that the Bible and Christianity are bad for women. **For all the positive points however, Christianity's role in degrading women and holding back their progress can't be ignored or forgiven if equality-minded contemporary Christians are ever to** move their religion beyond its tendency to provide cover for men who treat women poorly. No Christian can simply say its in the past and Christianity now values women as much as men, because there are still millions of Christians worldwide who prefer the traditional view of women as second-class human beings. It should not be news to anyone, but some Christian leaders still cite the Bible as proof of women's inferiority and proper role as servants to men. (122)

If Christianity is to be indicted for how it views women, it should at least be on the basis of what it actually says, not a generic accusation against unnamed "Christian leaders" who claim the Bible teaches that women are inferior. I do not doubt there are some who identify as Christian and have a personal view of women that is deplorable. That does not make such a view either Christian or biblical. Every worldview has its outliers.

To prove the Bible is down on women, the skeptic cites several Bible passages.

> Gen. 3:16 *Unto the woman he said, I will greatly multiply thy sorrow and thy conception; in sorrow thou shalt bring forth children; and thy desire shall be to thy husband, and he shall rule over thee.*

> I Cor. 11:3 *But I would have you know, that the head of every man is Christ; and the head of the woman is the man; and the head of Christ is God.*

> 1 Corinthians 14:34-35 *Let your women keep silence in the churches: for it is not permitted unto them to speak; but they are commanded to be under obedience as also saith the law. And if they will learn any thing, let them ask their husbands at home: for it is a shame for women to speak in the church.*

> 1 Corinthians 11:8-9 *For the man is not of the woman: but the woman of the man. Neither was the man created for the woman; but the woman for the man.*

> Ephesians 5:22-24 *Wives, submit yourselves unto your own husbands, as unto the Lord. For the husband is the head of the wife, even as Christ is the head of the church: and he*

*is the savior of the body.Therefore as the church is subject
unto Christ, so let the wives be to their own husbands in
every thing.*

Skeptics reply, **Clearly, ideas and words like these are best left in ancient
times.** (123)

Generally speaking, the objection is that the Bible puts women in
a subservient and inferior role to men. But is this kind of analysis really
true? Let's look at these passages in light of what Christianity teaches
and what the Bible actually says about women. Then, if turnabout is fair
play, we'll examine just how well women fare in the modern antithesis of
a Christian culture.

Gen. 3:16 is part of a series of verses where God pronounces the curse
upon the serpent, and upon Eve and Adam for their sin of disobedience.
Apparently, before the arrival of sin in the human race, Eve's role was to be
a helper to Adam but not necessarily subservient to him. She was not told
that her husband *shall rule over thee* until after the act of sin. Sin always has
consequences, even for those who don't believe there is such a thing. One
result was that Eve, and all women, would have travail in childbirth and
that the husband would be more authoritative in the marriage relationship.

In a sense, the skeptic may be right about the unfairness of husbands
ruling over wives. However, if he is going to use the Bible to prove the
point, then he must also accept the Bible's reason for it. The man was not
given a position of authority over the woman until sin entered the picture.
So if someone does not like the idea from the Bible of the husband being
the head of the wife, he has to acknowledge that according to the same
Bible the reason for man being given headship is sin. Christianity did not
exist in Gen. 3:16, so it cannot be the original source. Had Adam been the
first to disobey God, perhaps the headship role would be reversed.

In fact, there is much in the Bible to support the idea that equity is
righteous and that sin gives rise to inequity. Sin has produced inequity
from the beginning. Critics have no logical basis to object to the Bible's
statement of the husband's headship, then fabricate their own interpretation to justify the objection. Additionally, this headship of the man applies
only to marriage, not social hierarchy in general. As we shall see later,
the husband is also charged with the responsibility to provide for, protect, and sacrifice for his wife, hardly a view of a woman as a second-class
human being.

I Cor. 14:34-35 commands women to *keep silence in the churches*. Depending on your presuppositions, this verse may clearly sound discriminatory. Men can speak in church, women cannot. But like so much of atheistic thinking toward Christianity, it is too simplistic and inaccurate. Scripture passages must be read and interpreted in their given context, the same as you would any other literature. The Bible is not just a collection of random sayings. The New Testament is filled with letters to real people who lived in actual cities and were dealing with specific problems. When those are understood, the real meaning of passages becomes more clear.

Paul was writing to the church at Corinth, which he had founded. After his departure, it had deteriorated into chaos and disorder. Just as Tyre was like the New York City of the fourth century BC, so was Corinth in the first century AD. This fledgling church, with its new converts from wildly diverse cultural backgrounds, was in desperate need of instruction, direction, and order. The verse cited comes in a long discourse about the gift of speaking in church meetings in a language the speaker had not previously learned, something which the Bible says occurred occasionally among early New Testament believers.

Some people were trying to imitate this special gifting and were babbling things that could not be interpreted, an indication it was not from God. Apparently, women were particularly inclined to do this, so Paul instructs them to remain quiet. Incidentally, Paul also instructed any men who were doing this to be quiet too. I Cor. 14:27-28 *If any man speak in an unknown tongue, let it be by two, or at the most by three, and that by course; and let one interpret. But if there be no interpreter, <u>let him keep silence in the church</u>; and let him speak to himself, and to God.*

After God tells men who were doing this to remain quiet, he instructs women to do the same. This sounds pretty equitable to me once you understand what is really being taught. Also, women were being argumentative. In the interest of keeping order, Paul tells them to talk about questions with their husbands at home rather than disrupt the service. He concludes this chapter with a statement that places the reason for the whole teaching in context, *Let all things be done decently and in order.*

Given the opportunity, women seem to be more inclined than men to dominate a service. My Dad was a Baptist preacher for 40 years. It was his custom to take prayer requests from the congregation prior to a pastoral prayer. On one such occasion, a woman offered a prayer request for her health needs which soon turned into a long soliloquy of ailments that he feared would take over the service. Not knowing how to gracefully get out of the dilemma, he listened patiently as the minutes passed and the rest of the congregation grew restless. Finally, the woman said she just wanted God to have the glory in all her struggles. Dad seized the opportunity. "Do you really want God to have the glory," he asked? "Yes," the woman replied. "Well," Dad said, "let's all stand and sing, To God Be the Glory." After the song, Dad's leadership and control of the service was restored without hurting anyone's feelings.

Few churches interpret the I Cor. 14 passage as forbidding women to speak at all while at church. In most evangelical churches, women teach Sunday school classes, sing specials, or help in children's programs. The emphasis in I Cor. 14 is order, not unilateral prohibition. In context, it is applied equally to both men and women.

What about I Cor. 11:8-9 which says the woman was created for the man? Critics perceive this as meaning the woman is the property of, or servant to the man. But that is not what the verse says at all. It is merely a statement of fact according to biblical history. God created man, then he created a woman to be his companion and helper. To view this as oppressive or demeaning is like saying that marriage is demeaning to women because the woman becomes the companion and helper of her husband. It is the basis for all of societal structure. Curiously, as we shall see later, it is really the non-Christian culture that views women as being made for men, I mean in a demeaning sort of way.

The idea of wives submitting to their husbands, as Ephesians 5 commands, is particularly egregious to the modern, progressive mind. How dare God, or anyone else, suggest that a woman should submit to her husband? What kind of ancient barbarism is this?

Let's say you have a husband and wife whose marriage is based on equality. Each has equal say and neither's opinion outweighs the other. That is fine as long as they both are in agreement, but what happens when they disagree? Former atheist turned Christian apologist, and Oxford scholar, C.S. Lewis, observed that in the above scenario, "one or other of them must have the casting vote,"[1] The Bible simply states that the casting vote goes to the husband.

All of civilization is based on a similar hierarchy of rule. Governments run this way. Businesses, schools, and organizations all operate on the basis of someone being the head. Families operate this way too. Either the man will be the authority in the relationship or the woman, but they cannot be equal any more than a corporation can have multiple equal heads. A football team may have several coaches, but it has only one head coach. Ultimately his decisions prevail.

God designed the family to be operated with the man as a servant leader. Notice in the same passage cited from Ephesians 5 where women are to *submit to their own husbands,* we find, *husbands love your wives even as Christ also loved the church and gave himself for it.* The husband is to sacrifice himself for his wife. I'm not a woman so I can't say for sure, but I think if a woman had a husband who was ready to sacrifice himself (that is, his time, his ambitions, even his very life) for his wife, she might not have a big problem with following his lead. I don't really know, just a hunch.

To skeptics, this passage evokes images of a domineering husband who always has his way and a timid, mousy wife who can't say, "Yes sir" enough, but that's not reality. My wife will tell you that I am the head of our household. Ultimately, what I say goes, but she often has her say.

I have learned after 40 years of marriage that I should listen to her when she diagnoses a problem with the car, even though she knows little about the mechanics of an internal combustion engine. It's not that she is always right, just usually. Once, she identified a slight rattle in the engine as the water pump. I had replaced water pumps and I disagreed. Weeks passed and the noise got worse. Finally, I took the car to my mechanic, who diagnosed a bad water pump!

In many cases, I will take her advice over a doctor's. Not that I distrust doctors, I have just seen her be right too many times. I sometimes tell people I am married to a housewife, a teacher, a nurse, a doctor, a pharmacist, and a mechanic. Oh yeah, she also has a degree in dental hygiene, so I listen to her about teeth too. If she offers advice to me on how to frame a wall or repair a leaking water pipe, I'll probably follow my own intuition.

When the Bible tells wives to submit to their husbands, it is not telling them to check their brains at the marriage altar. In proper balance, which isn't always easy, Christian marriage allows each partner to play off the strength of the other. Husbands take the lead and wives willingly follow. A smart wife will let her husband lead and a wise husband will listen to his wife's advice. Of course, this is the biblical ideal. Life throws in a lot of variables that offer their own unique challenges. When the entire teaching of the Bible as it relates to women is taken in context and in its entirety, particularly the New Testament, which is the founding text of modern Christianity, women are to be loved and sacrificed for (Eph. 5:25), provided for (I Tim. 5:8), and honored (Rom. 16:1-2).

It is also noteworthy, despite the fact that in the Jewish culture of the New Testament era a woman's testimony was not valid in court, that Jesus chose to have announced first to women, entrusting to their witness alone, that he had risen from the dead. Here is the most significant event in all of Christian history, and the validation of Jesus' entire earthly message, and he entrusts it to two women. That speaks volumes about Jesus', and thus, Christianity's view of women.

Contrast this with the skeptic's citing of Ruth Hurmence Green, the late writer and critic of religion.

> **As long as women fail to denounce the Bible, they are in danger from it, for it has long been and continues to be their greatest oppressor. Its scriptures demean her and deprive her not only of her self-respect, but of veritable control over her body. The body makes her a slave, a piece of property and the mercy and whim of the male and in a state of total submission to her husband, who may even act as her abuser. She is regarded by the scriptures as the receptacle of the male seed and the means of reproducing the human race, and this is her only function. [2] (124)**

Nothing in this statement accurately reflects the teaching of the Bible. It does illustrate the tactic of passionately accusing your opponent of the very thing you are guilty of yourself. Keep this quote in mind as we move on to examine how our non-Christian culture actually views and treats women. Critics who charge that women are in danger from the Bible of being demeaned or deprived of self-respect, and are at the mercy and whim of the male, are throwing boomerangs. While there may be examples of some poor Christians who view women this way, it is rampant, blatant, and normative in the secular culture.

How do women fare in a non-Christian culture?

Christianity is often criticized as being oppressive or demeaning to women, but how are women treated in the non-Christian culture that pervades American society? I contend that it is here we see the demeaning treatment of women, merchandising and exploiting them for personal and corporate gain. Here are just a few examples.

Twenty-six of the thirty-two pro football teams in the NFL feature cheerleaders on the sidelines, most dressed in gratuitously revealing outfits. Anyone can recognize that these women in no way resemble a pro version of the high school cheerleading squads that promote team spirit and often compete with each other for state and national recognition. Women who want to be an NFL cheerleader must first go through the equivalent of a dairy cattle auction, where they are examined for weight, appearance, body form and structure as well as performance. If selected, the main compensation for performing in front of millions in what amounts to little more than underwear in most cases, is the privilege of being part of the male-dominated NFL experience.

> Cheerleaders make $1,000-1,500 a month at the absolute most. The vast majority make far less... A lawsuit by the Oakland Raiderettes filed in January and later joined by the Cincinnati Ben-Gals says that NFL cheerleaders are broadly expected to fund their own travel expenses and buy their own team-mandated cosmetics. According to the lawsuit, pay is illegally withheld until the end of the season. A January tell-all by a former Ravens cheerleader on Deadspin revealed that in addition to all this, cheerleaders are essentially treated like pieces of meat, subject to arbitrary rule enforcement, constant weigh-ins and mandatory visits to expensive salons at cheerleader expense."[3]

> The Raiderettes lawsuit "alleged that the Raiders broke a raft of state labor laws, including failing to pay minimum wage, withholding wages for months and refusing to reimburse cheerleaders for their business expenses." They won a 1.25 million dollar settlement. The Oakland Raiders also agreed to triple cheerleaders pay to a whopping $9 an hour.[4]

In 2014, the Buffalo Bills disbanded their "Jills" cheerleading squad after members sued the organization for what they described in a New York Times report as a "nightmare scenario." Here is the lawsuit's account of a charity golf tournament.

The Jills Annual Golf Tournament–Select Jills were required to wear a bikini, and then go into a dunk tank, where they were dunked in water by the golf tournament participants. Jills cheerleaders are also "auctioned off" like prizes at this event, and had to ride around with the winning bidder in his golf cart for the duration of the tournament. While serving as a "bought person" they were subjected to additional demeaning treatment, including degrading sexual comments and inappropriate touching. Oftentimes, the Jills were forced to sit on participants' laps because there was not enough seats in the golf carts. The golf tournament also featured a "Flip for Tips" component, wherein participants paid gratuities to watch select Jills do backflips and acrobatics for the gratification of the crowd. The Jills did not receive any of the tip money.[5]

There are even more spurious details to this story which I did not care to print. I think the point should be well taken. Such abuse, manipulation, and harassment are rampant and have prompted numerous other lawsuits, yet for some unexplainable reason the big gripe is that these cheerleaders don't get paid enough.

A transcript from a Sept. 23, 2014, NPR interview entitled, "Cheerleaders' fair wage lawsuits adds to NFL's woes,"[6] mentions nothing of this abominable treatment of women. In light of the fact that the above description of sexual harassment in the lawsuit by Buffalo Bills cheerleaders was public news four months prior to the NPR interview, and that reports of such manipulative harassment is commonplace, not even mentioning such demeaning and abusive treatment of women leaves one wondering just how much concern there is about how these women are treated beyond issues of pay. With news of this kind of control and coercion pervasive on the internet, it is also unfathomable that women still pay a fee to try out in the hopes of getting the privilege of participating in the NFL experience, potentially at the expense of their own dignity and self respect.

The fact is, NFL cheerleaders main function is to be eye candy for male fans and generate money for the franchise. If cheerleaders suddenly disappeared from the sidelines, it would have no effect whatsoever on a game's outcome or the team's performance throughout the season. The one effect it would have is that approximately one million dollars less would flow into team coffers, and that is the reason they are there.

To put this in proper perspective, imagine any other corporation subjecting its female employees to requirements for weight, hair color, skin tone, and willingness to pose for provocative photographs for the company calendar as well as showing up for work in skimpy, revealing, company-mandated uniforms. In any other venue, such treatment would be considered nothing less than sexual harassment —in spades! It is true that as far as dress requirements go, women know what they are getting into and are willing to submit, but as many lawsuits testify, that is only the beginning of the gratuitous demands.

When a skeptic says, **It should not be news to anyone, but some Christian leaders still cite the Bible as proof of women's inferiority and proper role as servants to men,** we have a right to ask, "Are not these women being used as servants to the larger interest of secular enterprises?" You may find oppressive and exploitative treatment of women in some professing Christian organizations, but you will not find a defense of such self-serving tactics like this in the teachings of the New Testament. Christianity, when practiced as it is taught in the Bible, treats women with dignity, honor, and respect.

Professional sports is not the only place we find the despicable exploitation of women to generate corporate profits. Go through the checkout at any department or grocery store and you are accosted with magazines, which feature women dressed in revealing attire designed to attract male attention. The cover banner often advertises sex as the lure to see what is inside.*

Such debasing of women as sexually useful tools is pervasive in American culture. Despite the inarguable evidence of this, quoted skeptics like the late Ruth Hermence Green insist that when it comes to women, it is the Bible and Christianity that **demean her and deprive her not only of her self-respect, but of veritable control over her body. The body makes her a slave, a piece of property...** [7](124) Such willful blindness only serves to perpetuate our culture's exploitative use of women. Ask the cheerleaders of professional football teams who have sued their employer for sexually harassing behavior if the above quote is an accurate description of treatment they have received. One former Bills cheerleader said, "I ended up feeling like a piece of meat."[8]

To underscore this point, consider that magazines in a typical checkout almost never feature Sports Illustrated, that is until the swimsuit issue comes out. Suddenly, Sports Illustrated magazine is worthy of premium space in the checkout line. Once again, women are used for their willingness to expose themselves in a magazine which has nearly 80% male readership.[9] I could be way off, but my guess would be the gratuitous swimsuit issue spikes the profits for Time Inc., SI's owner. All of this to provide a majority of male readers with yet another opportunity to gawk at women who are paid to exhibit themselves for consumer pleasure and corporate profits.

If there is a bigger money maker in American culture than professional sports, it is probably Hollywood. In a scathing expose' entitled, "How to Make Money in Hollywood, Don't Be a Woman Over 34," author Kevin Lincoln cites, "Age, Gender, and Compensation: A Study of Hollywood Movie Stars," a study published by Irene E. De Pater, Timothy A. Judge, and Brent A. Scott in the *Journal of Management Inquiry*. This study considers the question of how female and male actors' earnings keep pace with each other as their careers progress.

> For men, [actors] average yearly earnings increased until the age of 51, at which point they leveled off and remained steady for the remainder of their careers. For women, [actresses] it's an entirely different situation: Earnings increase until the age of 34, then rapidly decrease afterward.

> With men so thoroughly dominating the creation of films, a woman's performance of sexuality, it would seem, becomes a greater part of her brand as an actor. As that element of what she has to offer fades in the view of male creators (i.e. as she gets older), so does her value and role in the stories they are telling.[10]

Whatever the reasons may be, this fact highlights a glaring difference between the value Hollywood places on aging women and the New Testament's repeated positive portrayal of women, especially older women, as key players in the development of Christianity. The skeptic notion that Christianity and the Bible demean and oppress women could not be more wrong.

It was not Jesus Christ, but Charles Darwin who said,

> The chief distinction in the intellectual powers of the two sexes is shown by man attaining to a higher eminence, in whatever he takes up, than woman can attain —whether

requiring deep thought, reason, or imagination, or merely the use of the senses.[11]

You will not find such demeaning doctrine in Bible.

In contrast, the New Testament, where Christianity first appears, presents numerous women in prominent roles. Mary, the mother of Jesus, (Luke 1); Mary Magdalene, Joanna, Susanna, and Salome gave Jesus provisions and traveled with him in Galilee, (Luke 8); Mary Magdalene was one of several women who were first to be told of the resurrected Christ, (Matthew 28); Martha, her home was open to Jesus whenever he visited Jerusalem, (Luke 10); Elisabeth, mother of John the Baptist, the forerunner of Christ, (Luke 1); Lydia, a businesswoman, (Acts 16); Priscilla, an instructor of the preacher Apollos, (Acts 18); Phebe, some scholars believe she hand delivered Paul's letter to the Romans, (Romans 16); Dorcas, a benevolent Christian "full of good works," (Acts 9); Anna, an aged prophetess who announced publicly that Jesus was the promised redeemer, (Luke 2); Lois and Eunice, grandmother and mother to Timothy who were commended by Paul for their genuine faith, (II Timothy 1); and there are many more. The value of women in the development of Christianity, especially older women in the New Testament, shines in stark contrast to the disgraceful, manipulative and exploitative use of women in our progressive, so-called, "liberated" culture.

Finally, for skeptics who love evidence, here is one more example of how non-Christian society has degraded and used women as disposable tools for increasing corporate earnings. If you are over 50, you remember the advertisements in the 60's and 70's featuring an attractive and smartly dressed woman smoking a cigarette, or at least looking like she was. The ad line said, "You've come a long way baby." The message was directed at girls and women to persuade them that smoking was a sign of being liberated and they no longer need to be excluded from this male-dominated habit. They had just as much right to smoke as men.

It worked, but it had a price tag. Women were sacrificed on the altar of business profits under the convenient pretense of equality. According to the U.S. Department of Health and Human Services, "Tobacco Facts and Figures," "...approximately 80% of lung cancer deaths among women are due to smoking." And in the same report, "Women smokers are up to 40 times more likely to develop COPD (Chronic Obstructive Pulmonary Disease) than women who have never smoked."[12]

None of these examples are representative of a Christian or biblical view toward women. They are however, the tip of a very menacing iceberg that has decimated the decency, modesty, and respect which the New Testament teaches are to be hallmarks of women and how they are to be treated.

Here is a small sampling of Bible passages that illustrate Christianity's stark contrast with our American culture's merchandising use of women.

I Timothy 5:1-2 *Rebuke not an elder, but intreat him as a father; and the younger men as brethren; The <u>elder women as mothers; the younger as sisters, with all purity</u>.* Young women are to be treated like a decent man would treat his sister, and older women the way you would want your own mother to be treated.

I Timothy 2:9 *Also, the women are to dress themselves in modest clothing, with decency and good sense, not with elaborate hairstyles, gold, pearls, or expensive apparel.* (Holman Christian Standard Version) Would anyone care to argue that if a woman refused to expose her body for male spectators she would have no chance of cheering in the NFL, or the NBA. And don't get sidetracked by the apparent jewelry prohibition. That's a whole different question. We are addressing Christianity's alleged advocating of abusive treatment of women.

Titus 2:3-5 *The aged women likewise, that they be in behavior as becometh holiness, not false accusers, not given to much wine, teachers of good things; That they may teach the young women to be sober, to love their husbands, to love their children, To be discreet, chaste, keepers at home, good, obedient to their own husbands, that the word of God be not blasphemed.* Notice that in New Testament Christianity, as women age their value increases, the exact opposite of the attitude toward women in so much of our non-Christian, sex-appeal oriented culture.

Skeptics, Bible critics, and many women may bristle at the command for wives to submit to their husbands and be obedient to them. Oddly, women who may object continue to put themselves in demeaning and subservient roles to men. We have already seen that Hollywood treats women as disposable once age makes them less useful for its purposes. It seems to me the New Testament model of being a lifelong partner to a loving and sacrificial husband, mother to children who desperately need her nurturing care, and being treated with honor and respect offers women a far better deal.

I am fully aware that some Bible passages conflict with the modern view of the liberated woman. As the cigarette ads of past decades exemplify, just because a view is current does not necessarily make it good for women. While some of the gains women have made are praiseworthy, many have been for business enterprises who gladly exploit them for corporate benefit and at women's ultimate expense.

Finally, I would not begin to defend the attitude toward women of every professed Christian organization, church, or Christian leader. I have known some whose views are deplorable and treatment of their own wives despicable, but we are talking about what the Bible, and particularly the New Testament teaches, not how some poor example of a Christ follower disavows the teaching of his own book. As the skeptic points out, Christianity is sometimes unrecognizable in some of its own adherents, but it is in the New Testament where we find what true Christianity's attitude towards women should be.

All things considered, it is the secular culture that cheapens and dishonors the purity and chastity the Bible says women should exemplify and the dignity with which they should be treated. Instead, in the name of equality and opportunity, the non-Christian culture often uses women as exhibitionists and pawns to fatten the wallets of corporations by gratifying the insatiable, sensual appetite of male consumers.

*Just a few days before this manuscript was submitted for publishing, CNN reported on the recent decision by Walmart to remove Cosmopolitan magazine from its checkout lines. In a statement, the National Center on Sexual Exploitation lauded the "significant policy change." "Walmart's removal of Cosmo from checkout lines is an incremental but significant step toward creating a culture where women and girls are valued as whole persons, rather than as sexual objects,"[13]

NINETEEN

IS IT SMARTER TO BELIEVE OR NOT BELIEVE?

Religion is not a vast domain for the dumb, and atheism is not some exclusive club for the brightest among us. (126) Quotes like this from a skeptic are refreshingly objective and fair-minded. Many atheists think that Christianity is a reservoir of shallow thinkers and superstitious, religious nuts. It's nice when a skeptic acknowledges that being religious, and especially Christian, does not make one an imbecile.

Nevertheless, skeptics think the creationist view as it is given in the book of Genesis **is about the most absurd and extreme antiscience position anyone could hold** (126) even though held by someone like David Dewitt, **a biochemist and neuroscientist with a doctorate from Case Western University.** (126-127) What is fascinating about the skeptic's devotion to evolutionary theory is that here there is no skepticism whatsoever. From a big bang some 13.8 billion years ago,[1] to the first appearance of modern man about 200,000 years ago,[2] skeptics "believe" without a doubt, despite the impossibility of scientific observation of these supposed facts.

Remember that scientific method we all learned in 8th-grade? Notice that it starts with an observation. Fundamentally, anything that happened before there was someone there to observe is not in the domain of science. We can examine results of what happened using the scientific method. We cannot make unequivocal statements about something that is supposed to have happened, but which cannot be verified by observation, and call it a scientific fact.

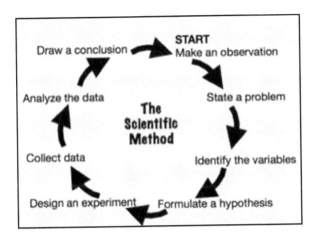

Evolutionists who are considering the origins of the universe, or even man, by necessity must omit the first step of the scientific method because there was no one there to make the observation from which the scientific method begins. They can make use of other aspects, like formulating a hypothesis, experimentation, and analysis of data, but none of this originates from an observation. Consequently, results of employing parts of the scientific method are interpreted in light of a previously held conclusion — everything evolved from an original "Big Bang."

I think we can get the hang of it if we work our way backwards in the scientific method beginning with the conclusion. If you draw a conclusion from analytical data, resulting from an experiment, designed to test a hypothesis, formulated to examine a problem, resulting from an...ooops! There was no observation 13 billion years ago, or 200,000 years ago. At the very least, we don't have anything even approaching written records that can be dated more than 6000 years ago![3]

So when evolutionists cite evidence obtained using the scientific method to explain events that happened 200,000 years ago, or 13 billion years ago, they must start by stating a problem, replacing observation with a conclusion, and interpret the data in light of the conclusion, then restate the conclusion as if it was now a proven fact. But this conflicts with the very definition of what a fact is. "A fact is a truth known by actual experience or observation; something known to be true."[4] Therefore, what is being stated as a fact is really a belief cloaked in scientific jargon.

I am not trying to provoke the ire of skeptics. Rather, I am trying to demonstrate that skepticism, by necessity, must omit God as a factor in anything, leaving it with a predisposition to interpret information according to the dictates of that lack of belief. Christians do the same thing when considering the same subject. So in an attempt to be truly objective, we must acknowledge two other factors.

First, believing involves bias. Second, trust does not necessarily require proven facts. Skeptics, and Christians demonstrate this all the time.

I think the Big Bang is too unmanageable and too subject to a preconceived view to get an impartial grasp on the relevance of bias and trust and how they dictate what we believe. So let's consider something on a far lesser order of magnitude, "The Little Bang."

In chapter 8, I told you about escaping unscathed from a gas explosion in our small cabin. I'll call this "The Little Bang." If you are a skeptic, get ready to see if you are really objective by answering this question honestly. Did you believe it? I mean, did you believe the first-hand account I told was factual?

If you did, your belief was based on trust that someone you do not know and whose honesty you could not verify, had told you a rather incredible story which you believe to be true. If you are a Christian and believed the story, you did so on the very same basis of trust. Neither the skeptic nor the Christian had any proof the story was true, but you believed it anyway; at least I hope so.

Let's make "The Little Bang" a micro version of the Big Bang by removing one detail, observation of its occurrence. Everything you know about "The Little Bang" comes from someone who was there. But what if all the other details remain the same except there is no witness to tell you what happened? Then you have something a bit more like the Big Bang, at least as far as observation goes. There is evidence, but what you believe about the evidence can lead you in any number of different directions that may or may not be right. With this background, consider again "The Little Bang." With no observation, and no one to tell you what actually happened, try figuring out what did happen.

As you start your investigation, you come to the small cabin. The heavy sliding glass door is laying on the patio, frame and all, still intact. A kitchen window is shattered with a thousand pieces scattered 30 feet away. Paint is blistered on the walls of the living room and carpet is singed into plastic throughout the cabin. There is a bit of charred paper in the corner of the living room. A gas line valve is open, but the valve from the tank outside is off. The kitchen stove is pulled from the wall. The burners and oven are all off. A table is in front of the kitchen door. No one saw or heard anything. What actually happened is entirely up to you to determine.

As you try to recreate what could have happened, you are immediately confronted with an inescapable fact. You are biased. You already know what happened, so you cannot honestly imagine any other scenario that makes as much sense as the one you already believe. Because of your bias, you cannot help but begin from the conclusion you already believe to be true. Anyone else's interpretation of the evidence, who had not read the account in chapter 8, would also be hopelessly subject to your bias.

However, what you believe really happened is totally dependent on your trust in the account of someone who was there and provided you with the details, even though you have no proof. Furthermore, you do not know this person. For that matter, you believed the story without even verifying that the one who told it actually exists! I hope this helps you to see that what we believe about anything for which we do not have first-hand observation is ultimately based on trust, the key component of faith.

The skeptic says, **many thoughtful and sensible religious people are able to hold onto and defend unproven, extraordinary claims without flinching. But if someone wants to sell these people a house or a lawn-mower, they suddenly spring into super-skeptic mode.** (129) It is fair to turn this around. The skeptic suddenly becomes a "super-believer" in something like evolution, despite the fact that scientists readily confess that they lack answers to fundamental questions. In other words, skeptics also **hold onto and defend unproven, extraordinary claims without flinching.** (129)

Despite the inability to logically and scientifically answer the following simple yet profoundly troubling questions, the evolutionist still "believes" in the absence of any observation-based evidence.

1. What exactly went "bang" in the big bang and where did it come from?
The unproven nature of the very essence of evolution, how it all began, is plain in this explanation from the Harvard Smithsonian Center for Astrophysics.

> Although astronomers understand what the universe was like just a few seconds after the Big Bang, no one yet knows what happened at the instant of the Big Bang - or what came before. What powered the Big Bang? Where did all the stuff in the universe come from in the first place? What was the universe like just before the Big Bang?... The leading idea is called the "inflationary universe" model. The key assumption of this model is that just before the Big Bang, space was filled with an unstable form of energy, whose nature is not yet known. At some

instant, this energy was transformed into the fundamental particles from which arose all the matter we observe today. That instant marks what we call the Big Bang.[5]

A moment ago I said that evolutionists start with a conclusion based on their bias, then work backwards before restating the conclusion as a proven fact. Along the way, proofs and evidence are substituted with presumptions and assumptions. See how this plays out in the above description.

It begins with an unobserved conclusion, there was a Big Bang. Then there are a series of suppositions. "The leading <u>idea</u> is...," "The key <u>assumption</u> of this model is...," "space was filled with an unstable form of energy, whose nature is <u>not yet known</u>." Then we get to the observation, "this energy was transformed into the fundamental particles from which arose <u>all the matter we observe today</u>." Finally, the conclusion is restated as a fact. "That instant marks what we call the Big Bang." It all sounds very scientific, but it turns the scientific method on its head.

The evolutionist may argue that science is using the scientific method by making observations in the present to draw logical conclusions about what happened in the past. However, this doctrine, known as uniformitarianism, is selectively employed by the evolutionist. For example, spontaneous generation, something necessary for evolution to be true, was disproved scientifically by Louis Pasteur in the nineteenth century. So when it comes to the origin of life itself, evolutionists must say they believe something happened in the past which has never been scientifically observed in the present. Incidentally, so do creationists. But while creationists believe something which cannot be proven by science, evolutionists believe something which science has proven cannot be. At the conclusion of his award winning discovery, Louis Pasteur said, "Never will the doctrine of spontaneous generation recover from the mortal blow of this simple experiment!"[6]

At their most foundational level, both creation and evolution are "beliefs." There is simply no observed evidence that life arose from non-living matter, or that a human being was created out of the dust of the earth. Michael Ruse, an atheist with an impressive resume, opponent of intelligent design, self-proclaimed "ex-Christian," and professor of philosophy at Florida State University said,

> Evolution is promoted by its practitioners as more than mere science. Evolution is promulgated as an

ideology, a secular religion — a full-fledged alternative to Christianity, with meaning and morality. I am an ardent evolutionist and an ex-Christian, but I must admit that in this one complaint — and Mr. Gish [Duane T. Gish the Creation Scientist] is but one of many to make it — the literalists are absolutely right. Evolution is a religion. This was true of evolution in the beginning, and it is true of evolution still today.[7]

And no less a philosophical giant than David Hume, whose general views are not Christian said,

> The whole frame of nature bespeaks an intelligent author; and no rational enquirer can, after serious reflection, suspend his belief a moment with regard to the primary principles of genuine Theism and Religion.[8]

In the absence of observed phenomena at its most foundational point, honest scientists and philosophers must concede that evolution originating from a Big Bang is a belief, not a fact.

2. How does evolution explain the necessity for simultaneous evolution of male and female in every sexually reproducing species?

Keep in mind that as the male gender of a species evolved, its female counterpart had to also be evolving at precisely the same rate, at the same time, and in the same place, and this simultaneous evolutionary development had to all take place within the lifespan of each species or it becomes extinct before it even gets started. And this has to have happened millions of times for all male/female species! Many evolutionists recognize this as no small problem.

> Sex is the queen of problems in evolutionary biology. Perhaps no other natural phenomenon has aroused so much interest; certainly none has sowed as much confusion. The insights of Darwin and Mendel, which have illuminated so many mysteries, have so far failed to shed more than a dim and wavering light on the central mystery of sexuality, emphasizing its obscurity by its very isolation.[9]

In addition, although human's closest ancestor is supposed to be the ape, there is no known instance of humans and apes interbreeding. What scientific evidence is there that a sexually reproducing specimen can propagate itself if there is no complementing gender, or that a species propagates a different species? Furthermore, what benefit to natural selection and survival of the fittest is the development of sexual reproduction in the first place, when asexual reproduction of simpler "less evolved" single-celled organisms is far more efficient?

If we take everything that science has observed in the past, that is, begin where the scientific method begins, with observation, we discover every species can breed only within that species. This is what the Bible says as well. For evolution to be true, this observed fact has to not have been true for millions of years in the unobserved past, a totally unscientific speculation.

Consider also that reproductive systems are irreducibly complex — times two. The male and female systems of each species have to be fully functional in order to be useful in procreation. How did reproductive systems for both genders of a species gradually evolve parallel to each other so they could be useful?

Christians are not trying to be obstinate. We simply find the notion preposterous that such intricate, complex systems, along with the required instincts to use them, took millions, or even thousands of years to develop. Where is the evidence that this occurred? Surely in their heart of hearts evolutionists, if they think about such things, find their position tenuous at best.

3. *How did humans develop the ability to speak in a language?*

> After millions of years of evolution there are no animals that are in a transition phase from non-speaking to speaking and no languageless community has ever been found.[10]

How humans developed the ability to communicate in languages is another major problem for evolutionists. Notice how the backward approach to the scientific method applies to the following evolutionary explanations of man's ability to speak.

> Physically, a deprived physical environment led to more meat-eating and, as a result, a bigger brain. The enlarged brain led to the premature birth of humans, and in

consequence a protracted childhood, during which mothers cooed and crooned to their offspring. An upright stance altered the shape of the mouth and vocal tract, allowing a range of coherent sounds to be uttered.'[11]

It all started with an ape that learned to speak. Man's hominid ancestors were doing well enough, even though the world had slipped into the cold grip of the ice ages. They had solved a few key problems that had held back the other branches of the ape family, such as how to find enough food to feed their rather oversized brains. Then man's ancestors happened on the trick of language.[12]

In the previous chapter, skeptics may have gotten a laugh from my explanation of I Cor. 14:34-35 when I stated, "The verse cited comes in a long discourse about the gift of speaking in church meetings in a language the speaker had not previously learned, something that occurred occasionally among early New Testament believers." People spoke in a language they never learned? Really? However, when it comes to the gift of language itself, evolutionists must accept that apes, or ape-like men, somehow learned to speak, either suddenly or gradually, in an intelligent language previously unknown to them. I think Christians are entitled to smile here. God definitely has a sense of humor. In the following explanation, note again the use of suppositions, "My own view," and "may have."

My own view is that language developed much more gradually, starting with the gestures of apes, then gathering momentum as the bipedal hominids evolved. The appearance of the larger-brained genus *Homo* some 2 million years ago may have signaled the emergence and later development of syntax, with vocalizations providing a mounting refrain. What may have distinguished *Homo sapiens* was the final switch from a mixture of gestural and vocal communication to an autonomous vocal language, embellished by gesture but not dependent on it.[13]

In each case, the researcher begins with a conclusion — that man evolved the ability to speak in a language. And in each case, either an unsubstantiated statement is made to support the hypothesis, or a personal view (opinion) rather than an actual observation, becomes the basis for the conclusion. When evolutionists try to explain the origin of human speech the scientific method once again gets turned backwards.

4. When did evolution stop?

This is a question everyone pondering evolution should ask. If evolution has been going on for billions of years to produce all of the diverse species we see today, why don't we see some of the transitional forms now — the in-between forms? The leap from apes to men, a development which supposedly occurred some 200,000 years ago, seems to have stopped just about 6000 years ago, leaving us with humans and apes, nothing in-between.

In 1972, Niles Eldridge and Stephen Jay Gould developed the hypothesis of punctuated equilibrium to explain the gaps between species in the fossil record. This idea states that species appear suddenly, then remain stable throughout their geologic history before splitting into a new species.[14] It demonstrates the "conclusion first" pattern for implementing the scientific method. Evolution has occurred, so science must find a way to explain the obvious jumps from one species to another in the absence of fossils that would document that leap. But like gradual evolution, it remains nothing more than an idea which has never been and cannot be observed or proven correct or false by science. It is simply a means of explaining an apparent phenomenon in light of the "fact" of evolution. The fancy word for this is unfalsifiable, meaning there is no conceivable way the hypothesis can be shown to be false. Creationism is also unfalsifiable.

These four simple questions are not insignificant, nor are they by any means the only ones that give evolutionists pause. They are foundational to the concept of evolution and origins. Though speculations abound, proof does not. Yet skeptics believe anyway. Many prominent evolutionists readily, if not regrettably admit this.

> When it comes to the origin of life there are only two possibilities: creation or spontaneous generation. There is no third way. Spontaneous generation was disproved one hundred years ago, but that leads us to only one other conclusion, that of supernatural creation. We cannot accept that on philosophical grounds; therefore, we choose to believe the impossible: that life arose spontaneously by chance![15] (George Wald)

> My attempts to demonstrate evolution by an experiment carried on for more than 40 years have completely failed... It is not even possible to make a caricature of an evolution out of paleobiological facts...The idea of an evolution rests on pure belief.[16] (Heribert Nilsson)

> The absence of fossil evidence for intermediary stages between major transitions in organic design, indeed our inability, even in our imagination, to construct functional intermediates in many cases, has been a persistent and nagging problem for gradualist accounts of evolution.[17] (Stephen J. Gould)

> I can envision observations and experiments that would disprove any evolutionary theory I know.[18] (Stephen J. Gould)

My reason for focusing on evolution in this discussion on believing versus not believing is to demonstrate that at the most basic level, how all things began, both Christians and skeptics are believers in something which cannot be scientifically verified. I do not say that to antagonize skeptics, or evolution-believing professing Christians for that matter. It is merely an objective reality necessitated by the impossibility of any observation-based evidence for events which occurred before there were humans to observe anything. Though testable hypotheses are not possible to prove either, in the case of evolution and its necessity of non-living matter spontaneously generating life, science itself has proven it impossible.

It is the individual's presuppositions that incline them to interpret any scientifically obtained evidence one way or the other. One thing is certain however, we cannot both be right. But observation of present realities and the history of real science tip the scales heavily in favor of the creationist view. Six-thousand years of written human history correlates well with the biblical timeline. The Bible records that species can only reproduce after their own kind, exactly what we observe scientifically in the natural world. Life has never been scientifically observed to come from non-life. Further, if you want to accept that language evolved gradually in apes, or ape-men, that is your privilege, but skeptics should be honest enough to admit that this is an unproven and unobserved belief, not a fact. So when the skeptic asks Christians if it is smarter to believe or not believe he is presenting a false choice. Skeptics believe too.

TWENTY

IS THE BORN-AGAIN EXPERIENCE IN CHRISTIANITY UNIQUE?

I t is a given that skeptics would doubt the Christian experience of being born again. There is something supernatural about a person's life being dramatically changed when they surrender to Jesus Christ, but a skeptic rejects the supernatural. In response to descriptions like these from Christians who were describing their born-again experience; **It's powerful. I don't have any doubts whatsoever. I felt pure joy. I know him [Jesus] as well or better than I know any of my friends and family members**, the skeptic says, **I felt like I was debriefing an astronaut who made first contact with an advanced extraterrestrial life-form.** (132-133)

Skepticism from unbelievers about spiritual rebirth is not surprising to the Christian. Paul said in I Corinthians 2:14 *But the natural man receiveth not the things of the Spirit of God: for they are foolishness unto him: neither can he know them, because they are spiritually discerned.* The word "discerned" in this verse, comes from a Greek word that means "to investigate, examine or question." This is exactly what a good skeptic tries to do. He wants to investigate the claims of Christians being born-again to see if they are legitimate or if they can best be understood by some other explanation.

Because this event is so important to many Christians, it warrants analysis and challenge. Is being born again a real or imagined event? (132) **In order to make a fair assessment about whether or not we can trust born-again experiences as evidence of a god's existence, we have**

to consider how reliable and consistent we are at separating fact from fiction in our own heads. (133) That's why the scientific method is invaluable. It's a way of discovering, learning, and confirming reality above and beyond many of the natural human frailties such as bias and the capacity for delusion. (133)

It is fascinating how perfectly this attempt by an unbeliever to evaluate the Christian born-again experience fits into what Paul wrote in I Cor. 2:14 where he describes the futility of trying to explain spiritual things by natural means. Because the natural (unbelieving) man does not receive (accept) the things of the Spirit of God. When he tries to explain them by natural means, they just seem foolish. The Bible not only describes the spiritual element of man but the futility of the one who rejects spiritual things while still trying to understand them. The comparison of the born-again experience of many Christians being like an astronaut describing contact with extraterrestrials only confirms what the Bible says.

How then can a skeptic ever come to the point of accepting Christ? His reasoning will not allow it because he thinks he is being asked to accept something that defies reason. Are skeptics then consigned to an eternity without Christ, unable to be saved? Of course, the answer is no. Many atheists have been born again. Dr. J. L. Wile maintains a list of recent skeptic converts to Christianity along with their story. You can read about these and others at blog.drwile.com.[1]

- Dr. Sarah Salviander, Ph.D. in astrophysics and currently a research fellow at the University of Texas Department of Astronomy
- Dr. Wayne Rossiter, Ph.D. in ecology and evolution from Rutgers University
- Douglas Ell graduated from the Massachusetts Institute of Technology (MIT) with degrees in math and chemistry. He then went to the University of Maryland, where he earned a Master's degree in theoretical mathematics. He also went to law school and graduated magna cum laude. After that, he began his career as an attorney.
- Guillaume Bignon is a French theologian who used to be an atheist. He was a student of math, physics, and engineering. He graduated from engineering school and now works as a computer scientist.
- Dr. Holly Ordway, author of, "Not God's Type - A Radical Academic Finds a Radical Faith," has a Ph.D. in English literature

from the University of Massachusetts, an MA in English litera-ture from University of North Carolina, and an MA in Christian apologetics from Biola University.

- Rosaria Champagne Butterfield, English professor at Syracuse University, former atheist, lesbian, and Christian antagonist, is now a pastor's wife.
- Alister Edgar McGrath, Ph.D. in molecular biophysics and Doctor of Divinity, both from University of Oxford, is author of "The Dawkins Delusion."

If you read the stories of these and many other former atheists, you find highly educated and intellectual people who employed scientific perspective and objective analysis to do exactly what the skeptic says we should do as **a way of discovering, learning, and confirming reality above and beyond many of the natural human frailties such as bias and the capacity for delusion.** (133) Reading the stories of these one-time unbelievers exposes the fact that skeptics too can be guided by delusion, bias, and human frailty and that reasoned and objective thinking can and has led many to accept Jesus Christ and become a Christian.

Such conversion however, is not exclusively one directional. There are numerous cases of those who once professed Christianity converting to atheism. These people have been persuaded of the truthfulness of an atheistic worldview in contrast to a Christian one. At the very least, when a person converts to atheism from Christianity, it is no less an "experience" than being born again into Christianity from atheism. Why does one highly intelligent and well-educated person reason their way to Christian belief and another seem to reason their way from it? The question alone could spawn an entire book. But it is fair to say that many people who were biased in one direction have found some reason to convert to an opposing belief system.

I said earlier that in atheism all roads lead back to evolution. Even in a discussion about being born-again, skeptics default to a naturalistic origin for everything. **None of this is meant to disparage the human brain. It's an amazing product of the indifferent and unintelligent creative force of evolution. Thanks to this magnificent three-pound firestorm of neurons that we carry around in our skulls, our species has been able to create languages, mathematics, science, music, art, ice cream and so on. Of course, these powerful brains also enable us to exploit and kill one another in creative ways too, so it's a mixed bag.** (134)

Having said that, notice this amazing, though perhaps unintended admission by a skeptic. **Even in light of that downside however, our brains can be described as wonderful machines of calculation and imagination.** (134)

Somehow, it completely escapes an atheist that we have never seen even a simple machine produced as a result of indifferent and unintelligent creative force? No such phenomenon has ever been observed. Yet a skeptic still makes this imperative evolutionary statement as if it is a scientific fact. No doubt, it is the honest and objective analysis of a simple observation like this, coupled with an eventual open-minded approach to the actual message of the Bible that led many of the above atheists to become born-again Christians. As we have already observed, when an atheist claims that a 3-pound firestorm of neurons developed the capacity to create language, music, or mathematics through an undirected, purposeless evolutionary process, he is making a statement of sheer faith in the absence of any evidence. It is the overwhelming power of personal belief that prevents skeptics from acknowledging this reality.

In supporting the contention that a born-again experience is not unique to Christianity, skeptics offer examples like: **trances of prehistoric shamans, prophecies made by the priestess Pythia on Mount Parnassus,** and **contorted spasms of a "possessed" animist** or **when a holy man prays away an evil *jinn* who had possessed the body and mind of a Muslim.** (136) However, none of these even vaguely resemble the concept taught by Christ himself when he said to Nicodemus three times in the same conversation, *Ye must be born again.* (John 3)

Yes, being born-again is unique to Christianity, but let's define just what being born-again actually is and what it is not. It is not merely a mystical experience. Jesus Christ, the founder of the Christian faith, said in John 3:3, *Verily, verily, I say unto thee, Except a man be born again, he cannot see the kingdom of God.* And I Peter 1:23 says, *Being born again, not of corruptible seed, but of incorruptible, by the word of God, which liveth and abideth forever.*

Those who do the hard work of studying, like the former atheists mentioned earlier, discover that the word of God teaches that Jesus Christ died on the cross as the substitute for our sin. He took our punishment. Sin separates us from God and places us at enmity with him. Remember, holiness and sin are mutually exclusive. In a similar way, breaking civil laws places us at enmity with the authority of civil law. The rule of law and lawbreaking are also mutually exclusive. By definition, the one is at odds with the other. The Christian story is that God became a man in order to take the sentence for our sin. Just as a criminal can be pardoned, God offers to pardon us through the sacrifice of Christ. Chapter one explains why this sacrifice had to be so harsh and why it is complete and the ultimate act of love.

As converts to Christianity, we realize we have broken God's law and are therefore under his condemnation. Through Jesus Christ we can be forgiven and not have to pay for our own sin because Christ paid for us. Accepting this is what we call being saved, or born-again. John 3:16 puts it as simply as it can be stated, *For God so loved the world, that he gave his only begotten Son, that whosoever believeth in him should not perish, but have everlasting life.* Sometimes the decision to accept what Christ has done is accompanied by significant emotions. Being forgiven an overwhelming debt you are unable to pay can have that effect. Often however, the decision to accept Christ is unemotional.

I know a Chinese man whose wife had prayed for him to be saved for many years. He was an outspoken critic of his wife's Christianity and referred to the things she was hearing at church as "garbage." Eventually, he became persuaded of the truth of the gospel message and accepted Christ. On a Sunday morning, he walked the aisle to make his acceptance of Christ publicly known. There were no tears, no expressions of joy, no emotions whatsoever. He simply made a conscious, informed and reasoned decision based on what he now understood was the truth.

The representation of being born-again as a mystical experience may reflect the expression of some, but that is far from normative and is entirely absent in the Bible. Once again, if we are going to examine what being born-again really is, then we should go to the source and see what the experience was like for those in the New Testament.

In the book of Acts, following a sermon by Peter, some 3000 people *gladly received his word and were baptized.* (Acts 2:41) There were no mystical feelings, no goose bumps, no euphoria, just a reasoned decision after coming to an intellectual understanding of who Jesus is and what he did for them. In fact, if you scour the New Testament, the most dramatic conversion you will find is that of the apostle Paul.

According to Acts 9:5, Jesus spoke personally to him. *I am Jesus whom thou persecutest.* Scripture tells us Paul *trembled,* and was *astonished.* Although the term born-again is not used in this account, the change in Paul was consistent with others whose life has been changed by a personal acknowledgment of Jesus Christ as savior. It was not **a psychological**

phenomena brought on by strongly held beliefs, fueled by cultural influences and peer pressure. (135) It should be obvious that a person like Paul, or a modern-day unbeliever, who up to the point of conversion had neither strong belief nor peer pressure, cannot be influenced by a something he does not yet accept as true. In fact, Paul was a chief antagonist of the belief he was about to embrace himself.

In a moving and heartbreaking testimony, the skeptic describes his own attempt at being born-again. **When I was around the age of thirteen, a devout and devoted Christian who was apparently working his way through the phone book called my house. The telemissionary asked if I had accepted Jesus into my heart and been born again. When I told him that nothing like that had ever happened to me, he explained that when I died, I would not be able to go to heaven and would have to suffer in hell forever. He said it was crucial that I immediately get myself properly born again to be safe. He told me that in order to live again after I die, I only had to invite Jesus into my heart, ask him to forgive me for all the terrible things I had done in the first thirteen years of my life, and then say the Lord's Prayer. At first, I was just being respectful to a stranger, but then I thought, "Hey, why not?" Spurred on by that anonymous missionary who phoned me, I tried my best to initiate the born-again experience. I had doubts and couldn't fake absolute belief, of course, but I said the words and thought the thoughts with the utmost sincerity possible — and nothing happened. It was like pulling the trigger on an unloaded gun. No belief, no born-again experience.** (137-138)

This account is particularly poignant for me because I once did something very similar, except I was on the missionary end. One day, while serving as an assistant in the church my father pastored, he received a call from a young man who picked our church's number out of the phone book to ask for help with some moving he had to do. Dad sent me on the errand to see if I could help this guy and perhaps be a witness to him.

When I arrived he only needed help moving a couple heavy things from the house to a truck. We were done in several minutes, so I began talking to him about Christ and salvation. He listened politely and agreed with what I said about Jesus dying on the cross for his sin. I finally asked him if he wanted to accept Christ. He said, "Well, it can't hurt anything?" I led him in a sinners prayer and went home feeling quite happy that I had led someone to accept Christ.

In hindsight, and having a little more mature understanding of leading someone to Christ now than I did then, I realize that while my effort was sincere, his response was much like what the skeptic's missionary told him. Being born-again was a way to "be safe." It is unfortunate that so many, including myself at the time, think that we can help someone to be born-again by getting them to answer correctly, and say the right prayer. I am afraid there is still far too much of this kind of thinking pervading the Christian church today. It has no parallel in scripture. Not a single convert in the New Testament said a prayer in order to be saved. That doesn't mean doing so is wrong, it is just not a biblical prerequisite.

The skeptic says it all - **No belief, no born again experience**. Interestingly, this admission of unbelief reinforces what the Bible says about what it takes to be saved. In Acts 16, the Philippian jailer asked Paul and Silas, *Sirs, What must I do to be saved?* Paul answered, *Believe on the Lord Jesus Christ and thou shalt be saved and thy house.*

No other religious system of belief offers forgiveness from the consequence of sin through the sacrificial death and ensuing resurrection of God himself. Among all the religions in the world, Christianity's offer of pardon for sin and from eternal separation from God, paid for by God on our behalf and offered to man as a free gift is unique.

TWENTY-ONE

IS FAITH A GOOD THING?

Nobody, Christian or non-Christian should rely on faith as a way to think. (141)

With that, the skeptic sets out to demonstrate that **faith is both flawed and undesirable because it asks people to sacrifice sound thinking in order to leap to unwarranted conclusions.** (141) **If there is evidence for something, then I'll accept it as real or true. But if there is none, I won't, simple as that.** (142)

Skeptics distinguish between two kinds of faith. One is the kind of faith that places trust in someone or something, like your wife, or the chair you are about to sit in. But that's not the kind of faith the skeptic is arguing against. The second definition of faith is offered as **believing/ knowing that a god is real even if proof or good evidence is lacking or absent.** (141)

This definition is worthy of careful analysis. Defining faith in this way stacks the deck against Christian belief by suggesting that such faith is without proof or even good evidence. Faith is defined as a blind leap in the absence of any good reason to make the jump. The premise is hardly accurate.

Of course, there certainly are many Christians, and no small number of non-Christians, who believe in God without having done a lot of investigation or critical thinking. There is something to be said for child-like faith that trusts without requiring indisputable evidence or intellectual persuasion. This is faith based on believing in the integrity of another, even if it is someone you do not know and have never even met, like me and the story of the gas explosion. If you believed that, with no proof it was actually true, it was by faith, period!

On the other hand, a person may believe that the moon is responsible for ocean tides because someone who was knowledgable told him and he believed it without having to know all about gravitational attraction and earth's rotation. His knowledge may be lacking, but his belief is no less true than that of the astrophysicist who has proven it by empirical methods.

It is similar when it comes to believing in God. Many accept his existence without requiring all the theological knowledge, and if I may say, the practical evidence. The theologian however, like the astrophysicist, has studied the evidences of his field and is able to better articulate them to others who have not.

One who believes in the reason for tides may be ignorant of many of the scientific facts, but his belief is based on the authority of one who knows the facts and on realities he can see for himself. What the astrophysicist says about how the moon affects tides correlates to real life. Sometimes however, what we can see clearly by evidence can fool us into believing something that is not true.

Part of my job has been to transport Amish workers to their place of employment. One of them in particular liked to talk about matters of science. As we drove along to work one morning, he commented about the beauty of the sun rising over the rural New York landscape. Unable to resist, and curious about the science knowledge of an Amish man, I told him that the sun doesn't actually rise but only appears to because of the earth's rotation. I explained that we are the ones moving on a spinning sphere at about 1000 miles per hour. With the earth's circumference at about 24,000 miles, it makes one complete rotation every 24 hours.

"How do you know that?" he challenged. I told him that in the 1500s Copernicus figured out the planets actually revolve around the sun and that the earth rotates. I don't know if the Amish study such things, but he had a hard time accepting what I was saying because it conflicted with the physical evidence he could see right out the van window. The sun was coming up plain as day. "How do you know that scientists didn't just get together and decide that they would say the sun stays still and the earth rotates?" he asked. "How can you really know that what they say is true?"

I had to smile at his skeptic thinking. I'm sure he was partly just pulling my chain because he liked debate too, but he wasn't really convinced by my little science lesson either. And to a certain extent, he was right. I don't have the instruments or the capability to prove the sun does not move across the sky as it appears, or that the earth spins on its axis at 1000 miles an hour, despite the fact that I don't sense I am moving at all, much less at that speed. I never talked with Copernicus, and aside from relevant statements he is supposed to have made, I have to take the word of teachers who have studied the issue and scientists who have published the results of their own investigation. I believe on authority what I cannot prove myself and with what appears to conflict with physical evidence I can see. And that is the secret of Christian faith. It is believing based on the authority and credibility of another.

When the skeptic says, **faith is both flawed and undesirable because it asks people to sacrifice sound thinking in order to leap to unwarranted conclusions,** (141) he is presuming that faith precludes thinking. But that isn't what faith requires at all. This is critical to understanding the difference between blind belief and trust based on authority.

Ask a skeptic to prove the sun does not actually move across the sky and that the earth is spinning at 1000 miles an hour, and he will immediately appeal to an authority. If he is quite knowledgable, he may cite the heliocentric model of Copernicus or Kepler's laws of planetary motion. However, he will not be able to prove anything to you by empirical methods on the spot. You will have to take what he says based on the authority of those he cites, just like I was expecting my Amish friend to do. Incidentally, Johannes Kepler, who discovered the laws of planetary motion

> ...incorporated religious arguments and reasoning into his work, motivated by the religious conviction and belief that God had created the world according to an intelligible plan that is accessible through the natural light of reason.[1]

Kepler believed by faith that God intelligently created the celestial patterns he was studying. That belief guided him to the laws of nature he discovered. His faith led him to the light of knowledge. Christian faith does the same in relation to God.

The fact that we believe what scientists tell us about the earth's rotation and its relationship to the sun, despite what we can plainly see, is much the same as the Christian view regarding the existence of God and the truthfulness of the Bible. Eyewitnesses to long past events who wrote down what they saw, the places they visited, the experiences they had, some quite extraordinary, are no less authoritative than the work of Copernicus, Kepler, or ancient historians and scribes.

It may be true that these things cannot be proven empirically, but that is true of all ancient history. Just as the average Joe cannot prove Copernicus and Kepler were right, he believes what they discovered anyway based on authority, despite what he can plainly see with his own eyes. This knowledge was acquired because early scientists recognized order and precision in heavenly bodies as indicative of design, and it correlates with how the universe actually works.

One or more gods may be real-it's possible-but we can't just say faith settles the question and move on. We must rely on very good evidence to be sure, otherwise we set ourselves up to make mistakes and waste time believing in things that are not real. Choosing faith over reason to decide something dishonors the magnificent thinking machine inside your skull. (143)

As we have already noted, neither science nor history has documented a single machine coming into existence as a result of purposeless random processes, whether mechanical or biological. Machines, even simple ones, like a screw jack, or more sophisticated ones, like computers, pale into insignificance compared to the magnificent capacity of even a challenged human brain like mine. Yet with no evidence, much less very good evidence to rely on that such a "machine" has ever self-produced, the skeptic believes it did anyway. This belief without empirical data is nothing other than faith. But it is not the kind of faith that is based on the authority and credibility of others who have studied an issue or witnessed an event. It is a truly blind faith which accepts an extraordinary supposition with no examples, no experimental data, and no eyewitness documentation.

Remember, atheists say, **We must rely on very good evidence to be sure, otherwise we set ourselves up to make mistakes and waste time believing in things that are not real.** (143) I agree. Blind faith does that. Again, by blind I mean accepting something as true which has no eyewitnesses, no evidence, no documentation, and no corollary in the real world.

Look at the difference between faith that believes in the existence of God and believing that the human brain self-generated. The late Dr. Greg Bahnsen argued that one evidence for the existence of God is the impossibility of the contrary. He reasoned that we can believe in God on the same basis that we believe in other universal, immaterial, abstract things like the laws of logic, laws of morality and laws of science.[2]

These laws were not invented or developed but discovered. They were already operating, and as far as we have been able to discern, always have been. Science provides no example of when they were not operative. They are useful because they reflect reality. Even skeptics believe in these things, yet none can explain their origin. Apart from being given by an omniscient creator God, logic, morality, and universal natural laws that govern our very existence have no scientifically confirmed origin. We can believe that God instituted these things or that somehow they just happened to turn out that way. Both are positions of faith with no empirical evidence as proof. What we do know empirically from science however, is that no thinking or mechanical device has ever self-generated.

Romans 1 is also appropriate here. *Because that which may be known of God is manifest in them, for God hath showed it unto them. For the invisible things of him from the creation of the world are clearly seen, being understood by the things that are made, even his eternal power and Godhead, so that they are without excuse.* Don't let the fact that this comes from the Bible prevent you from fairly examining what it is saying. Skeptics don't have to believe it but should be willing to give it a fair hearing. Put simply, it means that what we can see in the world around us tells us all we need to know about God as far as his existence and nature is concerned. In fact, it means that this evidence is so persuasive that mankind has no excuse for missing it.

One of the facts evident in nature is that even simple order does not come into place by accident. We have never witnessed order and complexity arising out of chaos without input from some external intelligent source. Despite this fact, in his book, *The Blind Watchmaker*, Richard Dawkins cites the sieving effect of ocean waves sorting pebbles by size on the beach as an example of mindless nature producing order. While writing this chapter, I had the opportunity to see this for myself on North Carolina's Outer Banks. Sure enough, larger pebbles and shells were furthest from the water's edge while finer sand and smaller pebbles were closer.

Kill Devil Hills, NC photo by the author

Dawkins writes,

> A tribe living near the shore might wonder at this evidence of sorting or arrangement in the world and might develop a myth to account for it, perhaps attributing it to a Great Spirit in the sky with a tidy mind and a sense of order.[3]

However, as I observed and photographed this phenomenon, I noticed that the "sieving" effect was quite random and frankly looked anything but tidy. Further from shore were piles of broken clam shells and ocean debris. In some areas, where the beach undulates, there was no sign of this sorting effect at all. In some places, pockets of larger pebbles were scattered across large areas of the beach as if they had been broadcast randomly by hand. While overall you can see the effect, it hardly leaves you with a sense of order and neat arrangement and it is by no means consistent.

We were on the Outer Banks when hurricane Matthew came through in the fall of 2016. Thankfully, by then it was just a category one storm, but that was powerful enough. We could feel our house moving, the evidence of just how much could be seen in the sloshing water of the toilet bowl!

I went out to the beach the next day. Sand filled oceanfront swimming pools and was piled against beachfront homes like drifts of snow. Roads were closed due to sand and flooding. Debris littered the landscape. There was no tidiness anywhere.

Dawkins goes on to the astronomic scale of the solar system being just a larger version of what happens on the beach.

> The Solar system is a stable arrangement of planets, comets and debris orbiting the sun, and it is presumably one of many such orbiting systems in the universe. The nearer a satellite is to its sun, the faster it has to travel to counter the sun's gravity and remain in stable orbit. For any given orbit, there is only one speed at which a satellite can travel and remain in that orbit. If it were traveling at any other velocity, it would either move out into deep space, or crash into the Sun, or move into another orbit. And if we look at the planets of our solar system, lo and behold, every single one of them is traveling at exactly the right velocity to keep it in its stable orbit around the Sun. A blessed miracle of provident design? No, just another natural sieve.[4]

According to Dawkins, for the precision of the universe to which he readily admits, we can thank a purposeless process similar to that which appears to sort pebbles by size on the seashore. This is truly an amazing extrapolation! What happens if the cosmic "natural sieve" behaves like hurricane Matthew, sending chaos into the very place it had tidied up the day before? Dawkins did not take his analogy that far.

To illustrate the difference between faith based on evidence and authority, as I have suggested Christians believe, and a blind faith that simply says faith settles the question without any evidence, as the skeptic maintains, let's look at the difference between Kepler and Dawkins.

Kepler believed by faith that the universe was a reflection of an orderly God. Dawkins believes nature is the product of a "blind watchmaker" called natural selection that is "blind to the future and has no long term goal."[5] Kepler discovered laws that describe and govern planetary motion. It explained things as they really are. These laws have aided navigators and astronomers for over four centuries. Dawkins proposes concepts and ideas of how things might be. He proposes no law, only undocumented presumptions. Yet these have no consistent correlation to the real world. Kepler's discoveries are confirmed by the authority of reality.

Don't get me wrong. Dawkins has a brilliant mind. I find his books to be riveting reading. But being brilliant, engaging, creative, and persuasive, does not mean what is proposed rises to the level of a natural law, scientific fact, or even common sense. Shrouding possibility in a cloak of scientific verbiage does not make a scientific discovery. It only results in an imaginative idea and sometimes an interesting sci-fi movie. But if that idea is actually believed, then that belief is not rooted in a reality that documents and demonstrates it, but in blind faith that the idea is actually true, absent any real evidence to substantiate it.

The distinction between an imaginative idea and a scientific law is extremely significant. In an intelligently designed world, as Kepler believed, there can be laws. Laws imply governance. In a world resulting from undirected and purposeless events, there can be no laws. This is self-evident.

If our solar system functions as it does merely by fortunate cosmic accident, then it may not operate that way tomorrow. But that is not what we have seen in approximately 6000 years of recorded human history. Though Kepler did not discover the laws of planetary motion until the early 1600s, those laws were fully operating for millennia prior and for 400 years since. There has been no variation or disastrous cosmic hurricanes that untidy the laws governing the universe.

So far, Kepler appears to have been right. He discovered unchanging laws that govern the cosmos. If atheists like Dawkins are right, our perfectly tuned universe could be acted upon by random, mindless forces at any time. It cannot be governed by laws, only chance, and hopefully for us, a continued streak of good luck. If the laws which govern our solar system were as capricious as ocean waves, the destruction to the universe would be on an order of magnitude as outrageous as Dawkins' extrapolation from sorted beach pebbles to the laws of planetary motion.

And that is the difference between faith that God is real based upon evidence, like natural laws that regulate and produce order and predictability and allow for calculation and certainty, and a faith that blindly believes in something that is based on nothing more than an imaginative idea. One is rooted in the authority of reality, the other in an imagined concept wearing a scientific mask.

The same faith that is the foundation of belief in God and the framework for Christianity, also guided many of the early scientists who operated on the very logical premise that order and precision are evidence of an intelligent being who created an intricately balanced system. In the words of Richard Dawkins, "if we look at the planets of our solar system, lo and behold, every single one of them is traveling at exactly the right velocity to keep it in its stable orbit around the Sun."[6] An atheist sees this and attributes it to a purposeless but fortunate arrangement which happens to be beneficial for life on earth, so long as some other purposeless event doesn't come along and mess it up. It is an unsupported and unprovable supposition.

The Christian sees the same thing and observes that nothing in his field of experience regarding such precision ever occurs without being initiated and guided by intelligence. Both the atheist and the Christian are being guided by a belief, but the Christian's belief correlates to observed realities. The atheist belief is based on a supposition that is in conflict with reality. The point cannot be overstated. This is also a perfect example of Romans 1:19-20 cited earlier.

The matter of faith is so important, I want to provide one more illustration of the difference between evidence-based faith, and faith that is rooted in pure speculation. Skeptics ask, **If religion's version of faith is reasonable and if it works, then why don't scientists use it to explain various aspects of the universe? "I know extraterrestrial life is real because I have faith in its existence," says the astrobiologist. "Therefore there is no reason to search for it..."** (144)

Perhaps one of the best examples of totally blind faith is the SETI (Search for Extraterrestrial Intelligence) project. According to Wikipedia, "The Institute's SETI Researchers use both radio and optical telescope systems to search for deliberate signals from technologically advanced extraterrestrial civilizations."[7] Notice in the skeptic's statement above that if religious faith were applied to science, we could say there is no reason to search for extraterrestrial intelligence because we know it is there by faith. What should not go unnoticed is the supposition that extraterrestrial intelligence is real, otherwise why would anyone bother looking for it in the first place? It is supposed that a person of faith could say there is no need to look for it, just accept it by faith.

The "believer" in extraterrestrial intelligence however, would say we should look for it because we believe it is there, despite the fact there is no evidence. This too is faith. To be clear, most evangelical Christians I know do not believe in intelligent life anywhere other than on earth and see no reason to waste time and money looking for it. So far, this correlates with reality.

Frank Drake, the originator of Project Ozma, the predecessor of SETI and the first serious attempt to listen for alien radio signals, is the poster child for blind belief in extraterrestrial intelligence.

> At this very minute, with almost absolute certainty, radio waves sent forth by other intelligent civilizations are falling on earth...Someday, from somewhere out among the stars, will come answers to many of the oldest, most important, and most exciting questions mankind has faced.[8]

On what basis can such a thing be "almost absolute certainty?" On what authority can Drake say answers will come from these alien civilizations? Does he have faith that alien civilizations exist? Yuri Milner, a Russian billionaire, backed up his faith in extraterrestrial intelligence by donating 100 million dollars for a new initiative called "Breakthrough Listen." Well-known atheist and physicist, Stephen Hawking, signed on to the intensified search stating, "In an infinite Universe, there must be other life."[9] Even an atheist can have faith in the absence of evidence.

For over 50 years, scientists who believe without any evidence that intelligent life exists elsewhere in the universe have been searching for signs that someone or something is out there. What they are looking for are signals that have structure and order, something that is not just random interstellar noise but the equivalent of interplanetary morse code.

> SETI projects traditionally search for radio or optical signals that seem to be from an artificial source, for instance, because they are focused in frequency and repeat in a regular manner.[10]

Two instances of this are worth noting.

> On August 15, 1977, the Big Ear radio telescope at Ohio State University picked up a signal that resembled the frequency of hydrogen. It was immediately dubbed the

"WOW signal." The hydrogen line frequency is significant for SETI searchers because, it is reasoned, hydrogen is the most common element in the universe, and hydrogen resonates at about 1420.40575177 MHz, so extraterrestrials might use that frequency to transmit a strong signal.[11]

More recently, other signals have been detected that excite SETI observers.

For about the last decade, scientists have been detecting strange signals called "fast radio bursts" (FRBs) from deep space that have a suspicious mathematical pattern. The pattern is consistent enough that some scientists have even speculated that the signals may have a technological origin. In other words, it's possible they could be signals from aliens.[12]

What should not be missed in these examples is that scientists began searching for something for which there was no evidence of its existence, only belief. In addition, they continue searching for something based on the premise that some kind of regularity, order, or mathematical pattern may indicate an intelligent transmission. Why? If the order, precision, and mathematical patterns in our universe do not originate from intelligence, and are simply the result of a cosmic "natural sieve," why should signals in outer space with similar characteristics be perceived any different? There is something fishy here.

Significantly, after more than fifty years of technologically advanced search systems, no evidence of extraterrestrial intelligence has yet surfaced. Still, the search goes on. Clearly, looking and listening for intelligent life in outer space is a faith-based search, and a blind faith at that. It is a search based on belief alone with a total lack of evidence. Furthermore, this is the kind of evidence-lacking faith which the skeptic accuses Christians of holding.

So when a skeptic says, **If there is evidence for something, then I'll accept it as real or true. But if there is none, I won't, simple as that,** (142) it is reasonable to ask if he believes enough in alien intelligence to support searching for it, and if so, what evidence can he produce that supports that belief? If there is no evidence to support the belief, then is that not an evidence-less faith? To be fair, I don't really know if most skeptics are true believers in extraterrestrial intelligence, Stephen Hawking notwithstanding. But then again, what would be the point in spending time and money listening for something unless you actually thought it was out there — somewhere.

But don't these signals which SETI has discovered lend credibility to the search? Is not this at least evidence that something may be out there trying to get in touch with us? Shouldn't discoveries like these encourage us to keep looking?

Even if there were some kind of intelligence sending these signals, the initial search for them was based on a "belief," not founded on any evidence or scientific observation, only the imaginative idea that if life evolved here then it must have evolved somewhere else too. Discovering intelligent life forms from a distant galaxy would be confirmation that what was originally believed by faith is actually true, just like the believer in the moon causing tides initially believes by faith, based on some authority's say so, but may later confirm it with his own investigation.

For the record, in the case of extraterrestrial intelligence, that is not going to happen. SETI will continue to be a financial black hole that produces zero results in discovering real extraterrestrial intelligence. That's my opinion, but there are fifty years worth of fruitless search and a sizable book that has survived three-thousand years of critique to back it up.

The skeptic hits the nail on the head when he says, **We must rely on good arguments and very good evidence to be sure, otherwise we set ourselves up to make mistakes and waste our time believing in things that are not real.** (143) Over fifty years of high-tech searching have produced no trace of extraterrestrial intelligence. That seems like a pretty good argument that it does not exist, especially when there was not even a scintilla of evidence of its existence in the first place.

On the other hand, what if an intelligent, extraterrestrial being not only sent us signals but actually became terrestrial and lived here on earth? What if he provided us with, not radio signals to be interpreted, but an actual book we could read? What if he left a trail of witnesses and evidence that he was who he claimed to be? Would such evidence be convincing? It was to many. Others who witnessed the acts of Jesus Christ, heard his claims, or have since read about his message to the world, reject what he said and some even deny he ever existed.

Perhaps it was this kind of skepticism that prompted Mark Twain to say, "Faith is believing what you know ain't so." But that simply isn't true. Believing something you know isn't so is not faith at all, it is stupidity. People may mistakenly believe in something they think is true but really isn't. That is vastly different from believing in something you know is false.

Christian faith arises from evidence that is consistent with the realities of nature, from accounts of eyewitnesses, from non-Christian historians who corroborate the Christian story, from discoveries of archaeology, and from the Bible, unsurpassed in its consistency and credibility regarding ancient civilizations, historical accounts, scientific accuracy, prophecies and their fulfillment, and its uniform message written by forty authors over nearly 1500 years on three different continents.

Science, such as was done by Copernicus and Kepler, confirm rather than contradict the biblical record. There is abundant evidence to support the Christian faith and the existence of an intelligent, purposeful, and creative God. We simply have to examine what we can see as Kepler did, operating on the evidence-based faith that order and complexity do not arise from purposeless, random accidents. Therefore, as Kepler believed, "God... created the world according to an intelligible plan that is accessible through the natural light of reason." This is consistent with Christian faith in the God of the Bible and natural realities.

TWENTY-TWO

SHOULD CHILDREN BE CHRISTIANS?

Skeptics question the practice of evangelizing children. **It seems very much like intellectual bullying.** (149) **Why not let the religion stand on its own strength? Why not let children mature to the point that they are able to think for themselves about unusual and important claims?** (149)

While I am not in complete agreement with the skeptic's argument on this point, I do not totally discount it either. This may raise the ire of some Christians. In fact, we were the oddballs in our own church when it came to our children participating in programs like Vacation Bible School and Junior church. Perhaps I better explain.

Children will often do whatever they believe the teacher wants them to do. They like to please and are easily led. They will respond to an invitation to accept Christ because that is what they think the teacher wants them to do and it is what others in their class are doing. This is one reason we opted our children out of church programs when they were very young. We did not want them making a decision about becoming a Christian just because they thought that is what they were supposed to do. We certainly wanted all our children to become Christians, but we wanted them to understand what they were doing and why.

Being cautious about evangelizing young children put us in the minority in our own church and eventually led us to start a church where entire families were instructed together. I did not want some well-intended Sunday school teacher or Junior church worker talking one of our children into accepting Christ. That's almost heresy in most evangelical churches, but I wanted to be the one to determine when they were ready and able to comprehend God's plan of salvation. We know our children better than anyone else. As far as we are concerned, this is the most important decision a person makes in their entire life.

When I was twelve years old, I attended a Christian summer camp. There was preaching every night. Another boy I had made friends with went forward every time the preacher gave an invitation to accept Christ. After about the fourth time I asked him why he was doing that. "Two more nights," he said, "and I will have gotten saved every night." He was doing what he thought the preacher wanted without really having the first idea what it all meant.

This would be a good time to share my own experience of how I came to accept Christ as a young boy because it fairly illustrates both sides of this issue. Keep in mind, I was raised in the home of a conservative, fundamental, Baptist preacher. We attended Sunday school, Sunday morning and evening church services, and prayer meeting on Wednesday nights. The Bible, Christianity, and salvation were not strange to me.

I accepted Christ when I was around 9 or 10 years old. I don't remember the exact age. My Mom has told me prior to my accepting Christ that her or Dad often talked to me about it and I would cry and say, "I just don't understand." I don't remember that. What I do remember is not being able to accept that one person would die for another. I was a little boy. I could not imagine being brave enough to sacrifice my own life for someone else. How could anyone do that?

One night, when my Dad was away, Mom carried on the custom of family devotions. The scripture for that evening was John 15:13 *Greater love hath no man than this, that a man lay down his life for his friends.* The devotional story was about the sinking of the Titanic. It has been almost fifty years ago, but I clearly remember the light of understanding coming on for me that night. I realized what it meant for one person to give up his life so someone else could live. I also understood that even children die. The story of Jesus dying for me, taking my place, like many men did on the Titanic so a child or a woman could be saved, clicked for me that evening. My Mom did not have to ask me if I wanted to accept Christ. There was no persuasion or pleading. I went to her. I now knew what it meant for one person to die for another, and I understood that when Jesus died on the cross, he died for my sin. I cried again, this time because I did understand.

That doesn't mean that I understood all the theological ramifications about such things as atonement, or justification, I didn't. What I did know was that Jesus died for me. How could a nine-year-old know that? The same way he knows that a grandpa he never met loves him. He hears stories about him. He receives gifts from someone he has never seen. He believes the stories his parents have told him about grandpa are true. The stories could be made up. The gifts could have come from someone else. But he trusts in those who have told him. He believes it based on trust in an authority, just like so many other things we all believe but cannot prove ourselves.

And that is the other side of the issue of evangelizing children, which is why I said I am not in complete agreement with the skeptic's argument on this point. Yes, we do need to be careful not to take advantage of a child's desire to please, but we must also recognize that Jesus said, *Suffer little children, and forbid them not, to come unto me: for of such is the kingdom of heaven.* (Matt. 19:14) Jesus valued children and used them as an example of the kind of faith we must have. But is telling children Bible stories exploiting child-like faith?

The skeptic argues that **the stories in the Bible involving supernatural events or beings have not been confirmed by historians and scientists. They are not evidence based.** (150) But that is not true. Many of the stories in the Bible, even those that did involve supernatural events, have incredible supporting evidence, such as the Ipuwer Papyrus' accurate description of the plagues mentioned in Exodus.

We cannot prove every last detail empirically, but we can believe them because we trust the authority from which they come, just like a child would trust the authority of those who tell him about a grandpa he has never seen. As he gets older, he may still believe in grandpa but want to investigate further and even meet him if possible. This would not make him a "grandpa believer," but confirm a belief he already had. My own journey from childhood convert to analyzing skeptic criticisms of Christianity has not made me a believer but confirmed and matured a much simpler childhood understanding. An objective study of atheistic arguments and Christian apologetics leads to new and more persuasive discoveries.

We have already summarized the most remarkable supernatural event in history, the resurrection of Christ. The resurrection is very much evidence-based, yet skeptics simply reject the evidence as inconclusive or unreliable. When details surrounding a given story are corroborated by historians and archaeologists, it lends credibility to specific accounts for which there cannot be empirical evidence. We can believe them on the same basis we believe in the unseen grandpa, because we trust the integrity of those who had first-hand knowledge of the events and wrote about them, and in the truthfulness of those relating the stories to us, and the reliability of the research that confirms many of the details. Then, exploring further, we make new and exciting discoveries that reinforce the credibility of what at first seemed a fantastic story.

Let's look at just one example of this from the Bible to see how it works and why telling children stories from the Bible in Sunday-school classes is not as much like **dishonest marketing seminars designed to take advantage of innocent children** (151) as the skeptic would have us believe.

One of the most well-known stories in the Bible told to children in Sunday-schools is about David and Goliath. Almost everyone, irrespective of church upbringing, has heard of it. Let's take a more in-depth look to see if it meets the skeptic criteria of being evidenced-based.

How can we know this event actually happened and is not just a fable passed down from over 3000 years ago? Is it fair and reasonable to tell children a story about a Philistine warrior over nine feet tall who was killed by a young boy with a slingshot? Could this Bible story really be true?

All of ancient history is based on the writings of those who were there at the time or lived in close proximity to the time the event occurred. Archaeological discoveries add more clarity but do not really provide proof. Even if the skull of a giant with a stone embedded in its forehead were discovered in Jerusalem, that would not "prove" the story of David and Goliath. There could always be the possibility that the skull is a hoax, or it was a different giant, or that this particular one was killed in a different battle. All such legitimate discoveries are evidence which may be believed or not, depending on a person's presuppositions. But the story of David and Goliath has some very interesting corroborating evidence.

A July 11, 2011 FoxNews report entitled, "Archaeologists Excavate Biblical Giant Goliath's Hometown," details archaeological discoveries confirming that Gath, a Philistine city and the home of Goliath, according to I Samuel 17:6, actually existed.

> The findings at the site support the idea that the Goliath story faithfully reflects something of the geopolitical reality of the period," Maeir said -- "the often violent interaction of the powerful Philistines of Gath with the kings of Jerusalem in the frontier zone between them.[1]

Aren Maier, of Bar-Ilan University is the archaeologist in charge of the excavation.

An August 3, 2009 report titled, "Experts dig up dirt on David and Goliath," provides additional information on Maiers findings.

> I would say a Goliath-like people for sure existed here. You have evidence of an inscription which shows us two Goliath-like names at that time.[2]

And in yet another article referring to the finding of pottery with an inscription of the name "Goliath," Professor Maier is quoted.

> What this means is that at the time there were people there named Goliath ...It shows us that David and Goliath's story reflects the cultural reality of the time.[3]

Another report on the same dig states,

> Archaeologists in Israel have uncovered what they believe to be the enormous gates of Gath, the city of Goliath. The gate is part of enormous and extensive fortifications...[4]

While no giant skeletons have been reported, the data so far validates everything about the details surrounding the biblical story. But is it right to tell children stories of giants that are found in the Bible? Giants never existed, did they?

Anyone who is interested can search the internet or go to the library and find an abundance of reports and research which document the existence of giants. Some of these are undoubtedly spurious, taking advantage of photo editing to grab attention. One report, which proved to be a hoax, actually did claim to have found Goliath's skull, with a stone still embedded in the forehead. However, the more interesting and legitimate accounts are in journals from over a hundred years ago.

The Popular Science News and Boston Journal of Chemistry reported in 1890 on the work of anthropologist Georges Vacher de Lapouge. He discovered large human humerus bones in a Bronze Age cemetery in Castelnau-le-Lez France.

> If we judge of the height of this neolithic giant by the usual proportion of the parts of the skeleton to each other, he must have been between 10 and 11 feet high.[5]

Scientific American ran an article in August 1880 on the opening of a mound in Brush Creek, Ohio.

> The mound was opened by the Historical Society of the township, under the immediate supervision of Dr. J. F. Everhart, of Zanesville. It measured sixty-four by thirty-five feet at the summit, gradually sloping in every direction, and was eight feet in height. There was found in it a sort of clay coffin including the skeleton of a woman measuring eight feet in length. Within this coffin was found also the skeleton of a child about three and a half feet in length, and an image that crumbled when exposed to the atmosphere. In another grave was found the skeleton of a man and woman, the former measuring nine and the latter eight feet in length. In a third grave occurred two other skeletons, male and female, measuring respectively nine feet four inches and eight feet. Seven other skeletons were found in the mound, the smallest of which measured eight feet, while others reached the enormous length of ten feet. They were buried singly, or each in separate graves. Resting against one of the coffins was an engraved stone tablet (now in Cincinnati), from the characters on which Dr. Everhart and Mr. Bowers are led to conclude that this giant race were sun worshipers.[6]

So where are all these giant skeletons now and why don't we see them in museums? That is a very good question which has sparked lots of debate. From cover-up claims, to counter claims that confessions of a cover-up are a hoax, it is hard to tell where the truth really lies. But with reports from reputable, scientific journals going back a hundred years, it is apparent that giants did exist. I once had lunch with a paleontologist who had seen the bones of some of these giant skeletons himself.

Of course, all of this does nothing to prove the biblical story of David and Goliath, but it does provide evidence, if not proof, of the existence of giants. As far as scientific evidence supporting the biblical story goes; there were Philistines; they did occupy a city called Gath; the Philistines did war against the Israelites; there was at least one, and probably more, with the name Goliath; the dating of artifacts found at the site places the Philistines and Gath in the same time period as the biblical record indicates. In addition, the slingshot was a formidable weapon in ancient warfare capable of killing the enemy even at a great distance. All the details surrounding this common Sunday-school story can be substantiated by objective, scientifically supported evidence, including the existence of giants.

When all the data is objectively considered regarding this one Bible story, it becomes clear that the only part for which no empirical evidence exists is that a young boy named David killed a giant using a slingshot, placing the killing of Goliath in the same category as any other military exploit in ancient history. Considering that the slingshot was used as a military weapon at the time and that with practice incredible accuracy can be acquired, all that is left to believe is that David actually confronted Goliath and was enough of a marksman to kill him with a shot to the forehead. Watching videos of modern competitions using this ancient weapon make David's feat entirely believable.

The skeptic may argue that the story of David and Goliath does not involve supernatural events or beings, which is the basis for the objection to teaching such Bible stories to children as facts. That is true. Most stories in the Bible told in Sunday-school classes are not about supernatural events or beings. The story of Noah and the ark, Daniel and the lion's den, Joshua and the battle of Jericho, Samson, Esther, Jonah and the whale, the wise men at Jesus' birth, Paul, Silas and the Philippian jailer, the crucifixion of Christ, and many others include accurate historical context, real places, and actual people, and sometimes extraordinarily timed natural phenomenon but not a supernatural event or being.

While there certainly are events in the Bible that qualify as "supernatural," like the virgin birth, the resurrection, Jesus feeding the five thousand with 5 loaves and 2 fishes, calming the stormy sea by speaking to it, or walking on the water, these accounts in the Bible also involve the same characteristics of historical people, real places, and the corroboration of eyewitnesses whose credibility is substantiated by the accurate relating of other evidence-based historical facts. By objecting to teaching children stories that involve supernatural beings or events, the skeptic seems to be selecting what stories in the Bible could be appropriate for children based on his own prescription for believability. It seems when Bible authors are writing of actual places, real rulers, and documented historical events, they may be accurate, but when these same authors write of supernatural beings or events, they are either mistaken, delusional, or lying.

To address the question of whether children should be told Bible stories as if they were true, we have examined in some detail one of the most well known and often told stories in the Bible. What we find is that despite the incredible nature of the story of David and Goliath, most of the details surrounding this story can be scientifically and archaeologically verified. This may not be equally true of all other Bible stories, at least not with our present knowledge, but it does support the very reasonable position that when seemingly incredible accounts in the Bible have been proven true, or at the very least, possible, as much as any ancient event can be, there is very good reason to have confidence in the veracity of other accounts as well.

I should clarify here that Christian belief in the accuracy of the Bible is not because of external corroborating evidence. We believe the Bible is true first by faith and because *All scripture is given by inspiration of God....*(II Tim. 3:16) The corroborating evidence of its accuracy only confirms and reinforces what was already believed. In the last chapter, we will examine another example of how modern science has confirmed a biblical record that was once thought to be entirely imaginary.

So how should the Christian respond when a skeptic says, **I understand that some Christians might feel like they are under attack when I say that many skeptics think all those sweet and harmless Sunday-school classes are dishonest marketing seminars designed to take advantage of innocent children. But I simply want Christians to understand that many nonbelievers view imposing Christianity on a trusting child not only as unfair to the child but also as possible evidence of a perceived weakness in the religion by its own adherents. We wonder why, if Christianity is the ultimate truth, its teachings have to be pushed in such an advantageous manner so early in life. (151)**

The premise of this statement, of course, is that the story of Christianity is not really true and should not be presented as such to easily persuaded children. But when the Bible, from which Christianity comes, is examined thoroughly, we find no logic behind the notion that it is dishonest besides the skeptic presupposition that it has not been proven. As we showed in the chapter on prophecies, some of the Bible's most outrageous pronouncements, made hundreds of years prior to their historically documented occurrence, demonstrate the supernatural character and historical accuracy of this book of all books.

Such prophecies have been fulfilled exactly as they were predicted, defying any naturalistic explanation. Believing other historical accounts and unusual events becomes as easy as believing a well-researched history book. Children are taught history every day in schools around the world using books based on the written testimony of those who were witnesses to the events, or by those who have documented them through careful research. Why should the Bible be any different? Why should children not be taught its history, its people, its places, its events, and its meaning?

One last point illustrates the skeptic double standard when it comes to viewing Sunday-school classes as **dishonest marketing seminars designed to take advantage of innocent children.** (151) The skeptic asks, **Why not let the religion stand on its own strength? Why not let children mature to the point that they are able to think for themselves about unusual and important claims?** (149)

Ask a skeptic if creationism should be taught alongside evolution in schools and see how quickly he abandons the philosophy of letting children decide what they believe about both these important and unusual claims. Of course, the immediate response to this is that the two cannot be fairly presented on an equal basis because evolution is science rooted in fact, whereas creationism is a religious concept rooted in faith, not science. We have thoroughly refuted such an objection throughout this book, but let's level the playing field one more time.

At the very base of both creationism and evolution is a belief that something happened which has never been observed or reproduced by science. That something is the spontaneous appearance of life from non-living matter. The evolutionist must come to grips with the fact that this phenomenon has never been witnessed or reproduced scientifically. Believing that it happened cannot be based on any scientific evidence. Yet, it is the very core of the evolution of all living things.

Evolutionists generally explain how life began with a robust amount of "might haves," "could haves," and "may haves." By any definition, spontaneous generation is a violation of the natural laws science has observed and documented. This places the most foundational component of evolution, life from non-living matter, in the category of a miracle. Apple's Dictionary, version 2.2.1, defines a miracle as,

> a surprising and welcome event that is not explicable by natural or scientific laws and is therefore considered to be the work of a divine agency.[7]

Evolutionists simply replace "divine agency" with "luck." Richard Dawkins said, "...the origin of life could still be a staggeringly good stroke of luck."[8] If the spontaneous generation of life from non-living matter does not fall into the category of a miracle, what would? It has no confirmed naturalistic explanation, but skeptics still believe it.

From their belief-based positions on the origin of life itself, both evolution and creationism seek to use scientific principles and observations to support what neither can prove empirically. Whether you are an evolutionist or a creationist, the appearance of life on earth begins with a "surprising and welcome event that is not explicable by natural or scientific laws." This fact cannot be honestly rejected by either side of the origin of life issue.

So why should not the merits of both belief systems be considered on an equal basis in schools? Why has one belief been ruled unconstitutional in some states, and the other given free rein? Michael Ruse, Florida State philosophy professor and well-known evolutionist said,

> My area of expertise is the clash between evolutionists and creationists, and my analysis is that we have no simple clash between science and religion, but rather between two religions.[9]

It is at least honest to acknowledge that where there can be no scientific proof of an event, accepting that it happened anyway puts it into the category of faith. That is by no means a criticism, nor is it an opinion, but merely a statement of the obvious. So we end this chapter where it began. **It seems very much like intellectual bullying. (149) Why not let the religion stand on its own strength? Why not let children mature to the point that they are able to think for themselves about unusual and important claims? (149)** When this argument is turned back on skeptics regarding the evolution/creation controversy, it morphs into a science versus religion question. But with belief in a miracle at the root of both, it is as Michael Ruse said, a clash "between two religions."

We have examined one of the most common children's Bible stories for its legitimacy as an actual historical event and discovered that there is a great deal of evidence to support the biblical account. Relating events in the Bible that reflect real people, in real places, consistent with an actual historical timeline, and for which there is at least some archaeological evidence should hardly be considered intellectual bullying. Christians believe a similar approach should be taken in schools regarding the teaching of the only two possible views on the origin of life. Being exposed to the best arguments of both sides, let the students "think for themselves" about these unusual and important claims. It is time atheists acknowledge the "faith factor" in evolution and stop demanding that it be spoon fed to children, marketing seminar style.

TWENTY-THREE

DOES JESUS HEAL THE SICK?

I f Jesus can heal the sick, then why doesn't he? Why aren't his followers the most healthy people in the world? **People who are skeptical of Christian faith healing are only stating what should be obvious to all. If Jesus really cares about Christians and is able to cure them of any illness or injury, then something is clearly wrong. Look around. Our world is never short of sick and suffering Christians. (153) If one religion above all others were delivering a noticeably superior healthcare plan, there would be a stampede to sign up. . . It would be a colossal advantage, one the world would not ignore. (154)**

There are three key elements to understanding and answering skeptic thinking regarding this question. First, it reflects a lack of understanding of Christianity and why Jesus came. Second, hardship and suffering are integral to Christian faith. Third, according to the Bible, all healing comes from Jesus. Let's look at each of these in turn.

In chapters eight and nine of Matthew, Jesus heals a man of leprosy, another of palsy, Peter's mother-in-law of a fever, a man possessed of a demon, a cripple, a woman who had internal bleeding, raised Jarius' daughter from the dead, healed two blind men, and a man who was mute. And these are Jesus' healings in just two chapters. Skeptics may view these as mere fables, exaggerations, or possibly actual healings that occurred from some other cause for which Jesus took credit, but they are part of Christian history.

The point here is not to prove Jesus healed the sick by citing examples of his healing people in scripture, but to address the skeptic's contention that if Jesus healed Christians today, people would come flocking to churches to embrace this health-guaranteeing religion. And that is probably why Jesus did not heal every sick person he encountered, and why he does not do so today. This might be viewed as Christians evading the painful fact that Jesus simply does not heal people as described in the New Testament, however, we are first exposing the skeptic's lack of understanding of why Jesus came.

No one could honestly read the life of Christ in the gospels and come away with the impression that Jesus was a huckster who somehow performed tricks or perhaps even genuine miracles just to make a name for himself and get people to follow him. In the case of the man healed of leprosy in Matthew eight, Jesus told him, *See thou tell no man*. In fact, Jesus did this numerous times. Of course, the news still spread of Jesus' healing people. Many came to him to be healed, and many did become his followers. Others, especially the religious leaders who witnessed these miraculous healing events, did not. According to the Bible, Jesus' healing of sick people failed to convince them of anything.

If Jesus wanted to gain a following just because he could heal, there was one person in the New Testament that suffered incredible torment whom he could have healed but did not. Had he healed this one person, with many of his detractors looking on, he would have vindicated himself unmistakably. Even those who despised him would have had to fall at his feet in worship. Who was this unhealed person? Jesus himself.

No matter what you believe about the various healing accounts in the Bible, and particularly the life of Christ in the gospels, whether you are an atheist, an agnostic, or a Christian without answers, you would have to agree that if Jesus' goal was to get the largest following possible, and perform miracles of healing to prove he was worthy of being followed, walking away unharmed from a Roman scourging and crucifixion without even a scratch to show for it, would have been the ultimate healing. So if Jesus can heal any illness or injury, why didn't he heal himself and seal his position as the one and only Son of God he claimed to be?

When the skeptic says, **If Jesus really cares about Christians and is able to cure them of any illness or injury, then something is clearly wrong. Look around. Our world is never short of sick and suffering Christians,** (153) he is quite right. But what is wrong isn't that Jesus is not healing these sick Christians, it is the idea that Jesus healing people would cause a **stampede to sign up.** (154) The Bible transparently refutes that idea. If that were Jesus' motive, he missed his best chance on the day of his crucifixion. And that is why I say the first element of the answer to this question is that the skeptic does not understand why Jesus came.

Jesus' purpose was not to consign doctors and nurses to the dustbin of history and establish JesusCare as the world's health plan. In Luke 19:10, Jesus himself stated his reason for coming. *For the Son of man is come to seek and to save that which was lost.* Jesus' many healings served the purpose of establishing his identity as the Son of God.

Jesus did not heal people just so they would follow him. More accurately, he did it to convince people that he was who he claimed to be. Some believed, others did not. It is the same today. If not a single Christian ever got sick, or if he did, was healed immediately, it would not result in a massive turn to Christ. It would simply be viewed as a naturalistic phenomenon of how humans evolved the ability to self-heal, or be used to accuse God of not caring about atheists, who remain sick due to unbelief. For those who wanted to "sign up" just to be healed, it would not be because they recognized themselves as sinners needing to be saved, but because they wanted the benefit of good health without the cost of living the Christian life. Yes, Jesus healed many people. He also said, *If any man will come after me, let him deny himself, and take up his cross, and follow me.* (Matt. 16:24)

The skeptic stresses, **"scientific" confirmation because the scientific process is the only way we can reliably prove important or unusual claims. Dramatic stories about random incidents are not proof.** (154) If you place the skeptic in first century Jerusalem around A.D.30, he would have his scientific confirmation. He would have seen Jesus' healings with his own eyes. And as we have already noted, the key element of the scientific process is observation. But any reader of the New Testament could tell you, there were still skeptics who were unconvinced despite the irrefutable confirmation of being an eyewitness to repetitive healings by Jesus.

So what does this say about healings today and the skeptic observation that **Our world is never short of sick and suffering Christians**? (153) Anyone who has studied Christianity knows that suffering is a key element of the Christian life. Jesus did not establish a religion of health and perpetual happiness. The prophet Isaiah referred to the coming Messiah this way. *He is despised and rejected of men; a man of sorrows, and acquainted with grief.* (Isaiah 53:3) All of Jesus' disciples but one died tortured deaths, and we are promised, *all that will live godly in Christ Jesus shall suffer persecution.* (II Tim. 3:12) That is what *take up his cross* means in Matt.16:24.

Far from healing Christians of illness and injury, God allows suffering. But what kind of God would allow suffering if it is in his power to prevent it? The book of Job provides great insight into this question. It appears

God knew this would be a nagging problem for humanity through the ages, so in one of the oldest accounts in recorded human history he allows a righteous man to suffer unimaginable loss and hardship. And Job asked all the same questions of God about his suffering that people ask today. In the end, Job realized his complaints, as justified as they appeared to be at the time, were misdirected. *I uttered that I understood not; things too wonderful for me, which I knew not.* (Job 42:3) His experience with hardship allowed him to understand God in a way he never would have had he been allowed no suffering.

The interesting thing about illness, hardship, and physical or emotional pain is that it is in these times we learn life's most important lessons. During conflict, catastrophe, tragedy, and struggle we ask the important, probing and deeply relevant questions of life. The rich, fit and famous are not haunted by the question, "Why?" When all is well and the bills are being paid with money to spare, when we can't remember our last visit to the doctor, the children are all healthy, and we just got the big promotion, no one wonders why God is allowing these things to happen.

Indeed, it is when we are in the crucible of crisis that our core beliefs are tested and we discover what we truly believe, not when life is good. It is also when many people turn to God, if not in submission to his difficult will, then to accuse or question him, but at least their God-consciousness has been awakened. For many years I kept a sign posted in our kitchen. "Adversity is the trial of conviction, without it, you hardly know what you really believe."

I have had times when circumstances seemed wildly unjust and pushed me to outbursts against the God I claimed to love and who I thought was on my side. But it was also in these times that I learned the most important lessons of my life and come to a deeper understanding of the ways of God than I ever would have if I had never gone through the deep and dark valley of suffering. "No pain, no gain," is not just for athletes. We learn our best lessons when we are challenged. Those who think that if God can remove suffering then he should, are asking for a life of ease and comfort in which we face no personal challenges and never have the limits of our endurance tested by crisis.

And that's what is wrong with the skeptic notion that if God can heal all his sick and suffering followers, then he should. It is the very thing he uses to strengthen them and demonstrate the reality of their faith to a world that often cannot understand how a person who is suffering could still have faith in a God who could heal them but doesn't. He also uses sickness and suffering to expose imposters. Pretend Christians will buckle under the stress of hardship and trial, jettison their phony convictions, use the injustice of their circumstances to accuse God of not caring, and drift into the God-less life that was really in their heart all along.

When our son decided to make a career change, he soon found himself in the academy to become a Corrections Officer. The training for this is something like army boot camp, though not as long. However, it is quite brutal. Cadets are subjected to unreasonable demands, unquestioned instant obedience, strict regimentation, painful ordeals, and drill instructors that are, at the same time, your best friend and worst enemy.

The purpose for the seemingly unreasonable treatment and impossible expectations is to weed out the ones who are not suited for this career, and push the others to heights of personal achievement they never thought possible. These were the ones who were going to tough it out no matter what. The drill instructors knew what they were doing. On graduation day, the cadets who had been the object of their authoritarian demands and sometimes brutal verbal barrages were now their pride and joy. Sickness and suffering which God allows in the life of the believer work the same way.

The kind of god the skeptic seems to expect is like a wealthy parent who gives their pampered child everything he wants and puts upon him no burden or hardship. By not allowing their child to know demands, to risk injury to body or spirit, to never place upon them the yoke of what seems like unreasonable expectation, they ruin the child. He grows to be morally weak, lacking character, unable to stand rejection or imposition by others upon his self-centered world. His limits have never been pushed nor his will tested.

God loves his children and challenges them with trials to make them stronger than they ever thought possible. On graduation day, their endurance and faithfulness will be his pride and joy. This should make sense to any unbeliever because it mirrors the real world.

As his execution approached, the apostle Paul wrote to the young preacher Timothy. *But watch thou in all things, endure afflictions, do the work of an evangelist, make full proof of thy ministry. For I am now ready to be offered, and the time of my departure is at hand. I have fought a good fight, I have finished my course, I have kept the faith: Henceforth there is laid up for me a crown of righteousness, which the Lord, the righteous judge, shall give me at that day: and not to me only, but unto all them also that love his appearing.* (II Tim. 4: 5-8)

Hardship and affliction in the life of the professing Christian accomplish several things.

1. It tests our faith
2. It exposes shallow belief
3. It showcases the grace of God
4. It provides a platform for deeper instruction
5. It elevates spiritual maturity

I have to admit that a suffering Christian who has lived a life of devotion to God, yet is afflicted with some debilitating or demoralizing ailment does present a difficulty to our human reasoning. To us it makes no sense and appears to be grossly unjust. But the problem here is that this line of reasoning elevates human thought above God. If it does not make sense to us, then it just does not make sense at all. It sets man up as the pinnacle of understanding and justice and expects God to limit himself to that standard.

I am not just speaking generally. Like many of you, believer or skeptic, I have personal enigmas that, despite all I have said, still challenge my trust in God's goodness and justice. My father spent forty years faithfully and sacrificially preaching the gospel of Jesus Christ. For months before he died, at the age of ninety-two, his once sharp mind had grown dull. He could no longer write and had great difficulty articulating his thoughts. He could barely walk and required help with the most basic hygiene. His hearing was poor and his memory worse.

I have to wonder why God did not allow this choice servant, who had given his life in service for him, to spend his final months in the same dignity he had enjoyed throughout his years of ministry. Where was the reward for a life lived in devotion to Jesus Christ? I wrestled with it often. But then I remember that the great ones in the Bible: Paul, Peter, Elijah, Jeremiah, Joseph, Daniel, John, James, and others, suffered injustice, cruelty, sickness or worse. Being a follower of Christ never has assured us of health and success right up to our last day. So wherever the idea comes from that Christians should either be perpetually healthy, or able to quickly pray away disease, it does not come from Jesus or the Bible.

We have examined two of the three elements in answering the skeptic's question of whether Jesus really heals the sick, or why he does not. First, Jesus did not come to heal people but to save them from the eternal consequence of sin. Second, hardship and suffering in the life of the believer provide fertile ground for previously unrealized personal and spiritual growth, and evidence of faith despite struggle. The third element is that all healing, whether miraculous and unexplained, or resulting from the efforts of a skilled physician, comes from Jesus. How is that?

I have stated several times that when we discuss Christianity we have to frame the discussion by what Christianity really is according to the Bible, not interpretations of various sects, cults, or individuals. Nor should the suppositions of skeptic thinkers, who often isolate certain aspects of Christian belief for critical evaluation and may genuinely not understand what the Bible actually teaches, be the basis for understanding Christianity.

Colossians 1:15-17 refers to Jesus. *Who is the image of the invisible God, the firstborn of every creature: For by him were all things created, that are in heaven, and that are in earth, visible and invisible, whether they be thrones, or dominions, or principalities, or powers: all things were created by him, and for him: and he is before all things, and by him all things consist.* The Bible teaches that Jesus is the creator and sustainer of everything. Of course, skeptics don't believe that, but we are interested in giving answers that accurately reflect Christian doctrine.

What this means regarding Christian belief about healing is that Jesus is the author of life and all the knowledge that can sustain it. Thus, he is the author of all healing. So when a doctor performs brain surgery that removes a tumor and saves the patient's life, according to the Bible, his skill and knowledge ultimately come from Jesus. When pharmaceutical scientists develop disease-curing medicine, according to biblical Christianity, it is Jesus who makes that possible. This is consistent throughout the Bible as God often used real people to accomplish his purposes.

Skeptics will bristle at the idea of giving Jesus credit for human healing brought about through skill resulting from years of personal, diligent study. But we still have to address just how it is that the human brain can take in, process, and categorize information from a lecture, book, and microscope, transport it by the auditory and optic nerves in the ear and eye into the brain, compile and compartmentalize that information, store it, then, on demand correlate it to a specific problem, transfer that information from the brain, through nerves, into muscles that coordinate fine motor movements to precisely manipulate a scalpel and cut loose a tumor without damaging sensitive brain tissue.

To the skeptic, this is all due to a fortunate series of accidents that just happened to make man a brilliant learning machine capable of processing hundreds of stimuli in a single second, make instantaneous decisions, and

211

precision manipulations that can mean life, death or permanent disability to another human being. Christianity believes, and the Bible teaches that it was not a fortunate accident, but Jesus who is responsible for this marvelous, uniquely human capability. So in biblical context, we can say that all healings originate with him, regardless of what human instrument may be used. The skeptic's only argument against this is that the brain is a very beneficial accident that just happened to come together for humans in a way to allow for such amazing and complex function.

One last point is worthy of consideration. The skeptic says, **Imagine if Christians worldwide had an average life expectancy of thirty or forty years longer than non-Christians — regardless of income, living conditions, nutrition, exercise, and access to healthcare. This of course is not reality. The world as we find it does not seem to favor the health of Christians.** (155)

But is this really true? A May 5, 2011 report titled, "Medical Group: Christianity Leads to Longer Life, Health" offers interesting insight.

> There is extensive evidence that Christians live longer and remain healthier than other people, according to a new report. An 'overwhelming majority' of scientific studies highlight positive health benefits from practicing the Christian faith, says the Christian Medical Fellowship, which has looked at 1,200 studies and 400 reviews. The new report by Dr. Alex Bunn and Dr. David Randall, titled "Health Benefits of Christian Faith," says the benefits include protection from illness, coping with illness and faster recovery from it. The Christian faith is shown to increase life expectancy: in one study of 21,204 adults, those who attended church regularly had a life expectancy up to 14 years longer than those who did not.[1]

Another report highlighting the longevity associated with Christianity is entitled, "Christians Live Longer than Other Believers, Scientists Say," by Dr. Margaret MacKenzie. The report from Wyoming Institute of Technology comes to a similar conclusion as the one cited by the Christian Medical Fellowship.

> A team of scientists led by Dr. Richter DasMeerungeheuer, who is well known for his religious studies as related to science, developed a study with leading theologians

[sic] to determine which major religious group can claim the healthiest and longest-living worshipers. Dr. DasMeerungeheuer was able to narrow the groups down to only three: Judaism, Christianity and Islam, these being the three largest religions in the world.

Dr. DasMeerungeheuer's team of specialists spent long periods of time carefully observing each group to assess their habits and behavior, asking subjects and religious leaders a series of in depth questions about prayer, spirituality and group dynamics within the church community. They also examined the parish registers in order to ascertain the average age of death. At the conclusion of the study, it was found that Christians live approximately *fifteen years* longer than adherents to other faiths.[3]

Undoubtedly, you can find studies with contrary results. That is always the case. But there is compelling scientific evidence that the conscientious acceptance and practicing of the Christian faith can add years to a person's life on average and make them less susceptible to some diseases. Don't take my word for it. Try googling, "Do Christians live longer than atheists," and see what you find.

And what about protection from illness? Does following Christ keep a Christian from disease? The skeptic comments. **Want to save souls for Jesus? Just prove that praying to him can cure AIDS, and leukemia or restore amputated limbs. Do that and it's mission accomplished.** (155) Let's reiterate that according to the Bible, Jesus' mission was not to get people to follow him just because he could heal them. However, living according to Christian principles does protect from certain diseases.

For example, while homosexual sex increases the risk of contracting HIV (AIDS) by 40 times,[2] a person who follows the biblical pattern for monogamous, heterosexual sex within the confines of marriage, as well as avoiding other high risk and unbiblical behaviors, like drug use, has almost no chance of contracting HIV or other sexually transmitted diseases. Christian morality, even if practiced by a non-believer, avoids many such illnesses that are prolific among the promiscuous.

As for restoring an amputated limb, a preacher friend of mine lost his leg in a motorcycle accident when he was thirty-five. He is now in his eighties, wears a prosthesis, and continues to travel the world preaching the gospel of Christ. No, God did not restore his amputated leg. Bill Shade is remarkable precisely because God allowed him to lose a leg, and yet he continues to serve him long after most two-legged men would have retired to a life of golf and fishing. The skeptic's way would rob the man of triumph despite hardship and the privilege of serving others despite physical limitations himself.

Finally, I share the skeptic's view when it comes to popular "Christian faith healers." Frankly, I have had little exposure to this, but there is an immediate red flag that goes up when someone claiming to heal people uses their "gift" to enrich themselves. NBC Dateline did an expose' on a well-known faith healer, discovering a variety of techniques for keeping the truly sick from getting to the platform for healing. His organization also takes in an astronomical amount of money each year. All one needs to do is contrast this with the healings of Jesus and the apostles in the New Testament. There is no similarity whatsoever.

TWENTY-FOUR

HOW DO WE KNOW THAT THE MAN JESUS EXISTED?

A question that continues to surface in any discussion with atheists about Christianity is whether or not Jesus really existed. Atheists generally take the view that evidence for Jesus' existence outside the Bible is not credible nor proportional to what would be expected of someone who established a religion now claimed by some two billion people on earth. Statements within the Bible are disallowed because they are not objective. The following is typical of skeptic views regarding Jesus.

...we have no written firsthand accounts of Jesus having been a real man. This is a significant hole. (160)

...few scholars believe that anything in the Bible is a true first hand account by someone who knew Jesus personally. (160)

...all we have are stories about Jesus's [sic] life that were written down by people who never knew him. (160)

...What bothers me about these Jesus stories however, is that they are not histories. They are not official records that happen to mention a "Jesus." They are not letters between friends that drop the name "Jesus." No, they are "propaganda." I don't mean that in a negative way. What I mean by propaganda is that the stories about Jesus were written by people who said he was a god and wanted other people to believe it. The stories are nothing close to being objective and impartial accounts of past events that we can take at face value. They were produced by Christians with an agenda and could not have been more biased. (161)

Though I believe the New Testament is sufficient documentation of the life and ministry of Jesus Christ, skeptics would disagree. However, the internal coherence and consistent message of these books, written within one-hundred years of the time of Christ, provide unprecedented eyewitness account of real events occurring to real people in real places.

Many of these have been corroborated by modern archaeology. The April 2017 issue of *Biblical Archaeology Review* includes a report by Purdue University scholar, Lawrence Mykytiuk, citing fifty-three people in the Bible whose existence has been confirmed by archaeology.

> Mykytiuk writes that these figures mentioned in the Bible have been identified in the archaeological record. Their names appear in inscriptions written during the period described by the Bible and in most instances during or quite close to the lifetime of the person identified.[1]

It includes Israelite kings, Mesopotamian monarchs, pharaohs and other minor figures previously known only from their biblical reference.

If the Bible is accurate when it speaks of a Syrian king named Ben-hadad, or an Egyptian ruler named So, should we find it unreliable when it speaks of a man named Jesus? Is it reasonable to presume that when archaeology confirms the biblical reference to an obscure assassin like Adrammelech (II Kings 19:37, Isa. 37:38), the Bible is speaking erroneously or mythologically about its most central figure? This is tenaciously clinging to unbelief in the face of mounting secular evidence that biblical histories are actually true.

But these examples confirm Old Testament accounts and do little to convince the skeptic of New Testament reliability. After all, we are addressing the evidence for Jesus' existence, not ancient kings or assassins. So let's take a rational look at whether Jesus' life on earth was a real event or a contrived one.

Mark Eastman, author of "Historical Evidence for Jesus of Nazareth,"[2] offers some insightful thoughts relating to the Jesus question.

1. "Why would the Roman government brutally persecute peaceful followers of a non-historical figure?" This would be akin to any modern government attempting to exterminate believers in Santa Claus.
2. "Why would tens of thousands of first century Christians (almost exclusively Jewish believers in Jesus) who lived within forty years

of the "mythical events," willingly suffer the loss of all possessions and status and be murdered for a myth?"

It was stated earlier that Muslims who willingly die for their belief would be considered by Christians as dying for something that is not true. However, as we noted in chapter twelve, dying for something you believe to be true but is not is very different from dying for something that you know isn't true from the start.

Do skeptics who question the reality of Jesus' existence really stop to consider what they are suggesting? It would mean that one day in the ancient past someone started a rumor that a baby was born in Bethlehem to a virgin girl and that this baby was to become the long expected Messiah of Israel. Such news would have been very exciting, but no one actually sees this child because he does not exist. A story is then contrived that the parents take the child to Egypt to get away from Herod's plan to kill the baby. But this is pretty silly too. Why would Herod try to kill a child that was nothing more than a rumor? Apparently, Herod believed such a child did exist, was a threat to his throne, and was willing to massacre all boys in Bethlehem under the age of two to get him. But if Jesus never existed, there is no such child.

How do people begin following after a mere figment of their imagination who supposedly lives and preaches in their own hometown? How does someone who never existed become the central figure of history? Who were his followers following and why would they preach about and die for someone they had never even seen? These are simple but relevant questions those who doubt the existence of Jesus must answer.

When the skeptic says **few scholars believe that anything in the Bible is a true firsthand account by someone who knew Jesus personally,** and **All we have are stories about Jesus' life that were written down by people who never knew him,** (160) he is contradicting his own criteria for belief. Skeptics require evidence. In the case of Jesus' contemporaries and those who followed him, he simply discounts their testimony and arbitrarily says they didn't really know Jesus. The evidence that conflicts with a skeptic view is simply declared to be faulty. How do skeptics know that John the Baptist, Peter, or Matthew never knew Christ? Of course, some unbelieving scholars buttress such statements, but then the Christian can also cite scholars whose study leads them to conclude that the gospels were written by actual eyewitnesses of Jesus life and ministry.

Arguments like this can go on endlessly persuading no one, which is why I prefer to think rationally about what it would have actually meant for all these people to believe in, follow after, and die for someone that was entirely imaginary. To me, this reduces first century people, both Jews and Gentiles who either followed or opposed a Jesus who never existed, to mindless morons. We are talking about rulers in the most powerful empire on earth at the time and men who were obviously articulate and scholarly enough to compose a message that has endured 2000 years of critique. This places the argument that Jesus did not exist into the realm of the absurd.

The other argument, that Jesus did exist but was just a man and not the Son of God he claimed to be is probably more common among skeptics. But there is that persistent problem of making some kind of sense out of thousands of first century people following after a man who proved himself to be a liar and a fraud by not rising from the dead as he said he would. Even in the first century, we cannot rationally presume that Jesus' resurrection was faked to fool everyone. It cannot be overemphasized that if Jesus did not rise from the dead as he said he would then everything he taught, including what he said about himself was proven false. His closest followers would have known for certain that they had been duped and all Jesus' claims about being one with the Father (*he that hath seen me hath seen the Father,* John 14:9) were bogus.

In the area around Palestine, Jesus was a flashpoint for controversy, enough to be called before the Roman procurator Pilate for interrogation. But the skeptic says, **Roman histories of the time don't even mention Pontius Pilate, the most powerful person who lived during Jesus' era and in his region...** (162) Pilate is recorded by several contemporary historians. His name is inscribed on Roman coins and on a stone dug up in Caesarea in 1961 with the words, PONTIUS PILATUS PRAEFECTUS PROVINCIAE JUDAEAE.[3]

This doesn't prove that Jesus is the Son of God, but it does reinforce the credibility of the biblical account of his trial and subsequent crucifixion. Of course, this comes from the Bible, so it may appear to be suspect. But when other details of events are substantiated by evidence, on what logical basis can anyone say a given part of the account is fabricated with no evidence to support such a speculation?

The following quote summarizes the conflict skeptics have with acknowledging the existence of Jesus Christ and typifies the difficulty they have in objectively considering the real evidence and logical arguments that Jesus not only existed, but is exactly who he said he is. **I am not sure whether or not the historical Jesus existed. My hunch is that he probably did, simply because it seems more likely to me that a real preacher stirred up some trouble and was executed, and then a few people who liked him started a new religion in his name.** (163)

The tenor of this statement betrays the same attitude toward Jesus Christ that the Pharisees had. They considered him a troublemaker too. And even Jesus himself said,

> *Think not that I am come to send peace on earth: I came not to send peace, but a sword. For I am come to set a man at variance against his father, and the daughter against her mother, and the daughter in law against her mother in law. And a man's foes shall be they of his own household. He that loveth father or mother more than me is not worthy of me: and he that loveth son or daughter more than me is not worthy of me. And he that taketh not his cross, and followeth after me, is not worthy of me. He that findeth his life shall lose it: and he that loseth his life for my sake shall find it.* Matthew 10:34-39.

This doesn't sound like a very effective recruiting message to gain followers. "Hey, if you want to follow me, your own mother and father will stand against you. Your children will turn on you. The ones you raised in your own household will oppose what you stand for. Do you want to follow me? Get ready to bear a cross. Get ready to give up your preferred life because that is the only way you will find the life I have to offer."

Yes, Jesus openly acknowledged that those who follow him will suffer for it. He admitted that what he was teaching would stir up trouble for himself and his followers. Jesus words here also make it even more illogical to presume that, given such an undesirable promise to those who would follow him, they still would after he proves himself to be a liar by not being resurrected.

This is another reason I believe the Bible and the teaching of Jesus. He does not sugar coat his message. He teaches that being a Christian will become increasingly difficult as time goes on and only those willing to pay the price of rejection, slander, mocking and persecution are worthy to follow him. This is frighteningly prophetic of how things are going in the United States.

A report by two U.S.-based religious freedom groups says anti-Christian persecution is on the rise in America. The joint report by Texas-based Liberty Institute and Washington-based Family Research Council says groups like the American Civil Liberties Union aren't the only culprits. The report by Michael Carl entitled, "Persecution of Christians on Rise in U.S.," World Net Daily, 09/17/2012, says government agencies around the U.S. are trying to push Christian expression out the door.[4]

Among the violations listed in the joint report:

- A federal judge threatened "incarceration" to a high school valedictorian unless she removed references to Jesus from her graduation speech.
- City officials prohibited senior citizens from praying over their meals, listening to religious messages, or singing gospel songs at a senior activities center.
- A public school official physically lifted an elementary school student from his seat and reprimanded him in front of his classmates for praying over his lunch.
- Following U.S. Department of Veterans Affairs' policies, a federal government official sought to censor a pastor's prayer, eliminating references to Jesus during a Memorial Day ceremony honoring veterans at a national cemetery.
- Public school officials prohibited students from handing out gifts because they contained religious messages.
- A public school official prevented a student from handing out flyers inviting her classmates to an event at her church.
- A public university's law school banned a Christian organization because it required its officers to adhere to a statement of faith that the university disagreed with.
- The U.S. Department of Justice argued before the Supreme Court that the federal government can tell churches and synagogues which pastors and rabbis it can hire and fire.
- The state of Texas sought to approve and regulate what religious seminaries can teach.
- Through the Patient Protection and Affordable Care Act, also known as Obamacare, the federal government is forcing religious organizations to provide insurance for birth control and abortion-inducing drugs in direct violation of their religious beliefs.

- The U.S. Department of Veterans Affairs banned the mention of God from veterans' funerals, overriding the wishes of the deceased's families.
- A federal judge held that prayers before a state House of Representatives could be to Allah but not to Jesus.

The warning of Jesus to his would be followers of the cost of being a Christian is as relevant today as it was in the first century. We have not yet gotten to the point of calling for the execution of Christians, but the enemies of Christ in the New Testament first tried to silence his followers with legal threats to persuade them to cease public mention of Jesus and his teaching.

> *And when they had brought them [the apostles], they set them before the council: and the high priest asked them, Saying, Did not we straitly command you that ye should not teach in this [Jesus] name? and, behold, ye have filled Jerusalem with your doctrine, and intend to bring this man's [Jesus] blood upon us.* Acts 5: 27-28.

Not too far from the tone in some of the above-cited reports is it?

Almost everything we know about Jesus comes from the Bible. Denying that he existed at all seems a fool's errand. Denying that he was who he claimed to be dismisses some of the most educated, articulate, and powerful men of Jesus time as fools themselves. Meanwhile, skeptics nearly 2000 years removed from the time of Christ refuse the testimony of those who were either eyewitnesses or less than a hundred years removed from these events. This is somewhat like a 21st-century history student discounting first-hand eyewitness reports from soldiers of the American Revolution as biased or untrustworthy, or that the framers of our Constitution didn't even know George Washington.

For those who may find the biblical accounts of Jesus untrustworthy, there are many other extra-biblical sources that verify Jesus' existence. Following are several references by ancient historians who either mention Jesus directly in a manner consistent with the New Testament, or Christians who were followers of the teachings of a man matching Jesus' description.

REFERENCES TO JESUS OR HIS FOLLOWERS BY SECULAR HISTORIANS

Note - I use the dating system of CE here because that is how these sources are cited in the work from which they are taken. In my own writing, I still use BC and AD since BCE and CE are mere euphemisms for before and after the birth of Jesus Christ.

> **FLAVIUS JOSEPHUS** (37–100 CE) First-century Jewish historian captured by the Romans and put into service by them as a scribe and interpreter. Flavius was the name given him by his Roman captors.

Now, there was about this time, Jesus, a wise man, if it be lawful to call him a man, for he was a doer of wonderful works-a teacher of such men as received the truth with pleasure. He drew over to him both many of the Jews and many of the gentiles. He was [the] Christ; and when Pilate, at the suggestion of the principal men amongst us, had condemned him to the cross, those that loved him at the first did not forsake him, for he appeared to them alive again the third day, as the divine prophets had foretold these and ten thousand other wonderful things concerning him; and the tribe of Christians, so named from him, are not extinct at this day.[5]

From a 4th century Arabic version of Josephus' Antiquities of the Jews

At this time there was a wise man who was called Jesus. And his conduct was good, and he was known to be virtuous. And many people from among the Jews and other nations became his disciples. Pilate condemned him to be crucified and to die. And those who had become his disciples did not abandon his discipleship. They reported that he had appeared to them three days after his crucifixion and that he was alive; accordingly, he was perhaps the Messiah concerning whom the prophets have recounted wonders.[6]

Now some of the Jews thought that the destruction of Herod's army came from God, and that very justly, as a punishment of what he did against John, that was called the Baptist; for Herod slew him, who was a good man, and commanded the Jews to exercise virtue, both as to righteousness towards one another, and piety towards God, and so to come to baptism; for that the washing [with water] would be acceptable to him, if they made use of it, not in order to the putting away, [or the remission] of some sins [only] but for the purification of the body; supposing still that the soul was thoroughly purified beforehand by righteousness. Now, when many others came to crowd about him, for they were greatly moved by hearing his words, Herod, who feared lest the great influence of John had over the people might put it into his power and inclination to raise a rebellion, (for they seemed ready to do anything he should advise), thought it best, by putting him to death, to prevent any mischief he might cause, and not to bring himself into difficulties, by sparing a man who might make him repent of it when it should be too late.[7]

Jesus is not specifically mentioned in this last passage, but the manner in which John the Baptist is represented here is in complete agreement with the account in the gospel of John.

And yet one more reference to Jesus by Josephus

After the death of the procurator Festus, when Albinus was about to succeed him, the high-priest Ananius considered it a favorable opportunity to assemble the Sanhedrin. He therefore caused James the brother of Jesus, who was called Christ, and several others, to appear before this hastily assembled council, and pronounced upon them the sentence of death by stoning. All the wise men and strict observers of the law who were at Jerusalem expressed their disapprobation of this act...Some even went to Albinus himself, who had departed to Alexandria, to bring this breach of the law under his observation, and to inform him that Ananius had acted illegally in assembling the Sanhedrin without the Roman authority.[8]

THALLUS

What follows is quoted entirely from Mark Eastman, "Historical Evidence for Jesus of Nazareth," Appendix II.[9]

> Thallus was a historian who lived in the middle of the first century C.E. His writings focus partly on the historical events of the Roman empire of the first century C.E. We do not have his original works, written around 52 C.E., but we do have the writings of men who referred to his work.
>
> Julius Africanus, an early church father, writing in the year 221 C.E. wrote about the writings of Thallus. In a document written by Julius Africanus, there is a discussion about the darkness that was recorded by the writers of the New Testament at the time of the crucifixion of Jesus.
>
> *"Now from the sixth hour until the ninth hour there was darkness over all the land."*
>
> *[That is, from noon to 3:00pm.]* (Matthew 27:45)
>
> Now the skeptic might easily dismiss this event, recorded in the gospel of Matthew, as mere dramatics, an attempt to dress up the crucifixion event with some supernatural imagery. However, the darkness which occurred at the time of a full moon was recorded by Thallus.
>
> Africanus notes that Thallus had attempted to explain away the event:
>
> "Thallus, in the third book of his history explains away the darkness as an eclipse of the sun, unreasonably as it seems to me."[10]
>
> Africanus, writing in the year 221C.E., had access to the writings of Thallus. Thallus in his third book wrote that this darkness, which occurred during the reign of Caesar Tiberius, was a result of an eclipse of the sun. Africanus makes the point that this could not have been a solar eclipse because the crucifixion took place at Passover, which always occurs during a full moon. During a full

moon, there can be no solar eclipse, and Africanus recognized this.

An interesting aspect of this reference is that Thallus does not try to deny the existence of Jesus of Nazareth, the occurrence of his crucifixion nor the historical fact that the darkness occurred. He presents Jesus of Nazareth as an historical person, and the darkness as an historical event. His motive in writing about the darkness is to explain it as a natural event.

TACITUS (AD 116) Senator in the Roman government, writing about the burning of Rome and Nero's attempt to stop the rumor that he [Nero] was responsible.

Therefore, to scotch the rumor (that Nero had burned Rome) Nero substituted as culprits, and punished with the utmost refinements of cruelty, a class of men, loathed for their vices, whom the crowd styled Christians. Christus, the founder of the name, had undergone the death penalty in the reign of Tiberius, by sentence of the procurator Pontius Pilatus, and the pernicious superstition was checked for a moment, only to break out once more, not merely in Judea, the home of the disease, but in the capital itself, where all things horrible or shameful in the world collect and find a vogue...They [the Christians] were covered with wild beasts' skins and torn to death by dogs; or they were fastened on crosses, and, when daylight failed were burned to serve as lamps by night. Nero had offered his gardens for the spectacle, and gave an exhibition in his circus, mixing with the crowd in the habit of a charioteer, or mounted on his car. Hence, in spite of a guilt which had earned the most exemplary punishment, there arose a sentiment of pity, due to the impression that they were being sacrificed not for the welfare of the state but to the ferocity of a single man.[11]

LUCIAN OF SOMOSATA a Greek satirist, wrote a remarkable statement regarding the church in 170 C.E.

The Christians, you know, worship a man to this day-the distinguished personage who introduced their novel rites, and was crucified on that account... You see, these misguided creatures start with the general conviction that they are immortal for all time, which explains the contempt of death and voluntary self-devotion which are so common among them; and then it was impressed on them by their original lawgiver that they are all brothers, from the moment that they are converted, and deny the Gods of Greece, and worship the crucified sage, and live after his laws. All this they take quite on faith, with the result that they despise all worldly goods alike, regarding them merely as common property.[12]

The name of Jesus is not mentioned in this quote, however, the reference to him is unmistakable.

Mara Bar-Serapion a Syrian and a stoic philosopher, wrote this letter to his son from prison sometime after 70 C.E.

What advantage did the Athenians gain from putting Socrates to death? Famine and plague came upon them as a judgment for their crime. What advantage did the men of Samos gain from burning Pythagoras? In a moment their land was covered with sand. What advantage did the Jews gain from executing their wise King? It was just after that that their kingdom was abolished. God justly avenged these three wise men: the Athenians died of hunger; the Samians were overwhelmed by the sea; the Jews, ruined and driven from their land, live in complete dispersion. But Socrates did not die for good; he lived on in the statue of Plato. Pythagoras did not die for good; he lived on in the statue of Hera. Nor did the wise King die for good; he lived on in the teaching which he had given.[13]

The "Wise King" who was executed by the Jews is certainly a reference to Jesus. The writer could hardly be considered Christian however, since he puts Jesus on equal terms with Pythagoras and Socrates, and makes no mention of the resurrection, so the reference provides powerful evidence not only for a historical Jesus, but also as a testimony to him being considered both "wise" and a "King."

One final authority should confirm to even a skeptic reader that the New Testament is a reliable source of biographical, geographical, cultural, and historical information about the reality of Christ's existence, the development and growth of the Christian church, as well as political realities of the time.

> Sir William Mitchell Ramsay was a Scottish archaeologist and New Testament scholar. By his death in 1939 he had become the foremost authority of his day on the history of Asia Minor and a leading scholar in the study of the New Testament. Although Ramsay was educated in the Tübingen school of thought (founded by F. C. Baur) which doubted the reliability of the New Testament, his extensive archaeological and historical studies convinced him of the historical accuracy of the New Testament. From the post of Professor of Classical Art and Architecture at Oxford, he was appointed Regius Professor of Humanity (the Latin Professorship) at Aberdeen. Knighted in 1906 to mark his distinguished service to the world of scholarship, Ramsay also gained three honorary fellowships from Oxford colleges, nine honorary doctorates from British, Continental and North American universities and became an honorary member of almost every association devoted to archaeology and historical research. He was one of the original members of the British Academy, was awarded the Gold Medal of Pope Leo XIII in 1893 and the Victorian Medal of the Royal Geographical Society in 1906.[14]

This brief history is offered only to give credibility to Ramsay's view of Luke as an accurate historian. Some accounts indicate Ramsay set out to prove the Bible false, but instead was converted to Christianity. I could not confirm that story. However, his own words state,

> I may fairly claim to have entered on this investigation without any prejudice in favour of the conclusion which I shall now attempt to justify to the reader [i.e. the reliability of the book of Acts]. On the contrary, I began with a mind unfavourable to it, for the ingenuity and apparent completeness of the Tübingen theory had at one time quite convinced me. It did not lie then in my line of life

to investigate the subject minutely; but more recently I found myself often brought in contact with the book of Acts as an authority for the topography, antiquities, and society of Asia Minor. It was gradually borne in upon me that in various details the narrative showed marvellous [sic] truth. In fact, beginning with the fixed idea that the work was essentially a second-century composition, and never relying on its evidence as trustworthy for first-century conditions, I gradually came to find it a useful ally in some obscure and difficult investigations.[15]

Regarding the usefulness and accuracy of Luke, the author of the book of Luke and Acts in the New Testament, Ramsay stated,

Luke is a historian of the first rank; not merely are his statements of fact trustworthy; he is possessed of the true historic sense; he fixes his mind on the idea and plan that rules in the evolution of history; and proportions the scale of his treatment to the importance of each incident. He seizes the important and critical events and shows their true nature at greater length, while he touches lightly or omits entirely much that was valueless for his purpose. In short, this author should be placed along with the very greatest of historians.[16]

The argument for Jesus existence and the authenticity and accuracy of the New Testament is overwhelming. The logic of the argument that New Testament histories **were produced by Christians with an agenda and could not have been more biased,** (161) is threadbare. Jesus left no room for rational doubt of his existence, his deity, and the truthfulness of his message when honestly and objectively examined. In light of these historical references, go back and read the skeptic statements at the beginning of this chapter.

The writing of ancient historians, while not as detailed as the Bible, correlate well with the Bible's description of Jesus and those who followed him. It matches with other accounts of persecution against Christians who followed Jesus. In short, there is an abundance of historical references to Jesus that document his existence, reinforce the accuracy of the biblical record, and demonstrate the authenticity of the Christian faith.

TWENTY-FIVE

WHAT ABOUT ALL THE OTHER GODS?

Christians believe in one God in three persons. He is the God described in the Bible and he alone is worthy of worship. While there may be vast differences in practice among the many Christian denominations, there is broad agreement on this point.

Skeptics point out there are millions of religions and gods. Christians should at least be open to the possibility that perhaps some of these other gods are just as significant as their own. **Believing inside a protective bubble may feel good, but it's not worthy of anyone who values integrity and reason... I tend to believe that most Christians do not intentionally ignore all other gods and religions... I suspect their oversight is more a result of the confirmation bias that all of us labor with... My hunch is that thoughtful and honest Christians do not really want to operate under a ridiculous pretext that says 99.999 percent of all gods and religions don't merit a mention when discussing or thinking about the topic of religion.** (165)

No belief system worth holding onto would need to rely on the fraudulent assumption that it has exclusive rights to the god concept. And no self-respecting believer would want to pretend that his god is the only one humans ever claimed to be real. (170)

Neither the Bible nor Christians deny there are gods of other religions, past and present. The Bible makes hundreds of references to other gods. Some of these include: Amon, the chief god of Egypt (Jer. 46:25 ESV); Ashtaroth, a Canaanite goddess (I Sam. 31:10); Baal, a Canaanite god of fertility and rain (Jdgs. 2:10-13); Chemosh, the god of Moab (I

Kings 11:7); Dagon, a god of the Philistines (I Sam. 5:2-7); Molech, chief deity of Ammon (I Kings 11:7); Jupiter and Mercury (Acts 14:12-13), Castor and Pollux (Acts 28:11). The book of Psalms makes many references to "gods."

Among the gods, there is none like unto thee, O LORD. (86:8)

For the LORD is great, and greatly to be praised: he is to be feared above all gods. (96:4)

For I know that the LORD is great, and that our LORD is above all gods. (135:5)

Even God himself acknowledges these other gods.

...and against all the gods of Egypt I will execute judgment. (Ex. 12:12)

Thou shalt have no other gods before me. (Ex. 20:3)

Wherever skeptics get the idea that Christianity claims exclusive rights to the "god concept," it certainly did not come from what the Bible says. For centuries, Christian preachers have referenced these gods in sermons and acknowledged the reality of belief in their existence by pagan nations, particularly those who influenced the Israelites. Much of the Old Testament is about the Israelites forsaking Jehovah for these other gods.

The rub comes when we start talking about the existence of these gods as real historical entities. Good skeptics would, of course, immediately say that is the same issue they have with the Christian God of the Bible. He is just one of many gods created by a religious system of thought. Atheists like to say that the only difference between them and a Christian is they believe in one less god than the Christian does. This atheistic perspective is the real point of this chapter. How does the God of the Bible differ from the thousands of other gods? What makes him "above all gods?"

If nothing else, it should be clear by this point that we are a god-creating species. All these gods can't be real; that would be logically impossible based on their "divinely inspired" bios. For example, there can't be a few hundred or a few thousand gods who independently created the universe. The only options are that most gods

are the products of human fantasy or that all gods are the product of human fantasy. (167)

The skeptic is quite right here, as far as he goes. All these gods can't be real. But that is only an elementary starting point. The third option, that only one God is the true God and all others are merely human creations, is left out. But that should at least be recognized as another possibility.

The issue with all these other gods is that while God, the Bible, and Christians acknowledge that the concept of them exists, or did at one time, we maintain the reality of that existence is illegitimate. In other words, they never actually existed as a real entity, but only as an invented concept. All other gods, regardless of how ancient or current, had a beginning point. Somewhere in time, a priest, a ruler, a pharaoh, a witch doctor, or some other influential religious or political figure carved an image, deified a volcano, a river, or an animal, and a god was born. Where are they now? How many followers does Molech have today? What modern nation has temples to Baal? Who are the modern disciples of Pollux, Jupiter, Mercury, and Castor?

Is it not self-evident that if any of these gods were real they would not just fade into mythology or cease to exist when the empire that deified them is overthrown? Furthermore, books are not written to debate the pros and cons of the actual existence of these gods. Apparently, they are not worthy of serious intellectual analysis. The very fact that skeptics write books, host lectures, and participate in discussions over the Christian God says a great deal about the difference between him, and the other gods we learn about from mythology, or even ones that are mentioned in the Bible.

I do not pretend to be knowledgeable about other religions and their gods. I cannot discuss the particulars of any religious thought or book but Christianity and the Bible. One does not have to be an expert on Islam, Hinduism, or Greek gods to answer questions about his or her Christian beliefs and the God of the Bible. These other gods may be studied and discussed, but it is in the context of ancient mythology, not current social, political, and religious issues. In America, the separation of church and state mantra has never been about Molech, Ra, Anubis, Dionysus or Vishnu. It is always about Christianity and the Christian God.

But let's take a look at the Christian God and see how he compares to other gods. As you will see, it does not matter which ones we compare to or how much we know or don't know about them. To make a fair comparison though, let's choose two significant Greek gods: Zeus, considered the King of all gods, and Prometheus, who according to mythology made the first man from clay.

Immediately there is a stark difference between these two gods and the God of the Bible. Neither of these deities are considered to have communicated directly with humans in a cognitive way. No books are attributed to them. They reference no history that is confirmed by archaeology and/or ancient documentation. In this respect, Christianity and the God of the Bible have no equal.

What did Zeus teach about the Egyptians or the Romans? How many ancient cultures or people, confirmed by archaeology, did Prometheus cite? Are not the writings that refer to these Greek gods merely references to mythological entities and events never confirmed by hard scientific research?

The genealogies of the Bible on the other hand, are useful in identifying origins of people because entire nations today can be traced back to tribal groups in the Bible. There is an abundance of genealogical charts available documenting the origin of nations through the book called "The Word of God." For example, Persia was the nation that, along with the Medes, overthrew the Babylonian empire as told of in Daniel chapter five. In 1935, Persia officially adopted the name Iran, which is the literal meaning of the word Persia.[1] Is anything similar true of our two examples, Zeus and Prometheus, or any other gods? Do any of these gods have documented historical context? I have to wonder if any serious students of archaeology or ancient history invest their education in uncovering the ruins or tracing lineages told of in the myths of Prometheus?

We can debate the particulars of divine inspiration and the infallibility of the scriptures, but it is an exercise in futility to argue that the Bible is a book of fables, myths, and unproven accounts similar to mythological tales of Greek gods and their battles. That is not to say that every incident or individual mentioned in the Bible has external corroborating evidence. It does not, not yet. But as science and archaeology do their work, more and more of what was once thought fictitious in the Bible turns out to be true.

A stunning example of this is the account in II Kings 18 and 19 of Assyrian king Sennacherib's assault on the northern tribes of Israel, Judean cities, and his siege of Jerusalem around 701 BC. There was a time when Bible critics did not believe the Assyrian empire, or its capital city of Ninevah even existed. The Bible was the only reference to this ancient, war-like people. There was no trace archaeologically of its existence. The Bible was thought to be in error on this point.

In 1830, Colonel Robert Taylor discovered a six-sided clay prism in ruins of what was once Nineveh. The prism contained cuneiform writing detailing Sennacherib's conquests of Judean cities and his siege of Jerusalem in 701 BC, exactly what is described in II Kings. This artifact is housed in the British Museum. On Sennacherib's prism, he says this of Judah's king, Hezekiah.

> As for the king of Judah, Hezekiah, who had not submitted to my authority, I besieged and captured forty-six of his fortified cities, along with many smaller towns, taken in battle with my battering rams. ... I took as plunder 200,150 people, both small and great, male and female, along with a great number of animals including horses, mules, donkeys, camels, oxen, and sheep. As for Hezekiah, I shut him up like a caged bird in his royal city of Jerusalem. I then constructed a series of fortresses around him, and I did not allow anyone to come out of the city gates. His towns which I captured I gave to the kings of Ashod, Ekron, and Gaza.

Wikipedia elaborates on the comparisons to the biblical account.

> Some passages in the Hebrew Bible agree with at least a few of the claims made on the prism. The Bible recounts a successful Assyrian attack on Samaria, as a result of which the population was deported, and later recounts that an attack on Lachish was ended by Hezekiah suing for peace, with Sennacherib demanding 300 talents of silver and 30 talents of gold, and Hezekiah giving him all the silver from his palace and from the Temple in Jerusalem, and the gold from doors and doorposts of the temple.

> The tribute given by Hezekiah is then mentioned but in this account, nothing is said of Sennacherib capturing the city of Jerusalem. According to 2 Kings 19:32-36, this was the result of a miraculous event in which 185,000 of

the most valuable men in the camped Assyrian army were struck dead in their sleep.[2]

In II Kings 19:35-36 we are told, *the angel of the Lord went out, and smote in the camp of the Assyrians and hundred fourscore and five thousand: and when they arose in the morning, behold, they were all dead corpses. So Sennacherib, king of Assyria departed, and went and returned, and dwelt at Nineveh.*

> Although Sennacherib painstakingly recorded the cities he captured and destroyed, one city is conspicuously absent—Jerusalem. He speaks only of besieging Hezekiah in the city—not of taking it or Judah's king. What happened? The Assyrians, like other great empires of the time, left no records of their military defeats.[3]

Assyria was an irresistible force in the ancient world. Both the Bible, the Taylor prism, and subsequent excavations of Nineveh agree on this fact. It is especially interesting that while the Taylor prism details the events of Sennacherib's conquest of Judean cities, it makes no mention of accomplishing his ultimate goal of conquering the capital city of Jerusalem. The Bible gives the reason. Once again, the science of archaeology agrees with what was once thought by scholars to be a biblical myth.

So what does this have to do with the question of other gods? In the case of Christianity, God, and the Bible, we have a book which states it is inspired by God himself and therefore absolutely true in its history, which is in harmony with progressive archaeological discovery. That is not true of any other god of any religion ancient or modern.

The account of Sennacherib and the documentation of the existence and conquests of the Assyrian empire is just one of many historical incidences for which, at one time, the Bible was the only reference. Prior to the archaeological discovery of the Assyrian empire, Christians simply took what the Bible said by faith, holding to the Christian doctrine that despite a total lack of evidence, God's Word is true. This must have cast 18th and early19th century Christians as monumental fools, believing that a Bible story about a "non-existent" empire with a totally imaginary king named Sennacherib was accurate. I again quote my father. "The greatest friend of truth is time." However, neither time nor archaeological discovery has corroborated any of the myths surrounding Zeus, Prometheus, or any other gods.

What's more, following the Christian doctrine of the infallibility of scripture, Christians of the nineteenth-century had to argue that the reason there was no trace of the Assyrian empire was that God, through Old Testament prophets like Isaiah, Nahum, and Zephaniah, prophesied that it would be totally annihilated. How convenient! Can you hear the nineteenth-century skeptics laughing?

Once again however, it appears that the biblical account, including detailed prophesies about the utter destruction of Assyria are amazingly accurate. The prophet Zephaniah said, *he [God] will stretch out his hand against the north, and destroy Assyria; and will make Nineveh a desolation, and dry like a wilderness.* (2: 13) *...how is she become a desolation, a place for beasts to lie down in.* (2:15)

> In 612 BC Nabopolassar united the Babylonian army with an army of Medes and Scythians and led a campaign which captured the Assyrian citadels in the North. The Babylonian army laid siege to Nineveh, but the walls of the city were too strong for battering rams, so they decided to try and starve the people out. A famous oracle had been given that 'Nineveh should never be taken until the river became its enemy.' After a three month siege, rain fell in such abundance that the waters of the Tigris inundated part of the city and overturned one of its walls for a distance of twenty stades. Then the King, convinced that the oracle was accomplished and despairing of any means of escape, to avoid falling alive into the enemy's hands constructed in his palace an immense funeral pyre, placed on it his gold and silver and his royal robes, and then, shutting himself up with his wives and eunuchs in a chamber formed in the midst of the pile, disappeared in the flames. Nineveh opened its gates to the besiegers, but this tardy submission did not save the proud city. It was pillaged and burned, and then razed to the ground so completely as to evidence the implacable hatred enkindled in the minds of subject nations by the fierce and cruel Assyrian government.[4]

The predictable skeptic response would likely be the same as it was for the prophecy that Israel would come back together as a nation in the land promised to them by God. According to skeptic thinking, that was not done by God but by human intervention, just like the destruction of Assyria. Unlike the gods of mythology, whose supposed actions cannot be subjected to scholarly evaluation because they did not involve real people, God's actions can be analyzed precisely because he did work through human beings. What allows the Bible and the actions of God it documents to be subjected to scholarly analysis is the very thing that prevents Zeus, Prometheus, and all other gods from being subjected to the same kind of analysis — human historical context.

All of this represents just one example of the difference between all other gods and writings about them, and the God of Christianity and the Bible. Here we see actual histories given of real people, real empires, conquests of nations and fulfilled predictions of destruction which at the time they were given would have been unimaginable. The gods of other religions provide no such documented historical facts. The existence and fall of Assyria and Nineveh is just one of hundreds of examples of why the Christian God and the Christian book, with its historical context, is unparalleled among the mythological exploits of other gods.

Where are the writings attributed to Zeus? What accurate historical narratives are provided by Prometheus? Review the chapter on prophecies. Where do you find anything remotely similar to the precision of biblical prophetic statements and their fulfillment supported by modern archaeological discovery in the annals of deities of other religions?

Skeptics say, **Consider how much more difficult it becomes when one attempts to not only explain why their god exists but also why all the other gods do not.** (170) But the Christian can reply, "Show me a god that has revealed himself through intelligible and accurate historical narrative, fulfilled prophecy, archaeologically verified people, places, and events, useful genealogy covering thousands of years, first-hand eyewitness accounts of his teaching and miracles, actual service to mankind, suffering, martyrdom, and resurrection, and I will believe in that deity too."

Skeptics may say that all we "know" about the Christian God comes from the Bible, so using the Bible to show he is the one true God is circular reasoning. But even if you do not believe in the God of the Bible, the Bible still exists. It is a real book. It chronicles the kings of real nations, their warfare, their victories, and defeats. It names documented historical figures, and many cities and nations still in existence today.

It makes scientifically accurate statements before the science behind those statements was known. It describes evaporation and the water cycle (Eccl. 1:7, 11:3, Ps. 135:7, Jer. 10:13) thousands of years before it was discovered in the 1500s. The book we call "The Word of God" refers to "the paths of the seas." (Ps.8:8) But it wasn't until the middle 1800s that Matthew Maury, nicknamed "Pathfinder of the Seas," charted ocean currents. The Bible is useful in theological, genealogical, geographical, historical, political, and yes, even scientific discovery.

The examples could go on and on. The point is, what book (if there is any) of what god or gods makes scientifically accurate descriptions of natural phenomenon thousands of years before they are discovered? What scientific discoveries, like those of Kepler, were inspired or guided by any of the millions of mythological gods of ancient or modern civilizations? What useful information did any of these "gods" provide to advance discovery, science, technology, and medicine?

If the Christian God is just another invented god, then the Bible is just another human book. So did its forty authors, over 1500 years, just get lucky in composing a narrative written in three different languages, on three different continents, that articulates an accurate history of Israel, as well as other nations, that leads us right up to the present day, real world, middle east conflict? Was it a fortunate coincidence that its core message of redemption and a promised redeemer flowed from the quills of multiple authors separated by continents, centuries, and seas into a unified, coherent and complementary whole, unencumbered by contradiction or inconsistency? Is it not curious that while other gods have been consigned to the dusty libraries of mythology and fable, the God of Christianity is still worshipped and revered by believers, yet deemed worthy of continual critique, question, and analysis by skeptics? There must be something about the God of the Bible that is unique and makes him worthy of discussion and debate, while all the other gods are left to the fantasies of myth and folklore. The God of the Bible is, in fact, above all gods.

CONCLUSION

Sincerely asked questions deserve thoughtful and reasonable answers. That has been the objective of this book. If you are a skeptic, I hope you have considered these questions, and the response, with a fair and open mind.

For the Christian, this book is intended to help you recognize that challenges to your faith come in many forms. Some, like many of the questions answered here, may be sincere, coming from an unbeliever who genuinely finds Christianity curious and honestly doubts the reliability of the Bible. Others take the form of a direct assault on Christianity as a faith void of reason and logic. Answers to both have been rooted in reason and reality, as well as legitimate biblical interpretation.

Of all the religions of the world, and especially those with significant representation in the United States, Christianity seems the most targeted and most frequently vilified. Much of this animosity comes from a lack of understanding of the historical context of the Old Testament and the foundations of true New Testament Christianity. Some of it comes from a deep-seated contempt for all things religious, which in America, rightly or wrongly, equates to Christianity.

I have always found it most curious why Christianity, with its core message of grace and forgiveness, is so despised while the various other religions are, by and large, left alone. Why is the name of Christ frequently used as an expletive when the names of other gods are not? What is it about Jesus and his message of hope, repentance, and forgiveness that sparks such resistance from a secular culture?

Could it be that the quote of former president, James Garfield, illuminates the reason. "The truth will set you free, but first it will make you miserable." Skeptics who are honestly looking for answers from Christianity should be willing to self-examine their own unwillingness to accept reasonable answers that square with the Bible, true science, have real-world historical context, and directly address their own misgivings.

Christianity is not, and never was intended to be spread by force or edict but by persuasion, reason and the work of the Holy Spirit. It remains the same as it was in the first century, a belief that Jesus Christ, while he was on earth, was God in the flesh, that he lived a sinless life, died on a cross while having the guilt for the sins of all mankind imputed upon him, was buried according to the common practices of the day, and rose from the dead three days later. He now sits at the right hand of God the Father and will one day take to be with him those who have accepted his free pardon from the eternal consequence of sin. This faith cannot be forced on anyone. Millions however, have been persuaded of the truthfulness of its message, repented (changed their mind) about conflicting beliefs, and been born again. Acknowledging truth may be painful, even miserable at first, but it is the only way to be truly free.

The cover of this book depicts what has been happening for centuries as skeptics relentlessly assault the accuracy and authenticity of Christianity and the Bible. Some hope to bring an end to even the concept of God in society. It has been a futile pursuit. Perhaps the most famous skeptic in this effort was 19th-century philosopher Friedrich Nietzsche, who memorialized the idea that God is dead in his "Parable of the Madman." While it claims the dubious distinction of killing forever the notion of God, notice the dreadful hopelessness of the resulting void for humanity.

The Madman

Have you not heard of that madman who lit a lantern in the bright morning hours, ran to the market place, and cried incessantly: "I seek God! I seek God!" -- As many of those who did not believe in God were standing around just then, he provoked much laughter. Has he got lost? asked one. Did he lose his way like a child? asked another. Or is he hiding? Is he afraid of us? Has he gone on a voyage? emigrated? —Thus they yelled and laughed.

The madman jumped into their midst and pierced them with his eyes. "Whither is God?" he cried; "I will tell you. *We have killed him* -- you and I. All of us are his murderers. But how did we do this? How could we drink up the sea? Who gave us the sponge to wipe away the entire horizon? What were we doing when we unchained this earth from its sun? Whither is it moving now? Whither are we moving? Away from all suns? Are we not plunging continually?

Backward, sideward, forward, in all directions? Is there still any up or down? Are we not straying, as through an infinite nothing? Do we not feel the breath of empty space? Has it not become colder? Is not night continually closing in on us? Do we not need to light lanterns in the morning? Do we hear nothing as yet of the noise of the gravediggers who are burying God? Do we smell nothing as yet of the divine decomposition? Gods, too, decompose. God is dead. God remains dead. And we have killed him.

How shall we comfort ourselves, the murderers of all murderers? What was holiest and mightiest of all that the world has yet owned has bled to death under our knives: who will wipe this blood off us? What water is there for us to clean ourselves? What festivals of atonement, what sacred games shall we have to invent? Is not the greatness of this deed too great for us? Must we ourselves not become gods simply to appear worthy of it? There has never been a greater deed; and whoever is born after us -- for the sake of this deed he will belong to a higher history than all history hitherto."

Here the madman fell silent and looked again at his listeners; and they, too, were silent and stared at him in astonishment. At last he threw his lantern on the ground, and it broke into pieces and went out. "I have come too early," he said then; "my time is not yet. This tremendous event is still on its way, still wandering; it has not yet reached the ears of men. Lightning and thunder require time; the light of the stars requires time; deeds, though done, still require time to be seen and heard. This deed is still more distant from them than most distant stars — *and yet they have done it themselves.*"

It has been related further that on the same day the madman forced his way into several churches and there struck up his *requiem aeternam deo.* Led out and called to account, he is said always to have replied nothing but: "What after all are these churches now if they are not the tombs and sepulchers of God?"[1] (From Friedrich Nietzche's "The Gay Science")

The meaning of the title to Nietzsche's "The Gay Science" is "Joyous Wisdom," yet read how hopeless the Madman sounds and the ensuing chaos he envisions of a godless society while proclaiming the ultimate achievement of killing God. The line "Do we not need to light lanterns in the morning?" speaks of utter moral darkness. Of course, Nietzsche did not believe in God, so who or what was he speaking of when he said God is dead.

> What Nietzsche was referring to by "God is dead" is the general decline of Christianity that was taking place (and is still taking place, depending on who you ask) in the Western world. He explains "God is dead" later on in The Gay Science: 'the belief in the Christian God has become unbelievable.[2]

I have referenced the late Dr. Greg Bahnsen's argument that the proof of God is the impossibility of the contrary. "The Madman" highlights just what that impossibility would look like should Christianity ever be wiped from the public square. We see ghoulish glimpses of it now as schools, where God and the Bible are no longer welcome, have in their absence become killing fields. We see it in the hatred and intolerance toward those who revere Christian values and the God-ordained structure for the nuclear family as the foundation for a healthy society. Sadly, we even see it emerging in churches that are desperately trying to remain relevant by accommodating and even imitating a culture which is the very antithesis of the message of holiness and repentance it is supposed to be preaching.

For atheists who campaign for a God-less country, the book of Revelation provides meat on the bones of The Madman's skeletal image of such a world. Skeptics will have their day of a society without God, but it will be the result of God's temporary removal of the restraining influence of his Spirit (II Thess. 2:6-7). How much they will like it once they have it is an entirely different matter.

In the meantime, critics who refuse to consider the reality, reason, and logic of the biblical record, and the Christian faith, will continue the errand of The Madman. But as certainly as the Bible is true, one final time the God of all gods will be glorified. Every tongue will confess that Jesus Christ is Lord, (Phil. 2:11) and the book of all books will remain unbroken and unmarred as it has for thousands of years.

THE ANVIL

Last eve I passed beside a blacksmith's door
And heard the anvil ring the vesper chime;
When looking in, I saw upon the floor,
 Old hammers worn with beating years of time.
"How many anvils have you had," said I,
"To wear and batter all these hammers so?"
"Just one," said he, and then with twinkling eye,
"The anvil wears the hammers out, you know."
And so, thought I, the anvil of God's Word,
 For ages, skeptic blows have beat upon;
Yet, though the noise of falling blows was heard,
The anvil is unharmed — the hammers gone.
                                    -author unknown

THE END

Bibliography

Chapter One
1. Transcript of Ken Ham vs Bill Nye Debate. Monday, February 10, 2014, Q&A #2. youngearth.org.
2. Lewis, C.S. "Mere Christianity." Barbour and Company Inc., 1952, pg. 153.

Chapter Two
1. Fr. Copleston vs. Bertrand Russell. "The Famous 1948 BBC Radio Debate on the Existence of God." http://www.philvaz.com/apologetics/p20.htm.
2. The Works of Flavius Josephus. The Wars of the Jews or The History of the Destruction of Jerusalem. Book VII, Chapter 9. sacred-texts.com.

Chapter Three
1. "There's an Awakening in Our Country: A Q&A With Jimmy Carter." theatlantic.com. July 13, 2015.
2. Dictionary. Apple version 2.2.2, 2015-2017.
3. "HIV Among Youth in the US." Vital Signs. cdc.gov. Nov. 2012.
4. "HIV patients will spend $600K for lifetime care." nbcnews.com. Nov. 10, 2006.
5. "Deserting ObamaCare: UnitedHealth, nation's largest health insurer, bolts, fears huge losses." foxnews.com. April 20, 2016.
6. "Gay Related Immune Deficiency." en.wikipedia.org.
7. "HIV Among Gay and Bisexual Men." cdc.gov. last updated Sept. 27, 2017.

Chapter Four
1. O'Reilly, Bill. "Hitler's Last Days." Henry Holt and Company, 2015. pp. 81-85.

2. ibid. p. 85.
2. ibid. p.118.

Chapter Five

1. "The 35.4 Percent: 109,631,000 on Welfare." cnsnews.com. Aug. 20, 2014.
2. Weinberger, David. "What would the founders do about welfare." dailycaller.com, July, 5, 2015.
3. Rogers, Adrian. www.goodreads.com/quotes/167272.
4. John Adams. en.wikiquote.org.

Chapter Six

1. "America's Most (and least) Peaceful States." 247wallst.com. April 26, 2012.
2. Kirksey, Franklin L. "How Should We Then Live." sermons. pastorlife.com.

Chapter Seven

1. The argument that the laws of logic are evidence for the existence of the Christian God was used by the late Dr. Greg Bahnsen in his famous debate with atheist, Gordon Stein. "The Great Debate, Does God Exist." University of California, Irvine. 1985.
2. Hoesch, William, A., M.S. "How Coherent Is the Human Evolution Story?" icr.org.
3. Johanson, Donald C., Lenora Johanson, and Blake Edgar. "Ancestors: In Search of Human Origins." New York: Villard Books 1994, p. 60.
4. Johanson, Donald C. and Maitland A. Edey. "Lucy: The Beginnings of Humankind." New York: Simon & Schuster, 1981, pp. 257,258.
5. Donald C., Lenora Johanson, and Blake Edgar. p.28.
6. "Richard Dawkins Clashes With Giles Fraser On Radio 4 Over Atheist Poll." huffingtonpost.co.uk. Feb. 14, 2012.
7. ibid.
8. Washington, Harriet A. "Spectacle: The Astonishing Life of Ota Benga." by Pamela Newkirk", Sunday Book Review, nytimes.com. July 5, 2015.
9. Newkirk, Pamela. "The man who was caged in a zoo." theguardian. com. June 3, 2015.
10. ibid.
11. Washington, Harriet A. "Spectacle:...." nytimes.com.

12. Bohn, Lauren E. "Q&A 'Lucy' Discoverer Donald C Johanson." content.time.com. March 4, 2009.

Chapter 8.
1. Federer, Bill. "The fog that changed the course of American history." World Net Daily, wnd.com. Aug. 26, 2015.
2. ibid.

Chapter 9
1. Darwin, Charles. "Origin of Species." 2nd British edition, 1860, darwin-online.uk.org. p.189.
2. Dunkelberg, Pete. "Irreducible Complexity Demystified," talkdesign.org. April 26, 2003.
3. Miller, Ken. "The Flagellum Unspun - The Collapse of Irreducible Complexity." millerandlevine.com.
4. ibid.
5. "Ken Miller refutes the irreducible complexity of a mousetrap." youtube.com.
6. McIntosh, A.C. "Information and Entropy – Top -Down or Bottom-up Development in Living Systems?", Int. J. of Design & Nature and Ecodynamics. Vol. 4, No. 4 (2009), p. 351– 385.
7. ibid. p. 380.
8. ibid. p. 351.
9. Meyers, Jeff and David A. Noebel. "Understanding the Times." Summit Ministries, 2015, pg. 9.
10. ibid. p. 9.

Chapter Ten
1. Prothero, Stephen. "Religious Illiteracy: What Every American Needs To Know - and Doesn't." San Francisco: Harper, 2007, p.1.
2. "Romulus Breeder Gassed 93 Dogs." fltimes.com. Sept. 15, 2010.

Chapter 12
1. "Facts About the Resurrection of Jesus Christ." riverpower.org
2. McDowell, Josh. "Evidence for the resurrection." bible.ca. 1992.

Chapter 13
1. "Pliny the younger on Christ." mesacc.edu. see also: "Pliny the Younger on Christians." enwikipedia.org.

Chapter 14
1. "The Science Behind 'Interstellar's' Stunning Wormhole Voyage." dailygalaxy.com. Nov. 24, 2014.
2. Rabbi Mordechai Becher. "The Ten Plagues- Live from Egypt." http://ohr.edu/838.
3. Schulz, Matthias. "The Worst Ways to Die: Torture Practices of the Ancient World." Spiegel Online. spiegel.de. May 15, 2009.
4. Dr. Gordon Stein. "The Great Debate, Does God Exist." University of California, Irvine. 1985.

Chapter 15
1. LaHaye, Tim. "Prophecy Study Bible." AMG Publishers, Preface, Copyright 2000.
2. ibid. p. 829.
3. Butt, Kyle. "Tyre in Prophecy." ApologeticsPress.org. 2006.
4. ibid. Fleming, Wallace B. "The History of Tyre." New York, NY: AMS Press, 1966.
5. Byers, Gary. "The Biblical Cities of Tyre and Sidon." biblearchaeology.org. Jan. 26, 2010.
6. "Beyond All Religion." Buddha. beyondallreligion.net.
7. Isaiah Scroll. en.wikipedia.org.
8. Stoner, Peter. "Science Speaks." Online edition, Moody Bible Institute, revised 1976, Ch. 3.
9. "Six Day War." wikipedia.com.

Chapter 16
1. "Ten Commandments No Match for Big Mac." World Net Daily, wnd.com. October 8, 2007.
2. Hudson, David L. "Remember, profanity isn't always protected free speech." firstamendmentcenter.org. Oct. 6, 2011.
3. goodreads.com/quotes.
4. "About Relief Portraits Plaques of Lawgivers." aoc.gov.

Chapter 17
1. DeRouchie, Jason. "You Asked: Which is the Real Ten Commandments." thegospelcoalition.org. August 27, 2012.

Chapter 18
1. Lewis, C.S. Mere Christianity. Barbour and Company, 1952, pg. 95.
2. Green, Ruth H. "The Born Again Skeptics Guide to the Bible." Madison WI, Freedom From Religion Foundation, 1999, pg. 179.

3. McKay, Tom. "The U.S. Government Says NFL Cheerleaders Don't Deserve Minimum Wage — Here's Why." mic.com. April 2, 2014.

4. Abcarian, Robin. "Cheerleaders' wage-theft lawsuit to cost Oakland Raiders $1.25 million." latimes.com. Sept. 4, 2014.

5. Busbee, Jay. "Bills cheerleaders file suit against team over pay, harassment." sports.yahoo.com.April 23, 2014.

6. Green, Emily. "Cheerleaders' Fair Wage Lawsuits Add To NFL's Problems." Transcript All Things Considered, NPR, Sept. 23, 2014.

7. Green, Ruth H. pg. 179.

8. Powell, Michael. "Buffalo Bills Cheerleaders' Routine: No Wages and No Respect." NY Times, Dec. 10, 2014.

9. "Sports Illustrated." en.wikipedia.org.

10. Lincoln, Kevin. "How to Make Money in Hollywood, Don't Be a Woman Over 34." Pacific Standard, psmag.com. Sept 24, 2014.

11. Darwin, Charles. "The Descent of Man." Great Books of the World. Robert P. Gwinn, publisher, Encyclopedia Britannica, Inc., 1952, 1990, pg. 566.

12. "Tobacco Facts and Figures." US Department of Health and Human Services. betobaccofree.hhs.gov.

13. Horowitz, Julia. "Walmart will stop selling Cosmopolitan magazine in checkout lines." March 27, 2018, money.cnn.com

Chapter 19

1. Howell, Elizabeth. "What is the Big Bang Theory." space.com. June 22, 2015.

2. http://humanhistorytimeline.com.

3. "Recorded History." wikipedia.org.

4. dictionary.com

5. "A new form of energy may have powered the Big Bang." UniverseForum, cfa.harvard.edu. 2004.

6. Dubos, Rene J., Ph.D. and James G. Hirsch, M.D. *Bacterial Mycotic Infections of Man,* Fourth Ed., J.B. Lippincott Company, Philadelphia, Pennsylvania, 1952, p.3.

7. "Is Darwinism a Religion." Huffington Post. Sept. July 7, 2011.

8. Hume, David. "The Natural History of Religion." Introduction. 1757, en.wikisource.org.

9. Bell, Graham. "The Masterpiece of Nature: The Evolution and Genetics of Sexuality." University of California Press, Berkeley, CA, 1982, p. 19.

10. Comrie, Bernard, Maria Polinsky, and Dr. Stephen Matthews. "Atlas of Languages: The Origin and Development of Languages Throughout the World." Facts on File, New York, 1996, p. 7.

11. Aitchison, J. "The Seeds of Speech: Language Origin and Evolution." Cambridge University Press, Cambridge, England, 2000, p. 5.

12. McCrone, J. "The Ape That Spoke: Language and the Evolution of the Human Mind." William Morrow, New York, 1991, p. 9.

13. Corballis, M.C. "From Hand to Mouth: The Origins of Language." Princeton University Press, Princeton, NJ, 2002 p. 183.

14. "Punctuated Equliibrium." en.wikipedia.org.

15. Wald, George. "The Origin of Life." Scientific American, May 1954, 191:48.

16. Nilsson, Heribert. "Synthetische Artbildung." Verlag CWK Gleerup, Lund, Sweden, 1953, pp.1185 and 1212.

17. Gould, Stephen J."Is a New and General Theory of Evolution Emerging?" Paleobiology 6:119–130 1980, p.127.

18. Gould, Stephen J. "Evolution as Fact and Theory." Discover 2 (5):34-37, 1981.

Chapter 20

1. blog.drwile.com.

Chapter 21

1. Johannes Kepler. wikipedia.org.

2. "The Great Debate: Does God Exist." University of California Irvine, 1985.

3. Dawkins, R. "The Blind Watchmaker." W.W. Norton, 1987, pg 62.

4. ibid. p .62-63.

5. ibid. p.72.

6. ibid.p. 63

7. "SETI." wikipedia.org.

8. Drake, Frank. "Project Cyclops, A Design Study of a System for Detecting Extraterrestrial   Intelligent Life." ntrs.nasa.gov/archive, iii.

9. Merali, Zeeya. "Search for extraterrestrial intelligence gets a $100-million boost." nature.com. July 20, 2015.

10. ibid.

11. Krulwich, Robert. "The WOW signal." National Public Radio, May 29, 2010.

12. Nelson, Bryan. Mother Nature Network, mnn.com. Dec. 4, 2015.

Chapter 22
1. "Archaeologists Excavate Biblical Giant Goliath's Hometown." foxnews.com. July 11, 2011.
2. Barker, Anne. "Experts dig up dirt on David and Goliath." abc.net.au. updated Aug. 3, 2009.
3. Wheldon, Julie. "Goliath: The Proof." Daily Mail, November 12, 2005.
4. Berkowitz, Adam E. "Return of the Giants: Biblical Story of Goliath Proven True." breakingisraelnews.com. Aug. 16, 2015.
5. MacIsaac, Tara. "Did Giants Exist? Part 2: Where are the Skeletons Now?" theepochtimes.com. Dec. 19, 2014.
6. "Ancient American Giants." Scientific American, Aug. 1880. Volume 43 Number 07, p. 106
7. Dictionary, Version 2.2.1, Apple Inc.
8. "Richard Dawkins on The Origin of Life in the Universe." physics-astronomy.com. June 20, 2014.
9. Ruse, Michael. "The Evolution-Creation Struggle." Harvard University Press, 2005, p. 287.

Chapter 23
1. "Medical Group: Christianity Leads to Longer Life, Health." Baptist Times Staff. ethicsdaily.com. May 5, 2011.
2. "HIV Among Youth in the US." Vital Signs, cdc.gov. Nov. 2012.
3. MacKenzie, Dr. Margaret. "Christians Live Longer than Other Believers, Scientists Say." witscience.org. Sept, 9, 2014.

Chapter 24
1. Mykytiuk, Lawrence. "53 People in the Bible Confirmed Archaeologically." biblicalarchaeology.org. April 12, 2017.
2. Eastman, Mark. "Historical Evidence for Jesus of Nazareth." Appendix II. Blue Letter Bible.
3. "Pontius Pilate: Man behind the myth." BBC News World Edition, news.bbc.co.uk. April 13, 2001.
4. Carl, Michael. "Persecution of Christians on Rise in U.S." World Net Daily. wnd.com. Sept. 17, 2012.
5. Flavius Josephus. "Antiquities of the Jews." 18:5.
6. Pines, Shlomo. "An Arabic Version of the Testamonium Flavianum and its Implications." Jerusalem Academic Press, 1971.
7. "Antiquities of the Jews." book eighteen, chapter five, paragraph two.
8. "Antiquities." 20:9.

9. Eastman, Mark. "Historical Evidence for Jesus of Nazareth." The Search for Messiah, Word for Today, 1996, Appendix II.

10. Roberts, Alexander and James Donaldson. Africanus. The Ante Nicene Fathers. Chronography. 18:1, Wm Eerdmans Publishing Co., 1973 American Reprint of Edinburg edition, Grand Rapids, MI.

11. Tacitus. "Annals," Loeb editions 15.44.

12. Lucian. "The Death of Peregrine." 11–13, in "The Works of Lucian of Samosata." transl. by H.W. Fowler and F.G. Fowler, 4 vols. Oxford: Clarendon, 1949, vol. 4, as cited in Habermas, 1996. Lucian. The Death of Pregrine 11-13.

13. "Mara bar Serapion on the wise king of the Jews." textexcavation.com.

14. "Sir William Mitchell Ramsay." en.wikipedia.org.

15. Ramsay. "St. Paul the Traveller and the Roman Citizen." Putnam and Sons, 1904, p.8.

16. Ramsay. "The Bearing of Recent Discovery on the Trustworthiness of the New Testament." Hodder and Stoughton, 1915, p. 222.

Chapter 25

1. Name of Iran. en. wikipedia.org.

2. Sennachereib's Annals. en.wikipedia.org.

3. "A Staggering Archaeological Discovery: The Mighty Assyrian Empire Emerges from the Dust." Beyond Today, ucg.org. Dec. 9, 2010.

4. Padfield, David. "The Destruction of Nineveh." Lenormant and E. Chevallier, *The Rise and Fall of Assyria.* padfield.com.

Conclusion

1. Friedrich Nietzsche. "The Gay Science." (1882, 1887) para. 125; Walter Kaufmann ed. New York: Vintage, 1974, pp.181-182.

2. Lattier, Daniel. "What Did Nietzsche Mean by 'God is Dead?'" intellectualtakeout.org. April 12, 2016.

PREVIEW

Skeptics vs. Scripture
Book II

A Response to 25 **More** Skeptic Questions
About God, Christianity and the Bible

Skeptics have lots of questions for Christians. In Book II, the other 25 questions posed by Guy Harrison in, "50 simple questions for every christian," will be answered. Here is a sneak preview of some of those questions.

Is the United States of America a Christian nation?
How can we be sure that Jesus performed miracles?
What do evil atheist dictators prove?
What does archaeology prove?
Is the universe fine tuned for us?
Could we design a better world?
What is the problem with evolution?
Why do Christianity and science so often come into conflict?
Why do people go to hell?
Will the end times ever end?
Why does a good God allow so much suffering in the world?
Would you take Jesus' place on the cross?
Will Christianity endure?

Fads and styles have changed, but Bible principles have not. The author's first book deals with the volatile topic of dress and appearance for the Christian. It teaches timeless truths which, though unpopular in the Christian church, remain as relevant today as they were in 2005 when this book was first published. This is one of the most thorough scriptural treatments of the issue you will find.

The Fall and Rise of Christian Standards
by David Kidd

A gracious, honest and straightforward biblical analysis of a controversial issue

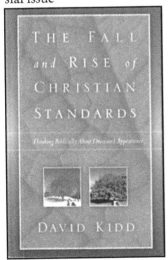

Biblical answers to common questions like these.
Are dress standards legalistic?
What about Christian liberty?
Is it wrong to make judgments of others based on dress?
How do you define modesty according to the Bible?
As long as the message is true, does how the messenger looks or acts matter?
What's wrong with tattoos and body piercing?
If God wants me to change how I dress, wouldn't he convict me about it?

Chapter Titles: *Ashes for Beauty* — Legalism, the Imaginary Giant — *Understanding Freedom in Christ* — What if I'm Not Convicted? — *Can We Be Too Different to Attract Others?*— Does Blessing Mean Approval? — *Understanding Biblical Modesty* — Understanding the Identity Principle — *What Does a Biblical View on Dress and Appearance Look Like?* — Understanding Bible Passages About Dress and Appearance

Available at <u>xulonpress.com</u>,
Amazon, <u>barnesandnoble.com</u>

CPSIA information can be obtained
at www.ICGtesting.com
Printed in the USA
FSHW01n1002060718
50085FS